Konza Prairie

Konza Prairie

A Tallgrass Natural History

O. J. Reichman

Illustrated by Teri Miller

University Press of Kansas

©1987 by the University Press of Kansas

Published by the University Press of Kansas
(Lawrence, Kansas 66045),
which was organized by the Kansas Board of Regents
and is operated and funded by
Emporia State University, Fort Hays State University,
Kansas State University, Pittsburg State University,
the University of Kansas, and Wichita State University

Library of Congress Cataloging-in-Publication Data

Reichman, O. J., 1947–

  Konza prairie.

  Bibliography: p.

  1. Natural history—Kansas—Konza Prairie Research
Natural Area. 2. Prairie ecology—Kansas—Konza Prairie
Research Natural Area. 3. Konza Prairie Research
Natural Area (Kan.) I. Title
QH105.K3R45 1987   508.315'8'09781   87-18903
ISBN 0-7006-0307-7

Printed in the United States of America

10 9 8 7 6 5 4 3 2 1

Contents

Illustrations / vii

Acknowledgments / ix

A Note about Konza Prairie / xi

1 AN INTRODUCTION
   TO KONZA AND OTHER
   GRASSLANDS / 1

2 ORIGINS / 9
   Evolution / 30

3 PATTERNS AND PATCHES / 36
   Disturbance / 49

4 GRASSLANDS / 58
   Photosynthesis / 76
   Fire / 104

5 FORESTS / 115
   Foraging / 125

6 SOIL AND THE BELOWGROUND
   HABITAT / 140
   Cycles / 158

7 STREAMS / 163
   Competition / 175

8 PATTERNS IN TIME / 186
   Weather on Konza / 196

9 KONZA TODAY / 202

Common and Scientific Names / 213

Index / 219

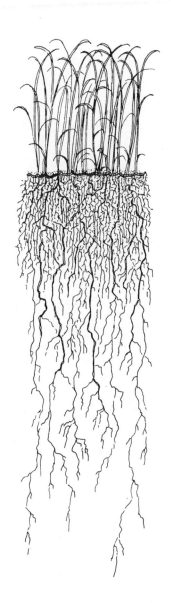

Illustrations

Map showing shortgrass, mixed-grass, and tallgrass prairies / 6

Map of Konza Prairie Research Natural Area / 7

Fossil fusilinids / 9

Geologic table / 12

Limestone strata / 16

Projectile points / 23

Ranch house and barn / 28

Mouse with young / 32

Nighthawk's nest / 36

Pollen / 42

Thistle / 45

Antlion adult and larvae / 48

Meadowlark / 54

Grass with roots / 58

Silica in grass / 61

Seeds / 66

Bluestem flower / 69

Buffalo gourd / 74

Chloroplast / 77

Grasshopper mandibles / 84

Tent caterpillars / 85

Chigger / 87

Bullfrog / 91

Collared lizard / 93

Cowbird's nest / 96

Prairie chicken / 97

Mouse jaws / 101

Shrew / 103

Mushrooms / 115

Acorns / 119

Poison ivy / 122

Thorn / 123

Praying mantis / 129

Aphid / 131

Wood-boring beetle / 132

Woodpecker / 136

Woodrat den / 138

Centipede / 140

Root hairs / 147

Cicadas / 154

Milk snake / 157

Crayfish / 163

Caddisfly / 171

Spirogyra / 178

Water strider / 181

Water beetle / 182

Fish / 184

Thunderhead / 186

Sunflower / 194

Bison / 202

COLOR SECTION *following page* 116

White flowers with upturned corollas

A yellow spider eating a fly on red flowers

A fire line on Konza

Kings Creek

A yellow crab spider on a variegated plant

A milkweed seed pod
Grass flowers
Smoke from a prairie fire
Close-up of a leaf
Brown prairie
Green prairie with
    white flowers
A limestone ridge on Konza

Fall colors
Winter on Konza
A small grasshopper on top of a
    ball-like flower
A damselfly
A bee on a white flower
A wave on the inland sea

Acknowledgments

As a relative newcomer to the tallgrass prairie, I relied on the knowledge and assistance of many colleagues while learning about Konza. My appreciation is extended to all of those researchers whose information I relied upon and to Derrick Blocker, Richard Elzinga, Greg Farley, Joe Gelroth, Barbara Hetrick, Sam James, Don Kaufman, Glennis Kaufman, Harold Klaassen, Patricia O'Brien, Clenton Owensby, Cathy Tate, and John Zimmerman, who taught me a lot concerning things I knew little about. I extend special thanks to Ted Barkley and Tim Seastedt for their assistance, and particularly to Elmer Finck, who taught me a lot about things I thought I already knew. Ted Evans, Elmer Finck, Rob Gendron, David Gibson, Marty Gurtz, Debbie Hayes, Tim Seastedt, Chris Smith, and Ron West contributed to the general information that went into the book; they also reviewed sections of the text that related to their interests. John Zimmerman reviewed the entire manuscript, and Bill Platt provided an extensive review which significantly improved the text.

Several colleagues contributed photographs to the book, and Teri Miller skillfully executed the illustrations, from grasshopper mandibles under a magnifying glass to complex grass flowers. Cindy Rebar helped locate specimens and examples for Teri to use, and I thank them both. My wife, Jessica, was the first to read the text, and her efforts as an interested layperson and skillful editor helped immensely. She also provided criticism so deftly that it seemed as though her suggestions were my original intent.

Special thanks from everyone concerned about the preservation of habitats go to Dr. Lloyd Hulbert, whose persistence eventually led to the establishment of Konza Prairie Research Natural Area. He died during the final preparation of this book; we will all remember that his knowledge of the tallgrass prairie was matched only by the grace with which he shared that knowledge.

The able assistance and encouragement from all of the professionals at the University Press of Kansas were greatly appreciated.

A Note about Konza Prairie

Both because of its fragility and because of the ongoing scientific research, Konza Prairie is not open to the public, although tours are occasionally given by the University for Man and by the Audubon Society in Manhattan, Kansas. A biennial open house is scheduled in the fall of every even-numbered year by the Division of Biology at Kansas State University. Information about Konza Prairie may be obtained by writing to the director, Konza Prairie Research Natural Area, Division of Biology, Kansas State University, Manhattan KS 66506.

Dozens of technical articles have been published concerning Konza Prairie. Lists of the plants and of many groups of animals are available in the *Prairie Naturalist*, a journal published by the University of North Dakota Press. The University Press of Kansas offers a variety of books that include information relating to tallgrass prairies and Konza, including *Kansas Geology: An Introduction to Landscape, Rocks, Minerals, and Fossils*, edited by Rex Buchanan; *Natural Kansas*, edited by Joseph T. Collins; *Edible Wild Plants of the Prairie: An Ethnobotanical Guide*, by Kelly Kindscher; and a beautiful photographic essay on prairies entitled *Prairie: Images of Ground and Sky*, by Terry Evans. The Museum of Natural History at the University of Kansas, Lawrence, has published a series of books on the plants and animals of Kansas, as well as *Archeology of Kansas*, by Patricia O'Brien.

Several books provide good overviews of prairies, including tallgrass prairies. The Audubon Society's nature guide called *Grasslands* presents the characteristics and distributions of many prairie residents. David Costello's *The Prairie World* (Minneapolis: University of Minnesota Press, 1980) and Paul Gruchow's *Journal of a Prairie Year* (Minneapolis: University of Minnesota Press, 1985) offer personal insights into the tallgrass prairie. *Where the Sky Began* (Boston, Mass.: Houghton Mifflin, 1982), by John Madson, is an intriguing account of the prairie, including the impressions of those Europeans who first set eyes upon it. The book also includes a helpful reading list.

1 / An Introduction to Konza and Other Grasslands

LIKE A DESERT OR AN OCEAN, THE TALLGRASS PRAIRIE IS A HABI-tat that may not immediately demand attention. But specific images persist in the subconscious until, as one builds upon another, the prairie's beauty and grandeur emerge.

A sense of the tallgrass prairie may first appear as a wind-driven ripple of grass hisses toward you and beyond, causing momentary fright, like an unseen serpent. The subtlety of the tallgrass prairie may register when the earthy smell of wet grass in summer is mixed with the sweet fragrance of that season's bouquet. The majestic expanse of the tallgrass can be powerful when you wander into a forest of big-bluestem stalks almost twice your height and find that your sole vista is straight up. Each perceptual double take contributes an impression, and bit by bit the tallgrass prairie becomes, first, alluring and, finally, irresistible. The passions that this habitat arouses are intensified with the realization that the once-vast tallgrass prairie is today rare and in danger of disappearing.

Slightly over a century ago, the tallgrass prairie in North America stretched over most of what is now Iowa, Illinois, southern Minnesota, northern Missouri, and the eastern edges of the Dakotas, Nebraska, Kansas, and Oklahoma; today only a fraction remains. In east-central Kansas, in a small corner of the original range of this grassland, lies Konza Prairie Research Natural Area, an 8,616-acre (3,487-hectare) protected tract established to preserve this vanishing habitat and to promote scientific research. It is not open to the public, but its value to all of us is immense. Konza Prairie is the result of thirty years of effort by Lloyd Hulbert, a biologist at Kansas State University, who recognized early on the ecological importance of the tallgrass prairie and the need to locate and preserve a remnant large enough to protect the habitat and to serve as a living laboratory. Hulbert's efforts also reflect an ethic that demands that parcels of undisturbed land be set aside for appreciation by future generations.

With the backing of the Nature Conservancy, a private foundation dedicated to preserving endangered habitats, and with the generosity of Mrs. Katharine Ordway, who made the land purchase possible, the Konza Prairie Research Natural Area has been set aside as a landmark area. Managed by Kansas State University, Konza Prairie provides both an area in which scientists can analyze the natural processes of the tallgrass prairie under relatively undisturbed conditions and a benchmark for comparisons to similar but unprotected areas. As the largest remaining tract of tallgrass prairie in North America, Konza Prairie is a living archive of this magnificent habitat.

At first glance, the tallgrass prairie appears monotonous. When seen from a passing automobile, the vast expanse is interrupted only occasionally by ribbons of forests that wind along streams and creeks. It is not until one peers into the prairie, rather than at it, that its true nature, its complexity and diversity, is revealed. In a tallgrass prairie, most of the action takes place on a small scale, within patches hidden under the canopy of grass. Some of the arenas of activity are so small as to be almost unimaginable, occurring under tiny stones or in the interstices of the soil. We are limited in our understanding of these processes by the physical constraints of our senses and by our inexperience with events on such a small scale.

At the other extreme, the prairie, with its big sky and few landmarks, is so vast as to be daunting. Those pioneers who set forth across its expanses must have experienced the same trepidation that European emigrants felt when they first gazed at the oceans they were about to cross on their way to the New World. The scope of the prairie can be awesome and incomprehensible.

Just as the spatial scales limit our ability to comprehend the prairie, so do the periods of time involved in its origin, development, and maintenance. We are relatively comfortable with years, months, weeks, and days; and we can perhaps visualize both our grandparents' and our grandchildren's generations, though not much beyond. But the North American continent has existed for billions of years, albeit not in its present location. This land mass has been subjected to all of the physical forces the earth is heir to, and these have set the stage for what we now see. The record is ever changing, a pattern that is likely to continue for billions of years.

These limits to our perception and understanding make many environments appear simple and uninteresting, but the prairie is especially susceptible to being unappreciated because on the surface it appears so uniform and static. There are no towering peaks on Konza, no shifts in the earth's crust rend it, and no glaciers loom on the horizon. But such features have occurred in the past as part of the heritage of Konza Prairie, even though their traces are imperceptible to most laypersons. These obscure patterns and processes, the boundaries of interactions between organisms and the physical world, are what draw the attention of scientists and reveal how the prairie evolved and where it is headed.

In one sense, it is curious that we are so limited in our perception of space and time. We inhabit the midpoint of the physical universe as we know it today—the smallest known objects, atoms, are billions of times smaller than we are, and the largest object, the universe, is that many times larger than we are. It is intriguing to wonder if this could be an artifact of our own intellect. If we were as small as atoms, would we still see approximately equal distances up and down the size scale? We also sit about in the middle of our time scale: the solar system is approximately 10 to 20 billion years old, our planet is about 4.6 billion years old, and life began on earth a little over 3 billion years ago. The sun is scheduled to shrink to near nothingness in approximately 10 billion years, freezing earth's inhabitants before expanding and consuming our planet. Why do we have such difficulty in perceiving and understanding the portions of our spatial and temporal world just beyond the close-by and the near term?

Perhaps this is because the more distant features have only recently begun to impinge on our lives. Until the last few centuries, only those objects and events closest to us were likely to affect us directly; what was under a rock or across the sea was probably of little importance to the survival of our primitive ancestors. Now, as we expand our horizons of interest and influence, it is important to understand things outside our immediate realm. Moreover, we are curious about our environment, and we have the time to satisfy that curiosity by exploring the unknown.

The ensuing pages contain descriptions and illustrations of the salient features of Konza Prairie, of the biological and physical forces that have molded it, and of its relationship with other grasslands and habitats. Some of the topics will be familiar—it is impossible to miss the grass on the prairie—but others, especially those dealing with scales of space and time outside the common frames of reference, will not. Process begets pattern, and so the patterns on Konza Prairie require explanation through an almost infinite array of physical and biological processes. Some of these occur sequentially; others occur simultaneously.

Ancient geologic events laid down a foundation for Konza, and erosion by wind and water have sculpted its face. Photosynthesis fuels the plants on the prairie, and natural selection has molded their responses to fire, grazing, and drought. Seasons regularly influence what survives on the prairie, and interactions such as competition for limited resources, predation, and responses to disturbances help to shape prairie patterns. All of the processes on Konza Prairie also occur elsewhere, but their unique arrangement and duration are responsible for the prairie patterns we now see.

The primary focus of this book is the patterns of Konza Prairie, but embedded within the chapters (and set off typographically) are descriptions of the important processes that generate these patterns. Only the common names of the organisms that are discussed are presented in the text, but there is a list of common names and their scientific counterparts at the end of the text.

Pattern and process intertwine in the real world: what goes on in one spot probably affects what can or will occur in another. But to understand many biological entities, it is essential to tease apart cause and effect, gaining generality at the loss of some accuracy, and such an approach is characteristic of this chronicle. While simplification promotes understanding, it is important to remember that there are emergent features of the interactions that defy simplification, and they are themselves part of the fascination of Konza Prairie.

Tallgrass prairies represent a relatively small portion of the grasslands that occur around the world on all of the nonpolar continents. Prairies tend to occur in the interior of large continental land masses and are characterized by a predominance of grass and an absence of trees (except along rivers and streams), by flat or gently rolling topography, and by periodic drought. Portions of eastern Europe and expanses of Asia are covered by steppes, fields of stubby bunch grasses that can survive the harsh environment; much of middle and southern Africa is wrapped in extensive velds that have existed for more than a million years; the interior of South America is covered by the pampas, thousands of square miles of relatively tall grass; and Australia retains fragments of grasslands in areas where conditions are too dry for forests and too moist for deserts.

For the last few thousand years in North America, grasslands have stretched from northern Canada to the southern United States and into Mexico. In the central Great Plains, prairies extend from the foot of the Rockies eastward to the Missouri River and northeastward past the Mississippi River into Illinois. As moist Pacific air approaches the Rockies from the west, it rises, cools, and relinquishes its moisture as rain or snow over the peaks. To the east, in the lee of the Rockies, the air has been wrung dry, and the sparse rainfall yields the arid shortgrass prairies of eastern Colorado and western Kansas. A little farther east the air flow descends and warms, regaining its capacity for moisture, and is rehydrated by a northerly flow of moist gulf air. The increased rainfall produced from this supplemental moisture is enough to generate the mixed-grass prairies of central Kansas and Nebraska. In the eastern quarter of Kansas, across Iowa, and into Illinois there is enough rainfall to support the luxuriant tallgrass prairie. Because it receives more than twice as much rainfall as the shortgrass prairie does, the tallgrass prairie is susceptible to invasion by forests, especially along its moist eastern flank. Thus, the tallgrass prairie is hemmed in on the west by the more drought-tolerant mixed- and shortgrass prairies and on the east by the smothering deciduous forests.

Like other grasslands, the tallgrass prairie is often visited by drought, and it hosts an array of grazing animals that have evolved

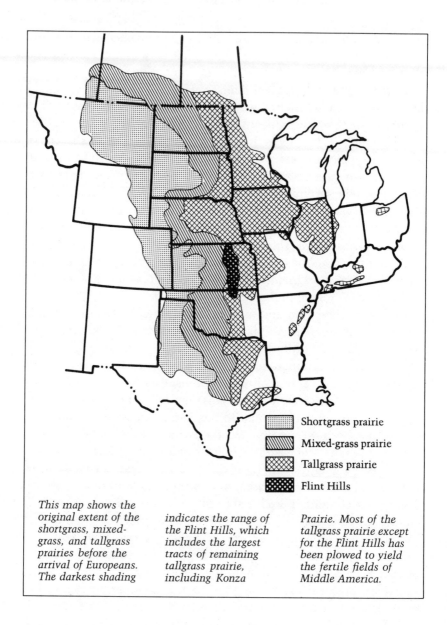

Shortgrass prairie

Mixed-grass prairie

Tallgrass prairie

Flint Hills

This map shows the original extent of the shortgrass, mixed-grass, and tallgrass prairies before the arrival of Europeans. The darkest shading indicates the range of the Flint Hills, which includes the largest tracts of remaining tallgrass prairie, including Konza Prairie. Most of the tallgrass prairie except for the Flint Hills has been plowed to yield the fertile fields of Middle America.

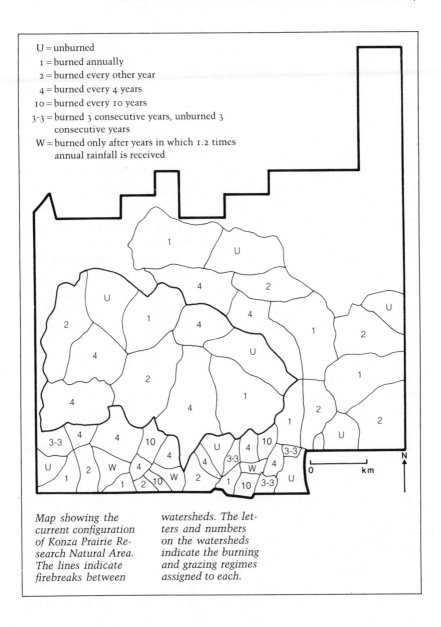

Map showing the current configuration of Konza Prairie Research Natural Area. The lines indicate firebreaks between watersheds. The letters and numbers on the watersheds indicate the burning and grazing regimes assigned to each.

to take advantage of the abundant and succulent summer vegetation. The plants that are not consumed become fuel for lightning-caused wildfires that can race across the surface, incinerating thousands of acres, killing trees and shrubs, and reestablishing the environmental conditions that favor grasses.

Although grasslands occur all over the world, the North American tallgrass prairie is special because of the magnitude of big bluestem grass, its dominant variety, which symbolizes the tallgrass prairie. In a good year, big bluestem sends up a flowering stalk over 10 feet (3 meters) tall, producing what has been described as an inland sea, complete with undulating waves, eddies, and the hiss of surf. During the growing season, the surface of the prairie writhes in response to the slightest breeze. When fall arrives and the grasses retreat into winter senescence, the stiff, erect skeletons of big bluestem and the beaten-down litter of that year's growth remain. This biotic clutter would accumulate forever were it not for grazing, fire, and the action of billions of tiny scavengers that regularly recycle the organic debris.

Ironically, the very conditions that promoted the development of the tallgrass prairie—good soil and adequate moisture—have also led to its demise. As settlers moved west during the nineteenth century and established homesteads, the native tallgrass prairie disappeared, much of it succumbing to the steel plow. Fortunately, a portion of the tallgrass prairie lies in the Flint Hills region of the Great Plains, and this has been its salvation. The Flint Hills are underlain by limestone, and their shallow, rocky soils made sodbusting a foolish venture. The region, which stretches in a 200-mile (322-kilometer) band from northern Oklahoma into southern Nebraska, resisted the agricultural invasion. Instead, the Flint Hills prairie became a tallgrass pasture as cattle replaced the nearly destroyed herds of buffalo. Grasses evolved to tolerate the effects of grazing, with the result that domestic cattle have been much less detrimental to the tallgrass prairie of the Flint Hills than plowing was. Although specific interactions between various components on the Flint Hills may have been altered by intensive agriculture designed to produce maximum forage, grazing has left many components of the tallgrass prairie intact.

2 / *Origins*

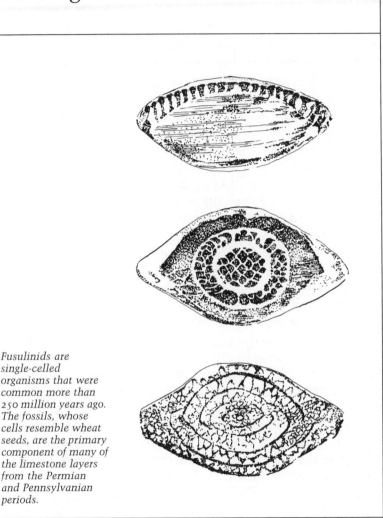

Fusulinids are single-celled organisms that were common more than 250 million years ago. The fossils, whose cells resemble wheat seeds, are the primary component of many of the limestone layers from the Permian and Pennsylvanian periods.

ALTHOUGH KONZA PRAIRIE NOW APPEARS PLACID AND BE-nign, it is the net result of dynamic processes that began several billion years ago. In the intervening epochs, Konza has been subjected to all manner of geologic change. The evidence for some of what occurred is forever lost to the inevitable forces of erosion, but major portions of the early history are exposed in the hundreds of feet of sedimentary rocks deposited while Konza was below the surface of ancient seas. These revealing strata and their fossils were laid down over millions of years so that each inch of depth provides a glimpse of the past, run in fast forward. The rocks disclose the ingredients for Konza, and the recipe involved in its birth and maturation.

The earth is constantly changing; except for catastrophic events such as volcanic eruptions or floods, most of the changes are imperceptible while they are happening, because they occur so slowly. Some changes are cyclical, such as variation in the position of true magnetic north, wobbles in earth's orbit, and changes in the circularity of its orbit. All of these alter the earth's relationship to the warming sun, thereby affecting the global environment. When the environment cools down sufficiently, snow and ice accumulate and form glaciers. Abundant glaciers tie up huge amounts of the earth's water, lowering the sea level world-wide, and when they melt, vast areas of land become submerged. In addition, mountains rise, thrusting the earth's crust to higher, colder altitudes, and the continents relentlessly wander around the globe, taking up residence at different latitudes through time. The net result of these processes is that any one spot on the earth has been subjected to repeated episodes of uplifting, erosion, sinking, deposition, inundation, and desiccation.

The crust of the buoyant North American continent, on which Konza is centered, has migrated over the face of the globe, floating on a subterranean sea of molten rock. The most dramatic geologic events today occur around the margins of continents, and so the central regions of North America have escaped the flamboyant collisions of the margins and the episodes of mountain building that flank the prairies to the east and west, although evidence from deep within the prairie suggests such activity in the past.

Igneous, metamorphic, and sedimentary rocks characterize the earth's crust. Igneous rocks are formed by the solidification of molten material that originates deep within the earth. The earth's core is a molten hearth, fired by the heat of radioactive decay. Continents are constantly moving and colliding in slow motion—one continent may ride up over the other, or if their masses are approximately equal, the collision produces uplifted mountain ranges. Overridden segments are pushed down toward the hot interior of the earth, where they melt and are reincarnated as igneous rock. The molten rock may rise to the surface during volcanic eruptions and may solidify or accumulate in subterranean spaces where it can be uncovered by subsequent erosion. As large portions of the earth's crust are subducted and recycled, most of the information contained in the ancient rocks is lost in the amalgamation and extrusion of the new material.

Metamorphic rock also loses much information as it is being formed. While rock near the earth's surface is being covered with more and more overlying material, it is subjected to extreme pressures, heat, and chemical assault. These processes change the configuration of the layers of the sedimentary sequence, intermingling the strata and mixing their constituent elements. Furthermore, the pressures actually change the chemical and physical properties, producing new minerals.

Fortunately, sedimentary rock releases its knowledge of the past much more freely; its strata are the incunabula of the earth's history. Erosion breaks down the emergent geologic features of the earth's surface, and the residue is moved about over the surface, primarily by wind and water. Erosion occurs at several scales of magnitude. It may be slow but eternal, such as simple wind friction that gradually abrades the surface of a granite escarpment; or it may be rapid and dramatic, as when massive floods scour away huge chunks of earth. Eventually, the largest mountains are broken into boulders, then to cobbles and pebbles, and finally to granules and dust. Regardless of how small these pieces are, they fall under the influence of gravity and work their way downhill and eventually settle in the low areas, where they are covered by succeeding deposits. As the deposition proceeds, the surface levels out, and thick layers of sediment accumulate. If this were the only process going on, the earth would eventually be uniformly flat, and all low places would be filled with the debris from all high places. But the earth is much more dynamic: new low spots are continually being produced by rents in the surface, and new mountains are being uplifted as the earth's surface crumples when continents collide.

Limestone is a conspicuous component of the globe's sedimentary rocks. Pure limestone is white or nearly so, but it is frequently contaminated with inclusions that alter its texture and color. Most of the limestones in Kansas are marine in origin, though some developed in fresh water. A substantial portion of limestone represents

GEOLOGIC TIMETABLE AND KANSAS ROCK CHART
(Not scaled for geologic time or thickness of deposits)

ERAS	PERIODS	EPOCHS	EST. LENGTH IN YEARS*	TYPE OF ROCK IN KANSAS	
CENOZOIC	QUATERNARY	HOLOCENE	10,000 +	Glacial drift; river silt, sand, and gravel; dune sand; wind-blown silt (loess); volcanic ash.	— 0.010
		PLEISTOCENE	1,990,000		— 2
	TERTIARY	PLIOCENE	3,000,000	River silt, sand, gravel, fresh-water limestone; volcanic ash; bentonite; diatomaceous marl; opaline sandstone.	— 5
		MIOCENE	19,000,000		— 24
		OLIGOCENE	14,000,000		— 38
		EOCENE	17,000,000		— 55
		PALEOCENE	8,000,000		— 63
MESOZOIC	CRETACEOUS		75,000,000	Limestone, chalk, chalky shale, dark shale, varicolored clay, sand-stone, conglomerate. Outcropping igneous rock.	— 138
	JURASSIC		67,000,000	Sandstones and shales, chiefly subsurface. Siltstone, chert, and gypsum.	— 205
	TRIASSIC		35,000,000		— 240
PALEOZOIC	PERMIAN		50,000,000	Limestone, shale, evaporites (salt, gypsum, anhydrite), red sand-stone; chert, siltstone, dolomite, and red beds.	— 290
	PENNSYLVANIAN		40,000,000	Alternating marine and nonmarine shale, limestone, sandstone, coal; chert and conglomerate.	~330
	MISSISSIPPIAN		30,000,000	Limestone, shale, dolomite, chert, oölites, sandstone, and siltstone.	— 360
	DEVONIAN		50,000,000	Subsurface only. Limestone, pre-dominantly black shale; sand-stone.	— 410
	SILURIAN		25,000,000	Subsurface only. Limestone.	— 435
	ORDOVICIAN		65,000,000	Subsurface only. Dolomite, sand-stone.	— 500
	CAMBRIAN		70,000,000	Subsurface only. Dolomite, sand-stone, limestone, and shale.	~570
PRECAMBRIAN			1,930,000,000	Subsurface only. Granite, other igneous rocks, and metamorphic rocks.	
			1,100,000,000 +		— 3,500

MILLION YEARS PAST

KANSAS GEOLOGICAL SURVEY   Eons not shown   *U.S. Geological Survey, Geologic Names Committee, 1980 the remains of calcium carbonate shells of animals such as crinoids (relatives of sea stars), fusulinids (extinct single-celled organisms), brachiopods, and mollusks such as snails and clams. Other lime-stones were caused by chemical processes that occur after carbon dioxide is removed from water by aquatic plants or by the mixing of currents, which causes the carbonates to precipitate and accumulate on the bottom. Several types of limestone occur on Konza, where they are usually interspersed with clay layers called mudstones, deposited when the water was turbid.

Geologists have divided the earth's history into periods, based on boundaries between major episodes of mountain building (see geo-logic table). The earth is estimated to be 4.6 billion years old, but most of what happened during the first 4.2 billion years (that is, during the Precambrian, up until 600 million years ago) has been obliterated by subsequent geologic activities. Thus, more than 85 percent of Konza's history is buried in igneous and metamorphic Precambrian bedrock that lies more than 1,000 feet below the cur-rent surface. These rocks have been significantly disrupted by past geologic events, but they are still sufficiently intact to reveal the evolution of the first hard-bodied organisms that may have inhabited what is now Konza, though there probably were earlier soft-bodied creatures that would not have been fossilized.

The geologic history of Konza Prairie after the Precambrian records the gradual deposition of numerous layers of sediments on the rela-tively stable basement complex of rock. Almost without exception, the layers under Kansas are flat, with older layers being overlain by younger ones. The oldest layers on Konza, which begin a thousand feet below the surface, were deposited about 600 million years ago, during the Cambrian period. The geologic record of the first tens of millions of years of the Cambrian, however, are missing across much of central North America, suggesting that rates of erosion during this period exceeded rates of deposition. Late-Cambrian rock layers offer some good news and some bad news. The material apparently was deposited above water; but because no life existed on land at that time, no fossils are included. By the close of the Cambrian, how-ever, the exposed land had been inundated, and the thick layers of limestone that were deposited include fossilized forms.

The ancient limestone layers suggest that almost all of the ani-mals we know about today, except for vertebrates, were present in the Cambrian, although usually in much simpler forms. The dominant creatures were trilobites, the extinct relatives of insects and crustaceans, which ruled the earth's seas during the late Cambrian. Their cohabitants included jellyfish, sponges, miscellaneous worms, brachiopods (ancient clamlike creatures), and primitive ancestors of sea stars.

Over the next 450 million years, from the beginning of the Ordovician period until the Tertiary, Konza experienced periods alternating between inundation beneath shallow marine seas and emergence above sea level. While the land was submerged, thick layers of sediment were built up from material washed or blown into the water and from the accumulation of billions of carcasses of dead organisms that lived in the warm seas. When the land extended above the water, it was eroded away by water and wind. These contrasting processes produced complex patterns of strata which are related to the relative amount of time the land was submerged or emergent, the intensity of erosional processes, and the nature of the depositional environment (that is, how clear or turbid the water was, and how many organisms lived and died there).

Each geologic period contained events that would be significant in the origin of Konza Prairie. For example, in the Ordovician, over 435 million years ago, the surface around what is now Konza Prairie became as turbulent as it ever has been. There were episodic earthquakes, shifts along fault lines, nearby volcanic eruptions, and oscillating marine inundations. Some of the surrounding seas were quite deep, harboring eurypterids (ancient predaceous arthropods) up to six feet long. Coral colonies lived along the shallower shores, and trilobites were still common. Primitive plants developed along the seashores, perhaps launching their initial invasions of land from these strategic positions.

During the two subsequent periods, the Silurian and the Devonian, large land plants evolved and grew over the emergent earth, including ancient Konza. The primitive plants developed strong stems that supported their quest for the sun and roots that could penetrate deep into the ground in search of moisture and nutrients. We would only barely be able to recognize these primitive forests, which were dominated by horsetails, ferns, and club mosses. The newly invaded terrestrial habitat was shared by only a few kinds of animals, primarily insects and their relatives. The Devonian is considered the age of fishes, because these early vertebrates diversified and ruled the earth's waters. The precursors to modern fish evolved muscular tails to propel them rapidly through the water. Steered by paired fins and armed with efficient jaws, the fish became major predators.

By late in the subsequent Pennsylvanian period, terrestrial habitats began to predominate in Kansas, and regional differences within the state developed. In the Konza area, the land rose above the highest water levels and was immediately incised by small creeks and streams that cut through the newly formed and emergent layers of sediment. Seams of coal from the Pennsylvanian are present around Konza, which suggests that the period was warm and humid. Thermophilic (heat-loving) plants, including tree ferns and horsetails, abounded on the land. These plants supported numerous insects and land snails, which would have supplied food for the first amphibians that ventured onto the land. Until this period, many animals, including all of the vertebrates, had been confined to the water. But amphibians, as their name suggests, spend a portion of their life cycle on land before returning to the water to breed. Invading the land was a major evolutionary step; it allowed amphibians to investigate the shoreline and to take advantage of the riches that might be found there. The water, however, still served as a magnet for life, recalling its wandering inhabitants during each breeding season.

The next period, the Permian, began with another major inundation of Konza by marine waters. The resulting depositions are the beds of limestone that are currently exposed on the rolling hills of Konza. Huge numbers of invertebrate fossils occur in these beds. Some of the later Permian strata have yielded fish and amphibian fossils, indicating that the warm seas were shallow and frequently near shores. The deposition of limestone, usually alternating with mudstones (from seas made turbid by suspended silt), continued for about 50 million years, producing layers over 200 feet (60 meters) in thickness. By the mid to late Permian, Konza was beginning to dry up. The effects of drying were exacerbated by massive reefs of sponges and algae that developed across Texas, damming up influxes of water from the Gulf of Mexico. As the seas dried up, they were probably thick, murky, and low in oxygen, much like a stagnant dying farm pond in August.

True land-dwelling animals had evolved around Konza by the Triassic and Jurassic periods. Reptiles were about to begin their rapid

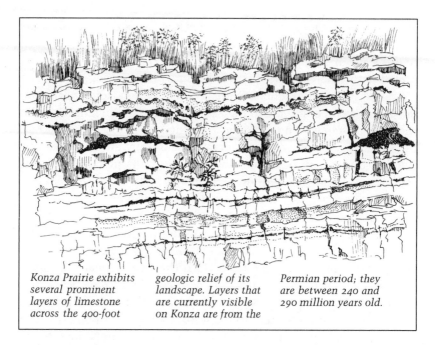

Konza Prairie exhibits several prominent layers of limestone across the 400-foot geologic relief of its landscape. Layers that are currently visible on Konza are from the Permian period; they are between 240 and 290 million years old.

and spectacular evolutionary spread on the earth that, over the next 100 million years, would make them the dominant life form on the planet. One of the primary reasons for the success of reptiles was the evolution of an egg that could develop away from water. Such eggs, which are called amniotic (for example, chicken eggs), freed reptiles to colonize and explore the vast continents. Among the dominant forms were the dinosaurs, the best known of the ancient reptiles. Although a few tiny fragments of dinosaurs may occur in the shales around Konza, the nearest major deposits of fossil dinosaurs are in western Texas.

During much of the Triassic and Jurassic periods, Konza protruded above water as the seas receded. These periods are characterized by erosion, although there were brief periods of flooding, and much of what had been laid down during the extensive depositions of the Permian was ground away and flushed into streams and rivers, to be swept off the edge of the continent and out to sea.

The last great marine invasion of Konza took place during the 75 million years of the Cretaceous period. An arm of the sea invaded from the northwest and eventually connected up with yet another inundation from the Gulf of Mexico, producing a broad sea basin centered in western Kansas. At some point during the Cretaceous, Konza must have housed a diverse terrestrial fauna on the shore of the invading sea. Ancestral mammals crawled about, and birds so primitive that they still had teeth flew in the skies along the shore. Dinosaurs diversified in spectacular fashion, taking over the skies, the seas, and the land. Giant mosasaurs and plesiosaurs plied the seas, and pterosaurs, including pterodactyls, glided on air currents. Clams and their relatives abounded in the sea, and early shelled relatives of octopuses and squid multiplied in abundance and diversity.

Significant environmental changes occurred world-wide at the end of the Cretaceous as the land rose and the seas drained to lower basins. These changes were accompanied by the massive extinction of large groups of organisms, including the dinosaurs. The emergent land was again subjected to long periods of erosion; as a result, all of the Cretaceous rocks and those of the Paleocene, Eocene, and Oligocene epochs of the early Tertiary that were laid down on Konza are now missing, even though substantial Cretaceous deposits still exist just west of Konza. The boundary between the Cretaceous and the Tertiary also marks the rapid growth of the Rockies, whose eroded rubble would eventually form deposits distributed over Kansas.

Sediments from the Miocene epoch of the Tertiary are absent from Konza, but where they occur in western Kansas, they reveal what Konza must have been like ten to twenty million years ago. If we could visit the Konza of the Miocene, we would recognize all of the components of the flora and the fauna. Although specific types of rhinoceroses and horses, for example, would look peculiar, we could easily identify them as relatives of modern forms. For contemporary Konza, however, a much more important evolutionary event was occurring during the Miocene. Grasses, which would come to dominate prairies, diversified and became common. Konza probably looked like some of the vast savannas of Africa, complete with scattered trees and large grazing mammals but with more ridges and draws. Once the land had emerged from the seas for the last time, the stage was set for the inexorable series of events and circumstances that led to Konza as we know it today.

Erosion, rather than deposition, has been the major geologic force on Konza for the last 60 million years. In the absence of broad bodies of water that ensnare the debris of a region, sedimentation occurs in small ponds and marshes and along stream courses. Thus, instead of having thick strata to analyze, paleontologists must rely on cores of sediments taken from ancient ponds. In the cores the layers are thin and cover short lengths of time compared to the massive marine deposits of earlier periods. Ponds trap pollen along with other airborne debris, so analysis of the cores can reveal the nature of the plant community in the vicinity of the pond while it was filling up with transported sediment. No cores for pollen have been taken from Konza, but those from adjacent areas indicate that as the Tertiary moved through its final stages, the Great Plains began an extensive drying period. This was due partly to the recession of seas, but also to the completion of the rise of the Rocky Mountains, which robbed east-flowing air of its moisture. Trees that had flourished across open, flat plains receded to more moist (or mesic) areas along stream courses or around temporary ponds, and grasses began to fill the expanses between drainages.

Grasses are adapted to deal with drought and grazing, and by the early Pliocene they had undergone an explosive diversification in the face of these dual depredations. The environments were seasonal, and rainfall occurred primarily during the warm seasons. The types of plants, reptiles, and mammals occurring in the Pliocene suggest that severe freezing was not common. In fact, subtropical conditions now characteristic of equatorial regions extended across Konza.

The Pleistocene—the first epoch of the Quaternary period—began 2 million years ago. It is extremely interesting because it is very recent in geologic time, and the evidence that it left behind is relatively fresh and exciting. More is known about what went on during this period than in earlier periods, so we can begin to understand details of the events that influenced Konza as we know it now.

Certainly one of the most intriguing features of the Quaternary is that it marks the beginning of the ice ages, during which four major glacial events occurred across the North American continent. Glaciations had occurred during earlier periods, but mostly in the southern hemisphere; those of the Pleistocene were the first to threaten Konza. The four glacial periods are named for the states in which their southernmost extension occurred. The Nebraskan glacial began over one million years ago; it was followed by the Kansan, the Illinoian, and the Wisconsinan, which began its retreat just twelve thousand years ago. Fitted in amongst the major advances and retreats were numerous minor extensions of ice southward and withdrawals north-ward. The leading edge of the Kansan glacier stopped its southward flow just a few miles from Konza Prairie, roughly along the present course of the Kansas River.

During the early Pleistocene, weather changes in the Northern Hemisphere allowed ice and snow to accumulate in layers that were hundreds of feet thick. The glaciers eventually reached thousands of feet in height, but when they were just over 200 feet (61 meters) thick, their own weight caused them to melt where they touched the ground and to ooze southward, scraping over the earth's surface, which was lubricated by their own juices. In some cases the crystalline bull-dozers manhandled immense boulders, pushing them thousands of miles before dropping them on Konza's doorstep. In other cases, glaciers ground large chips of the earth into dust, which then washed or blew miles away from their origins.

A major effect of glaciation was the alteration of the climate in adjacent areas. The spreading glaciers extended the polar regions, bringing cold, moist climates very far south. As the glaciers inched south, they pushed ahead of them the horizontal bands of habi-tats that form latitudinal belts across the continents. Not all of the habitats in North America were pushed southward, and not all of those that preceded the glaciers moved as uniform bands. Instead, the habitats tended to pile up in southern North America, with the habitat bands becoming narrower the farther south the glaciers trav-eled. During the Nebraskan glacial advance, which came within a few hundred miles of Konza, the tallgrass prairie was visited by oak woodlands as the local environment briefly became cooler and more mesic.

The Kansan glacial episode, however, brought the northern spruce forests with it, right onto Konza itself. At this time, which was probably the coldest period in the history of Konza, the landscape would have resembled the northern boreal woods of Canada, with their complement of plants and animals. The glacier must have been an imposing sight, glinting down at Konza from the northeast.

Two more major advances, the Illinoian and the Wisconsinan, fol-lowed the Kansan, then departed from the Great Plains less than twelve thousand years ago. The Illinoian probably came close enough to turn Konza Prairie briefly into the Konza Oak Woodland, but the Wisconsinan again pushed spruce forests onto Konza for a few thousand years. In the wake of the lingering death of the Wisconsinan glacier, Konza underwent a progression of changes characteristic of a region that is withdrawing from the effects of a nearby glacier. Glaciers advance and retreat slowly, integrating the climatic shifts that lead to their birth and death, but the succession of habitats in lands adjacent to the glacial fronts are quite rapid and abrupt. By analyzing pollen from core samples, scientists can calculate the "halflife" of each habitat as it passes through an area—that is, the time it takes for one half of the pollen in a sample to change from plants characteristic of one habitat type to those characteristic of the replacement habitat. Some of the changes were remarkably rapid. For example, core samples from sediments deposited during the retreat of the Wisconsinan glacier reveal that the halflife of the spruce-pine forests was on the order of 90 to 175 years, once the recession had begun. The subsequent transition to oak woodlands may have taken from 140 to 200 years, and the conversion to grasslands, another 150 years, making the total time for transition from a glacier-dominated boreal forest to a relatively arid grassland less than 600 years. In another area, the halflife of the transition from pine to oak was a mere 77 years, and the complete change to grasslands was accomplished in less than 200 years. Equivalent studies have not been done on Konza, but it probably sustained similarly rapid environmental changes in the face of the retreating glaciers.

As forests and woodlands disappeared from the central plains, the vegetation changed rapidly. In some cases, plants that had been subordinate members of the forest communities spread in importance and became dominant species. The region also became a magnet, attracting plants, especially grasses, that were adapted to take advantage of the newly created conditions. The flow of inhabitants into the tallgrass prairie was not, however, an orderly, smooth process. Some of the immigrants came from a thousand miles away, from the central Carolinas or the northeast, and had to negotiate for space in the new neighborhood. While the central plains were settling down after the glaciers had left, environmental conditions were very unstable. Over hundreds of years, immigrants flowed into and out of the central plains, with some transient species ending up in Wyoming and Colorado or flowing northeastward as far as Pennsylvania. Eventually, those with the greatest affinities for the region anchored the newly developing community. The tallgrass prairie, as we know it today, is very young and has acquired virtually all of its inhabitants from other areas; it has few natives among its flora and fauna. If the few tiny remnants of the tallgrass prairie can be preserved, we might see, in another million or so years, indigenous plants and animals that can rightly be called natives.

At the time of the retreat of the last glacier, many animals moved in to take advantage of the young grasslands. Dozens of species of grasshoppers flocked in to exploit the abundant food that the prairies offered. Many birds may have passed through, but few stayed, being deterred by the lack of trees in which to perch, hide, feed, or nest. A vast array of mammals could have been found in the grasses of primal Konza. Under the canopy of grass would have scurried voles, woodrats, and mice. Other rodents that are now found in Canada and Alaska would have found their southern limits near Konza. Coyotes, foxes, and weasels would have been in hot pursuit of the rodents. Deer and pronghorn would have grazed on the incipient prairie, along with bison and elk. Badgers and pocket gophers would have excavated the soil, looking for food, while muskrats and beavers might have busied themselves along stream banks and persistent pools of water.

Many of the animals, however, would have looked peculiar or out of place, even if we could recognize them as relatives of today's creatures. Camels and horses roamed the North American grasslands at this time, before migrating to other continents to continue their evolutionary radiations. Peccaries (wild pigs), musk ox, gigantic bison, and pronghorns that had four, rather than two, horns were present. Giant armadillos and predecessors of today's rabbits are known from fossil beds near Konza, as are large beavers, dire wolves, and ungainly sloths the size of small automobiles. Two of the most characteristic animals were the mammoths, which inhabited the grasslands, and their forest relatives the mastodons.

Some of the mammals remained in North America; pronghorns evolved here and still occur only in North America. Descendants of the giant beavers remain, as do the modern descendants of primitive rabbits. Others among these early residents migrated across temporary land bridges to South America or to Asia and thence to Africa, where they continued to flourish and experiment with new forms and habits. For example, horses, after arising in North America, emigrated to Africa, only to return in a domestic role with the Spaniards thousands of years later. Musk ox followed the glaciers' retreat north and now inhabit the circumpolar regions of the Northern Hemisphere. Camels became domesticated after reaching the Old World, and armadillos moved to South America before staging a return north during the last millennium. Giant sloths and the relatives of contemporary elephants became extinct.

A number of the mammals that were present on Konza during and after the last glacial advance found temporary refuge to the south and west, but most of them eventually succumbed, thus forming the pattern of massive extinctions that is characteristic of the late Pleistocene. A number of theories have been proposed to explain the disappearance of so many forms, especially large mammals, which met their demise between ten and fifteen thousand years ago. One of the most intriguing and controversial hypotheses proposes that the ones that died were associated with the initial invasion of humans into North America at about that same time. Tribes in northwestern Europe and Siberia had survived as mammoth hunters for thousands of years prior to arriving in North America. During the last glacial epochs, when huge amounts of water were tied up in glaciers and the sea level was low, these hunters traversed the Bering land bridge between what is now Siberia and Alaska, perhaps as early as thirty thousand years ago. These earliest immigrants may not have been able to move south because massive glaciers blocked their advance, although some may have skirted the glaciers in boats and moved south along the coast; hence, they may not have been as successful as later arrivals. Eventually, as the glaciers receded, the path southward cleared, and these primitive hunters flowed into a region replete with large mammals that were suitable to their needs. To these hunters, mammoths were what bison would be to Plains Indians many centuries later.

The earliest North Americans would have brought with them the skills they had developed in the Old World, skills that could have been directed against populations of naïve mammals that had never had to cope with such prudent predators. Under most natural circumstances, predators and their prey evolve counterstrategies to one another's ploys in the thrust and parry of the evolutionary process. But North America was rapidly invaded by hunters who had a new implement—a brain capable of developing the techniques and tools for the efficient killing of prey. Even if humans were not directly responsible for actually killing the last of these great beasts, they may

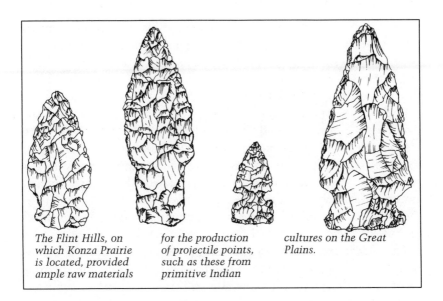

The Flint Hills, on which Konza Prairie is located, provided ample raw materials for the production of projectile points, such as these from primitive Indian cultures on the Great Plains.

have tipped the finely tuned balance in favor of extinction in a way that, when coupled with other natural forces, forced the extinction of a suite of large mammals.

There is almost no information that will allow us to make a characterization of all of the prehistoric peoples who inhabited Konza Prairie, though anthropologists have identified groups of natives who may have populated the region. We can use the "paintbrush" technique to deduce what natives in the area of Konza might have been like, beginning with the original immigrants ten to twelve thousand years ago. To do so, we must connect the dots between various sites that clearly represent the same cultures during corresponding time periods and "paint" in the range by assuming that the Indians in the appropriate habitats within the region would have exhibited similar traits. Of course, the farther back in time one peers, the less is known; so a broad brush and a good imagination must frequently be used in determining what the early natives on Konza might have been like.

It is important to be able to date materials that are excavated from sites. This can be done most accurately by using radiometric dating techniques. These methods take advantage of the uniform rate of decay of radioactive elements in substances such as charcoal from ancient hearths. A comparison of the ratio of unaltered material to decayed material reveals how old the charcoal is within a small range of error. Artifacts can also be dated by comparing them to other artifacts that already have accurate dates associated with them. For example, many geographic locations and time periods exhibit characteristic pottery fragments or projectile points that allow newly discovered items to be dated by comparison.

Even when a small amount of material is available for analysis, hypotheses can be proposed about the nature of the people who were responsible for the gathering or creation of the artifacts. For example, some ancient Indians in Kansas possessed ornaments made of sea shells that were native only to Florida. It would be reasonable to assume that these Indians either had traveled to the gulf to collect the shells or had traded for them. Either case would indicate travel or trade or both.

The oldest artifacts from the central plains are from the Paleo-Indian period, approximately 12,000 to 8,000 years ago. The environment in northeastern Kansas would still have been moist and cool, supporting a variety of ancient creatures, including mammoths, to attract the attention of immigrating hunters. Projectile points (spearpoints and arrowheads) characterize these early groups, because they are plentiful and persistent in the soil. These early immigrants used typical Clovis points. These spearpoints, which were first described from near Clovis, New Mexico, have been fluted by human hands along both sides of their entire length. Many Clovis points have been discovered in Kansas, but their origin is difficult to pinpoint, because most of them were found in stream deposits that originated far from their deposition site. Somewhat later, Folsom points, which are smaller and fluted only along the edges of the blade, are more characteristic.

A single archeological site in western Kansas includes evidence that a Paleo-Indian group killed and butchered at least ten bison. These early hunters were no doubt good naturalists, familiar with the habits of their prey. They may have been able to separate unwitting bison or mammoths from the main herd and then dispose of them one at a time. In some instances, the Indians may have driven large prey into deep mud or water and killed them as they foundered. Paleo-Indian sites provide some evidence of kills near water holes and of repeated visits to the same hunting sites.

The lance points that were used for hunting were attached to a bone shaft, which in turn was lashed to a wooden staff. As many as eight points have been found associated with the remains of a single mammoth kill, suggesting that it took that many projectiles to bring the animal down. Many items other than bison and mammoths were used as food, indicating that the hunter-gatherers were probably opportunistic in their feeding. Around Konza they may have sought seeds, nuts, and berries to augment their diet of fish, mollusks, and miscellaneous smaller mammals.

The size of these groups of natives may have been restricted to twenty-five or thirty (probably an extended family) by hunting practices that limited kills to one or a few animals at a time. Later in the Paleo-Indian period, hunting efficiency apparently increased, and groups may have more than doubled in size. These later groups also employed a greater variety of points and possibly the atlatl, a throwing stick used to increase the power with which a lance could be thrown. Mass kills and entrapments also boosted hunting efficiency. Sites in Nebraska and Wyoming indicate that from one hundred to three hundred bison could be killed at one time by entrapment or by running frightened animals off a precipice. It has been estimated that if three hundred bison were killed, the total yield would be almost thirty tons of meat, five tons of miscellaneous meat by-products (such as viscera and tallow), thousands of bones for tools, and enough hides to clothe an entire tribe.

The bands of Indians were probably nomadic, although they may have settled down for certain parts of the year. Many of the projectile points that are associated with these early tribes came from areas outside their normal range, which suggests that they traded with inhabitants of other regions.

Most of these early groups arrived from the northwest, but by late in the Paleo-Indian period, eastern Kansas came under the influence of Indians associated with the Dalton complex. These Indians came from the east, primarily from Arkansas, and were more typical of groups living in woodland rather than open areas. They were apparently quite mobile, so it is not unreasonable to imagine that they occasionally traversed Konza Prairie.

The next six thousand years represent the Archaic period, during which the environment around Konza probably reached its warmest and driest since the retreat of the Wisconsinan glacier. Such conditions would have made food gathering inefficient, perhaps forcing many of the Indians away from Konza. Indeed, population levels declined significantly during this time. The Indians that remained, however, were descendants of the earlier Paleo-Indian bands. They retained their hunting-and-gathering economy, but may have relied more on such game as deer, pronghorn, and fish; their reliance on bison and mammoths declined as the populations of their previous prey died out or retreated elsewhere during the long drought. The bands were apparently quite small, no more than a few families, and traveled between locales in patterns dictated by the seasons. Evidence from one site just north of Konza indicates that the Indians ate deer, bison, raccoons, skunks, squirrels, pocket gophers, woodrats, moles, and cottontail rabbits, along with ducks, geese, hawks, turtles, snakes, and fish, including catfish, suckers, and bullheads.

A variety of tools were produced from available raw materials, including awls, punches, knives, and scrapers. One major development by this group was the use of fire-forged chert for projectile points, a process that enhanced the stone's workability. Of course, the chert for which the Flint Hills are named was abundant on Konza, providing an ample supply of stones to be worked.

The next eighteen hundred years are known as the Ceramic period, which is broken into early, mid, and late segments. As the name implies, these periods included the development of ceramic technology and the widespread use of pottery. At the beginning of this period, Archaic people inhabited all of Kansas. About two thousand years ago, Hopewellian Indians, characteristic of eastern woodland tribes, moved into the region near present-day Kansas City, where they maintained a flourishing society. Splinter bands from this society probably moved along the Kansas River as far as Konza Prairie and mixed with the existing Archaic groups. The Hopewellians brought domesticated plants and primitive agriculture with them, and they continued to hunt a variety of prey. Long-distance trade was also a feature of this group, as evidenced by shell beads from Florida and ornaments made of copper from near Lake Superior.

Aspects of the Hopewellian influence were probably incorporated into the Archaic tradition to form the Plains Woodland group during the Early Ceramic period. By the Mid Ceramic period (500 to 1,000 years ago) the Plains Woodland group may have come under the influence of Caddo culture from Texas and Oklahoma; this mixture eventually evolved into the central-plains tradition. In the area of Konza Prairie the Central Plains Indians increased their use of agriculture and developed scattered farmsteads, small hamlets, and villages. Their dwellings were built on terraces overlooking major drainages or, frequently, up smaller side creeks. The tribes were primarily farmers, who had relatively little contact with people outside their local area.

Late in their tenure near Konza, the Central Plains Indians developed into the first distinguishable tribe in Kansas, the Pawnee, who, along with the Wichita to the south, were residents in Kansas as early as one thousand years ago. They tended gardens, raising squash, beans, and corn, and hunted bison during two major hunts each year.

It was the Pawnee whom the Kansa Indians (for whom Kansas and Konza Prairie are named) encountered when they first infiltrated the region around Konza Prairie about five hundred years ago. The origins of the Kansa are difficult to discern, but most recently they had moved west from what is now Missouri and Nebraska; prior to that, their native lands were probably in the upper Midwest. Arrowheads, pottery, and other household implements characteristic of the Kansa have been retrieved from sites within a few miles of Konza, so it is reasonable to assume that these tribesmen coursed over Konza during their travels and hunting trips.

Europeans first visited the central plains in the century after the Kansa arrived. Coronado entered western Kansas in 1541, and French traders came during the early eighteenth century. It is not clear what impact the earliest European visitors had on the natives, but the Kansa eventually were influenced by the waves of new settlers passing through their ancestral lands. In 1825 the Kansa were placed on a reservation that included Konza Prairie, and they remained there until they were deported to Oklahoma Territory in 1873.

Between 1850 and 1880 a series of military posts was constructed in Kansas to control hostile Indians and to protect major east-west trade routes. Fort Riley, 15 miles (24 kilometers) west of Konza, was constructed in 1853 and is still a major military installation. By 1871 the Santa Fe rail line extended west to Newton, and the link to Kansas City, with spurs to Manhattan, was completed in 1875. As American pioneers pushed westward, many settled in Kansas, and between 1870 and 1880 the population almost tripled (from 364,000 to 996,000); an additional 500,000 had swelled the population by the turn of the century.

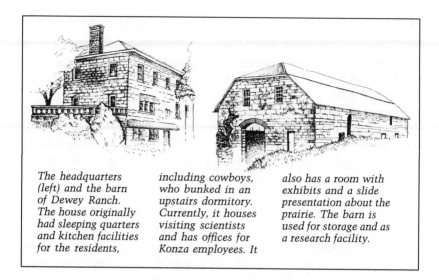

The headquarters (left) and the barn of Dewey Ranch. The house originally had sleeping quarters and kitchen facilities for the residents, including cowboys, who bunked in an upstairs dormitory. Currently, it houses visiting scientists and has offices for Konza employees. It also has a room with exhibits and a slide presentation about the prairie. The barn is used for storage and as a research facility.

Beginning in 1872, C. P. Dewey, a speculator who had quickly made a fortune buying and reselling property that had been devastated by the 1871 Chicago fire, began to buy large parcels of land in Kansas. Among the purchases was a 10,000-acre (4,048-hectares) plot south of Manhattan, much of which now makes up Konza Prairie. Dewey was followed by his son Chauncy, as the family continued its land acquisitions, eventually obtaining over thirty pieces of land by 1926. Almost three-quarters of the purchases occurred during the 1880s, most in 1887 and 1888. There had been a severe blizzard in 1886, and many of the local ranchers had been forced to sell their land at prices the Deweys could readily afford. The parcels were distributed among several Dewey family members and various holding companies, but eventually the owners succumbed to the same misfortunes that had brought them much of their holdings in the first place. In 1930, all of the Dewey land that is now part of Konza Prairie was transferred to the mortgage holder by the Riley County sheriff, and in that same year it was sold to W. D. Johnson and A. M. Clayton. Two years later the portion of Konza Prairie that lies in Riley County was sold to George Davis, and in 1957, its ownership passed to Frank R. McDermand III and the Pullman Cattle Company. McDermand sold Dewey Ranch to Dr. David McKnight in 1972.

In the late 1950s, Lloyd Hulbert of Kansas State University headed a group of nine faculty members from five departments who began to look for a parcel of land that could serve as a preserve and as a natural laboratory for research into the processes responsible for the origin and maintenance of the tallgrass prairie. Hulbert spent almost two years surveying different tracts that might be suitable, most of which had very little habitat in deep soils that had not been plowed. Eventually, after much negotiation, a parcel was purchased by the Nature Conservancy and was then traded to Mrs. Elizabeth Cobb Landon, wife of the former governor and presidential candidate, for the desired acreage. This original portion, consisting of 916 acres (371 hectares) in Geary County north of Interstate 70, was transferred to the stewardship of Kansas State University by the Nature Conservancy on 30 December 1971.

Several watersheds that ran across the original tract originated on the adjacent Dewey Ranch, so it became clear that the acquisition of the adjacent parcel was important for preservation and research efforts. In 1975 the Nature Conservancy began negotiations with Dr. McKnight in an effort to secure Dewey Ranch, which culminated in 1977 with a trade of Dewey Ranch for land in Oklahoma that was worth approximately $3.6 million. An additional 480-acre (194-hectare) segment was added in 1977, bringing the total to 8,616 acres (3,487 hectares). The donor for the purchases had wished to remain anonymous, but after her death in 1979 it was revealed that Katharine Ordway had been the source of support for the preservation of Konza, as she had been for so many other native-prairie tracts in America. A plaque near the ranch's headquarters now honors her support.

Today, Konza Prairie stands as a benchmark of preservation and research in a habitat that has virtually disappeared from North America. No one feature of Konza is unique, but the combination of its flora and fauna, the efforts made to preserve and maintain its original status, and the ongoing research efforts to understand the processes that occur on a tallgrass prairie make it a significant resource. Events beginning billions of years ago set in motion the long and meandering process that has created Konza as it is today. In attempting to understand Konza Prairie and to preserve it, we must be aware that if the past is any clue to the future, the tallgrass prairie will eventually erode away to the sea, be covered by vast oceans, and host a whole new array of creatures.

EVOLUTION

For centuries, people have been struck by the awesome diversity and integrity of the natural world. Over two million organisms are known, and at least that many have yet to be identified and classified. Attempts to explain why there are so many species and how they came to be so different have occupied the thoughts and efforts of naturalists since the early Greek and Chinese philosophers first delved into the subject. In 1859, Charles Darwin published On the Origin of Species by Means of Natural Selection, a summary of his explanations of what has come to be known as the theory of evolution. Darwin's curiosity about why there are so many species was stimulated during his five-year voyage around the world on the HMS Beagle in the 1830s. Everywhere Darwin disembarked he saw new and wonderful sights, and he felt compelled to attempt an explanation. For over thirty years he accumulated ideas and evidence; but he was prompted to write his book only when another naturalist, Alfred Wallace (who lived for one year in Manhattan, Kansas, early in this century), wrote to him expressing ideas surprisingly close to those Darwin had been contemplating for decades. Papers expressing the ideas of the two scientists were read consecutively at a meeting of the Linnean Society in London in 1858, and Darwin's book was published the following year.

The theory of evolution has become the cornerstone of modern biological thought. Biologists usually deal with proximal questions about nature by asking what patterns exist and how different processes work. The theory of evolution, however, stimulates questions about why things are the way they are—what are the ultimate causes of the diversity of life? Most scientists no longer consider these important questions to be mystical and religious ones, as they had before Darwin's theory explained the origin of species and the maintenance of biotic diversity on earth. Although scientists continue to debate the actual details of the evolutionary process and the origin of new species, most of them accept this simple and logically compelling theory.

There are three main components to the process of evolution. The first is that tremendous variation exists in traits among individuals of a species. The second feature is that many more individuals are produced each generation than can be supported by the environment. *The third is that those individuals that possess the most successful suite of traits are the most likely, on average, to survive and thus to pass those traits on to the next generation. The observation, therefore, that populations become better and better adapted to their physical and biological environment through time is merely a simple arithmetic consequence of variation, excess numbers of individuals, and the natural selection of the most fit. There is no goal to evolution; it is a passive process involving inherited traits that are forced through the natural sieve of overpopulation. It is conceivable that populations would continue to be refined by natural selection to the point of near perfection, but the environment is constantly changing, offering new barriers to individual organisms.*

To consider the first proposition of evolution, that of natural variation, all we have to do is look around us. No two individuals are identical, whether we are considering grasses, mice, or humans. There are two sources for this variation. The first originates in sexually reproducing organisms (asexually reproducing organisms form fairly exact copies of themselves). The traits expressed in each individual are governed to a large extent by the genetic information given to them by their parents. In sexual reproduction, the genetic complement of a male and a female are halved and doled out into gametes (eggs in females; sperm in males). When the gametes fuse at fertilization, the embryo has obtained one-half of its genome (genetic make-up) from each parent. The genes are randomly dealt into the gametes of the parents, generating some variation, and the mixing of genomes at conception causes further variation. Although any child may have its "mother's eyes" or its "father's chin," each individual is distinct, except for identical siblings.

Mutations are the ultimate source of variation in organisms. Mutations are changes in the basic genetic structure of a gene or series of genes that result in a genetic blueprint that is different from what it would have been had the mutation not occurred. Mutations can occur spontaneously (at an average rate of about one per million genes each time a cell divides), or they can be induced by a wide array of mutagenic agents, such as x-rays or certain chemicals. Mutations in ordinary cells rarely cause problems, because a single cell in a vast population of cells has little influence on the success of an individual. If a mutation occurs in an ovum (egg) or sperm that forms an embryo, however, it is passed on to all of the cells of the

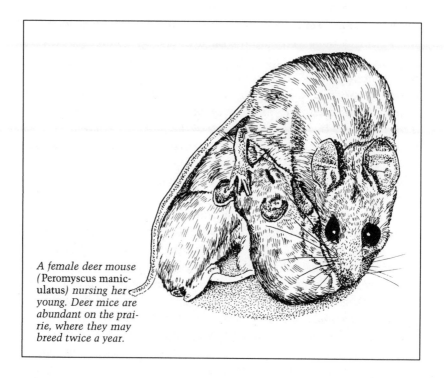

A female deer mouse (Peromyscus maniculatus) nursing her young. Deer mice are abundant on the prairie, where they may breed twice a year.

offspring of the next generation. The vast majority of such mutations are deleterious, as they occur in the midst of a reasonably competent set of genes. Occasionally, however, a mutation occurs that actually benefits an individual, increasing its chance of success compared to members of the population that do not have the new gene. If the new gene is sufficiently advantageous, it will gradually spread in the population over many generations as its proprietor outreproduces other less-well-endowed individuals.

The second feature of evolution relies on the fact that more individuals are produced each generation than can be supported by the available resources. There is a finite limit to the amount of biological energy that can be produced on earth. This limit is set by the abundance of green plants and their efficiency at converting the sun's energy into biological energy. If the availability of food in an area increases, it tends to increase arithmetically, following a sequence of one-, two-, or threefold increases. Population size, however, increases geometrically, following a geometric sequence such as 2, 4, 8, 16, and so forth (that is, two parents may produce two offspring, which, in turn, produce two each, and so forth). Clearly, in just a few generations a population that started at near zero would overwhelm the capacity of the environment to support it. For example, if one pair of mice produced four offspring, and each of those produced four, and so on, for just ten generations (as little as five years for mice on Konza), the total number of mice would be 1,048,576. Some attrition occurs because of death due to old age, but in natural populations, many will eventually die for lack of food or space or in interactions with competitors and predators. If each pair of parents produces two reproductively successful offspring, thereby replacing themselves, the population will remain at equilibrium (again, this is a mathematical phenomenon and does not reflect any intention on the part of the parents). Among organisms that have high mortality rates, those that produce thousands of offspring would be at an advantage compared to those that produce fewer offspring. For example, frogs on Konza may lay thousands of eggs in each clutch and may lay several clutches a year. Grasshoppers may lay 30 to 150 eggs several times a year, and some individual plants produce hundreds or thousands of seeds annually. Some animals, such as mammals and birds, beat the odds against producing successful offspring by having many fewer but by investing heavily in each one—nursing, feeding, and protecting their offspring until they can survive on their own. Even so, more are produced than can survive to breeding age.

The third feature of evolution is natural selection, a process by which less fit individuals are disproportionately eliminated from a population, eventually reducing the population size to a level that can be supported by the environment. Again, this is a passive process, with no goal. Simple arithmetic reveals that individuals with characteristics that give them even slight advantages (in such features as feeding, nesting, escaping predators, finding mates, etc.) over their competitors will tend to leave more offspring, and hence more of their successful genes, than those that do not possess such traits. Recall in the previous example of the mice, over one million offspring would be produced if each of ten generations had four successful offspring. If a competing mouse (i.e., one with a competing suite of genes) had only three successful offspring for each of ten generations, the total would be 59,049, a significant disadvantage compared to the more prolific mouse. This huge difference *within just ten generations illustrates the numerical advantage of successful individuals.*

Natural selection, therefore, tends to favor those individuals whose traits make them reproductively successful. This is true only if all else is equal. Numerous events in the environment can claim the lives of even the most successful individuals. For example, an especially swift rabbit might be able to easily escape from a coyote, but if the rabbit is pursued by a lightning bolt, no matter how swift the rabbit may be, it will be killed. Thus, the effects of natural selection are only obvious over many generations of countless individuals as the law of averages exerts its influence.

Humans have used an analog to evolution for thousands of years, artificially selecting among domestic plants and animals for traits deemed desirable. Ranchers, farmers, and plant and animal breeders regularly select from among the natural variation of organisms to choose the livestock, crops, or pets that are endowed with the most sought-after features. Ranchers seek to increase the productivity of their herds by choosing livestock that produce the most meat in the shortest period of time. Farmers select crops with high yields and resistance to disease. There are more than one hundred breeds of dogs, all of which came from a few progenitors that were artificially selected over the centuries for traits attractive to their owners. In evolution, natural selection replaces artificial selection, yielding individuals that are more closely adapted to the rigors of their environment than those individuals that do not make it through the selection process.

New species occur when interbreeding populations become reproductively isolated, perhaps as the result of mountain building or the widening of a canyon. The local conditions of competition, predation, and the physical environment that are experienced by the two subpopulations will eventually become quite different. As the two subpopulations change in response to their distinct local environments, they will gradually diverge in important characteristics. Subsequently, enough differences will accumulate between the populations to prevent interbreeding even if they were to be reunited, thus fulfilling the standard criterion for the definition of new species.

The general trend is to have more small species than large species of organisms: there are thousands of species of insects on Konza, somewhat fewer species of rodent-sized animals, and very few species of animals the size of dogs. This is probably because large organisms have broad requirements, whereas small species may be able to specialize on some tiny subset of the environment. For example, a bison requires a lot of space; it would be difficult to divide up the prairie into many subunits suitable for many species of this type of grazer. The greatest diversity of large grazers today occurs on the grasslands of Africa, but even there the number pales compared to the number of insect herbivores. Smaller herbivores, such as grasshoppers, can specialize on much-smaller niches; therefore, many more of them can be squeezed onto the prairie. One mouthful of forage for a bison on Konza could include several species of plants, while a similar bite for a grasshopper might include only a small part of one plant.

Evolution is an ongoing process. With no attainable goal, natural selection continues through the ages, sorting through each generation's nominees for success. On Konza Prairie, some of the important selective forces to which native species have adapted are drought, fire, herbivores, and predators, which are constantly impinging on the success of individual inhabitants. Over the next thousands and millions of years, these forces will continue to mold the prairie community, eliminating some evolutionary experiments while favoring others, leading to more and more prairie specialists. The residents can never relax, however, for as surely as Konza changed from a woodland to a prairie, it will eventually become something else, forcing the inhabitants to cope with a new array of selective forces.

3 / Patterns and Patches

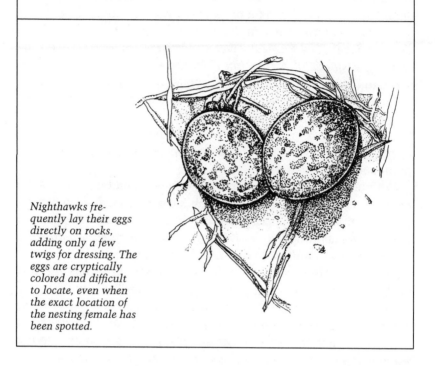

Nighthawks frequently lay their eggs directly on rocks, adding only a few twigs for dressing. The eggs are cryptically colored and difficult to locate, even when the exact location of the nesting female has been spotted.

A MAJOR FEATURE OF NATURAL HISTORY IS THE SEARCH FOR patterns. There are many recognizable patterns on Konza Prairie: the grasslands, the forests, and the streams, with their associated flora and fauna, and distinct seasons, characterized by changes in the weather. Other patterns, the ones that scientists spend most of their time investigating, are less obvious but just as significant and exciting. Physical and biological processes are responsible for generating the structure we see in the natural world; they are the independent driving forces that regulate and order the patterns seen on Konza and elsewhere. Humans are quick to discover underlying patterns in nature, and they seem to have an innate curiosity about what processes are responsible for the patterns. The recognition of structure usually precedes an understanding of the processes that are responsible for the pattern. Patterns frequently dawn on us when several features of the discernible world all of a sudden make sense in light of our past observations. Once a pattern is clear, once we have answered the "what" questions, we want to proceed to the "why" questions, ascertaining what physical and biological characteristics led to the observed pattern.

Patterns occur in both space and time. The primary habitat types of Konza (grassland, forests, and streams) overlap very little and occur in distinct configurations that are obvious, identifiable features of the landscape. Other patterns involve characteristic time frames, such as night and day or seasons of the year. Patterns in both space and time occur on a range of scales; they are only obvious when viewed in an appropriate frame of reference. Although we usually attempt to put our observations into a familiar frame of reference (e.g., "about as long as a football field"), much of what goes on in the universe is outside our normal guideposts. Patterns, both on a cosmic scale and on a microscopic scale, are difficult to grasp, and events that occur instantaneously or over immense periods of time are likewise incomprehensible. Nevertheless, patterns that exist on these scales are important to the natural world.

Konza Prairie is approximately 4 miles wide and 3.5 miles long (6.4 by 5.6 kilometers). Viewed from above, it would first be detectable from several hundred miles in space, within the distances that astronauts travel in orbits around the earth. From 20 miles (32 kilometers) up, Konza's actual boundaries are visible: roads outline it to the east, south, and north, and the western boundary is visible as a contrast between the heavily grazed pastures and the ungrazed prairie. The texture of the landscape is also visible as wrinkles in the surface that are dozens or even hundreds of feet high. A view from an airliner at between 30,000 and 40,000 feet (9,150–12,200 meters) in altitude reveals major habitat distinctions between the mottled grasslands and the precise rows in agricultural fields, as well as ribbons of water outlined by trees.

Humans are most familiar with the spatial scale of Konza Prairie that they see from a passing automobile. At this scale, Konza appears as thick brush strokes in impasto of grass stems, with shrubs and trees lining the dendritic water courses. Individual organisms are sometimes visible: a defoliated, arthritic oak might stand out against the winter sky, or a hawk might course over the prairie canopy in search of a meal. But we would still tend to view Konza as a group of indistinguishable individuals forming monotonous populations. It is not until one peers into the prairie, rather than at the prairie, that its major components become obvious. Patches are evident up close, and it becomes clear that the prairie is not composed entirely of grass, that the forests are not all trees, and that the underwater landscapes of the streams are exotic and unfamiliar.

Some of the patches on the prairie originate within the soil. The most barren patches occur where limestone is exposed as the surface erodes away. These rock faces serve as anchors for lichens, and dirt accumulates in small crevices and holes dissolved in the rocks. The dirt patches become microcosms of soil, where tiny plants begin life and attempt to survive, usually unsuccessfully.

Other types of patches occur at disturbance sites—spots that have been excavated or otherwise altered by physical or biotic forces. Depressions that may have served as buffalo wallows are still evident on Konza Prairie, even though it has been a century since bison could have bathed in these shallow basins. The soil beneath the wallows is more compressed and more moist; it also contains different nutrients than do the adjacent prairie soils, and thus hosts a distinct plant community. Excavations made by various mammals produce mounds of dirt whose soil characteristics change as they weather. These mounds also provide some of the few gaps in the grass canopy where seeds can germinate out of the shadow of their parents and other competitors.

Even smaller patches occur where a deer or bison leaves a foot-print, compressing the soil and perhaps altering the local micro-environment just enough to shift the ecological balance in favor of one plant or another. Nutritional hot spots occur where animals urinate or defecate, providing a rich point source of nitrogen and moisture in a depauperate soil. These small patches are usually ephemeral. Heaving caused by frost in winter rejuvenates the soil surface, obliterating signs of footprints except where animals, by continually passing along paths, have compressed the soil. Nutrient-rich patches are immediately utilized by microorganisms and plants in the vicinity; any remaining nutrients leach away, out of reach of most of those who seek them.

We know very little about patches smaller than these. Clearly, however, there are elaborate mosaics of tiny microhabitats beneath rocks and in the shade of a single grass stalk. At this scale, slight differences in exposure to sunlight or drying winds will directly affect localized environmental conditions, impinging on the interactions of microorganisms at the site. We have neither the technology nor the inherent understanding of biological, chemical, and meteorological processes at these levels to get a solid grasp on all that is going on. Interactions within patches at this level are very complex, and they occur between myriad species, many of which are not closely related. This further complicates any analyses, as scientists, who tend to specialize in one or a few groups of organisms, are forced to deal with unfamiliar groups.

The biological world continues into scales that we almost never actually see. All living tissues are composed of cells, the basic building blocks of life. Cells exist in a chemical milieu, and their membranes are constantly being bombarded by migrating molecules. Cells contain tiny organelles, which carry out vital functions. Even smaller than characteristic plant or animal cells are bacteria, fungi, and viruses. These primitive organisms live as parasites on cells, or they expropriate their cells' machinery to the advantage of the microbes. Some of these tiny organisms are well known in a medical setting, but on Konza Prairie they remain elusive and mysterious.

The most obvious spatial patterns on Konza are the major habitat types. True tallgrass prairie dominates Konza, making up 90 percent of its area, while trees cover approximately 6 percent (the remaining 4 percent is in plowed fields maintained by the Agronomy Department of Kansas State University). Creeks and streams form only a tiny portion of Konza Prairie, but their influence extends well beyond their actual path through the grass uplands and gallery forests of the lowlands. All of these habitats are underlain by the invisible underground environment. While this subterranean world is related to what grows above it, it is distinct enough to be considered a separate habitat. Furthermore, the belowground habitat is home to many of the most important and interesting creatures on the prairie. The separation of these habitats is somewhat artificial, because they all impinge on one another, but clearly there are enough differences to generate the patterns unique to each.

Over the last several million years, intermittent and perennial rills have eroded creases in Konza's landscape. These began when tiny rivulets discovered cracks or soft spots in the skin of Konza. Each succeeding rainfall provided water that, as if carrying a chisel and sandpaper, continued the perpetual erosion. As the incipient canyons got deeper and broader, they captured water from wider watersheds, amplifying the erosional effects. Some of the limestone strata that underlie Konza are more resistant to erosion than are others; these persist as flat uplands. They will eventually succumb as erosion flanks them on all sides and eats away at their soft underpinnings, but for the time being, they remain as mesas defining the highest horizons on Konza.

The terrain angles down from the uplands at about 20 degrees, except where bands of relatively resistant limestone jut out to form benches every several dozen feet along the face of the slopes. When viewed in silhouette, the hillsides appear to be giant stairsteps, with as many as ten benches emerging in the 150 feet (46 meters) of altitudinal relief on Konza. At the bottom of the slopes, small streams coalesce into larger ones, eventually finding the low, broad plains of the major drainages on Konza, such as Kings Creek. As the small tributaries course through the uplands and down the slopes, they provide ribbons of moisture to the grasslands. When the accumulation of water is sufficient, shrubs and trees begin to take advantage of that resource. The results are the gallery forests along the major water courses. In addition, numerous springs arise from between the alternating layers of limestone and shale. Water percolates through the shale, dams up above the impermeable limestone, and emerges from perched water tables to form seeps and springs along the limestone benches.

Each of the major habitats on Konza Prairie appears vast when viewed from a distant perspective. Seen edge-on, the prairie extends to the horizon. Viewed from within the gallery forest, the canopy of trees becomes the ceiling of the universe. This holistic view obscures a primary feature of the habitats, however. Close inspection reveals that habitats are composed of small-to-medium-sized patches or microhabitats, each dominated by specific kinds of plants and by a resident fauna, which tend to blend into the habitat when viewed from a distance. If habitats are the themes of the prairie, then patches are the variations, combining in an ecologically concordant fashion, that give the appearance of a unified whole. The patches, and the heterogeneity they engender, are where the action takes place on the tallgrass prairie.

What constitutes a patch depends on the scale of observation. Within the universe, the earth is a patch no larger than the size of the period at the end of this sentence compared to this entire book. On a global scale, the grasslands of the world are also patches that make up a relatively small proportion (approximately 5 percent) of the surface. Within Konza Prairie, patches range from an individual plant and its entourage to plots that are scores of yards square. Patches can be very small, such as shady spots under a small pebble or a crack in a limestone rock. Other patches are composed of amoeboid enclaves of bushes surrounded by the dominating grasses. The derivation of a patch ranges from underlying geological or pedological (soil) processes to the purposeful alteration of the environment by animals. The most dynamic patches on Konza are probably the incidental result of the activity of animals as they pursue their daily activities—a bedding site of a few deer or the cast excrement of an earthworm. Whatever their source and however long they exist, patches are responsible for much of the diversity displayed by the prairie.

The forces that generate patches, as well as the denizens that inhabit them, are not static. Habitats have been described as dynamic mosaics, with multiple, shifting patches making up the landscape. Some patches last for ages, such as the limestone ledges that bulge from Konza's surface. Other patches are ephemeral, from the shallow ponds that fill and drain in the course of one rainstorm to an individual flower that lasts one day. Most patches have life spans somewhere in between, lasting a year to several centuries from birth to death.

The smallest patches are tiny microsites whose characteristics are generated by their immediate physical environment. These sites are affected by minute shifts in the local conditions, such as changes in shade or prevailing winds. Each site possesses characteristics that are beneficial for some organisms but detrimental to others. Small, mobile animals can take advantage of shifting microsites, but less vagile organisms, such as microbes and the seeds of plants, have no real choice as to where they end up. Natural selection may favor anatomical structures that increase the chance of being picked up by the wind, but beyond that, these organisms are victims of fate. The pollen of most prairie plants is wind-borne, probably because the wind is such a reliable vehicle. Furthermore, many prairie plants

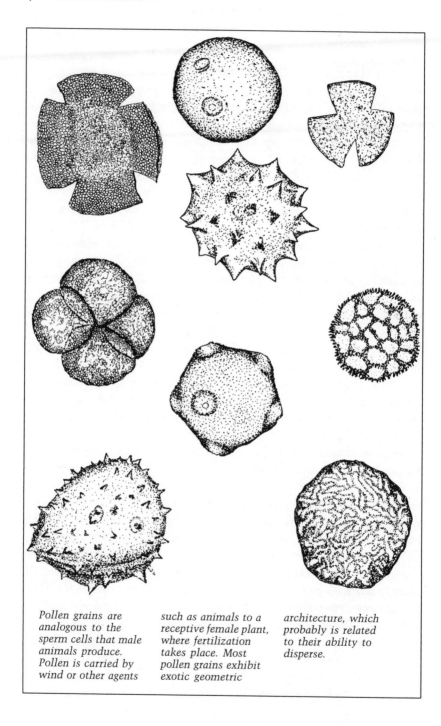

Pollen grains are analogous to the sperm cells that male animals produce. Pollen is carried by wind or other agents such as animals to a receptive female plant, where fertilization takes place. Most pollen grains exhibit exotic geometric architecture, which probably is related to their ability to disperse.

display a full range of passive techniques for dispersing their seeds on the chance that they will land at a beneficent site. Some seeds possess feathery plumes so that they can catch the wind and sail hundreds of feet, while others have evolved sticky coats, in order to hitch rides on passing mammals, who carry the seeds away before grooming them off at another location. Some seeds entice animals to serve as dispersal agents by wrapping themselves in a tasty fruit. These are all strategies that have evolved under pressure to disperse (that is, seeds that moved far enough from their parents and other competitors would be favored over time by natural selection) and to land in a site suitable for germination. In most cases on the prairie, the probability is very low that the seeds of any plant will reach microsites that have their specific requirements. Wherever a seed lands, it must cope with the environment in a small sphere around it. The conditions within that sphere—moist or dry, cool or warm— will determine the success of the dispersal effort.

Individual forbs (nongrass herbs) amidst the surrounding grasses function as small islands of habitat within the prairie. Each contains its own suite of residents, including herbivorous caterpillars and grasshoppers, siphoning aphids, and marauding spiders. Some of the residents spend their entire lives on a single plant, hatching from eggs and feeding on the host for weeks before reproducing. Others migrate to the plant after birth and spend a substantial portion of the remainder of their life cycle there. Still other animals are only brief visitors, stopping by for a sip of nectar or a bite or two of leaf before moving on. Some of these transients meet their fate in a spider web or in the jaws of a praying mantis. Multitudinous tiny herbivores and sucking insects take their toll on the plant. Actually, they are more like parasites than predators, because they usually do not kill the host. The difference between the quick and the dead is slight, however, for a single bison or deer can consume the plant and its occupants in one bite.

Individual plants produce patches of widely differing sizes—many individual plants are no more than a few inches high, whereas horizontal stems of buffalo gourd radiate dozens of feet in all directions. Sunflowers rise to 10 or 12 feet (3 or 4 meters), and tree foliage forms vegetated spheres dozens of feet in diameter. Such islands of habitat obey some of the same biogeographical patterns that oceanic islands exhibit. For example, larger patches house many more individuals than do smaller ones, as well as a higher diversity of species. This is partly due to the target effect—larger patches are going to be colonized more often than smaller ones simply because they make bigger targets. Bigger patches also encompass a greater range of microsites within their umbrella of vegetation, and hence can be utilized by a greater variety of specialists. Furthermore, bigger patches, whether biological or physical, tend to persist longer.

Although patches may consist of individual plants, most plants occur in relative proximity to others of their own species, producing somewhat larger islands of habitat. Several factors conspire to facilitate this arrangement. Plants usually do best on specific types of soil, either because that soil offers some critical nutrient or because it holds the correct amount of water, so plant distributions are often reflections of the underlying soil patches. Such soil patches exist on Konza where past geological events have concentrated soil elements of various types. These pockets of soil become sanctuaries for plants adapted to the specific conditions tendered by the soil at that location. Two basic soil types predominate on Konza: one in the low, moist bottomland; the other in the dry, cherty uplands. Each of these major soils hosts specific plant communities, and local modifications within each soil type generate discrete patches of soil.

Aggregations of plants might also reflect their reproductive and dispersal patterns. Even in plants that have evolved effective schemes to export their seeds, many still fall very near the maternal plants. Thus, once established in a suitable habitat, a single plant, such as a red cedar, may give rise to an island of habitat measuring dozens of yards across. Plants that reproduce by forming clones that send out aboveground or belowground runners are even more likely to produce coherent patches as they form clusters of tightly packed stems. Because the stems are from the same individual (that is, an asexually produced clone), they are technically a single plant, but in most aspects they function as a dense community of numerous individual plants. Big bluestem is the dominant clone on the prairie, as most of its reproduction occurs via underground rhizomes. It has been facetiously suggested that the entire tallgrass prairie is a single big bluestem cloned from an original progenitor. Clones do, however, yield discrete patches of vegetation that may be the entire universe for some of its residents. To newcomers, a clone may represent a resource bonanza. For example, a honeybee that is foraging for nectar

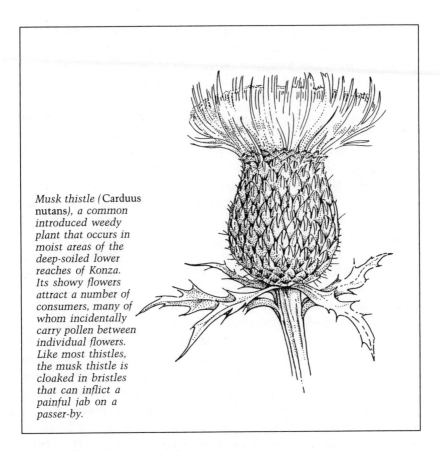

*Musk thistle (*Carduus nutans*), a common introduced weedy plant that occurs in moist areas of the deep-soiled lower reaches of Konza. Its showy flowers attract a number of consumers, many of whom incidentally carry pollen between individual flowers. Like most thistles, the musk thistle is cloaked in bristles that can inflict a painful jab on a passer-by.*

may fly long distances without finding any rewards, but once it encounters a large patch of flowers, it can fill its own needs and may even recruit other members of its colony to the patch to harvest the remaining resources.

An example of the complex interactions within a plant patch on Konza involves the relationship between the number and quality of individuals plants in milkweed patches and the number of seed bugs that inhabit the plants. (In this case, the term *bugs* is not slang for insects, rather it is a specific group of insects belonging to the order Hemiptera.) Of seed bugs that feed on milkweed seeds, the highest numbers occur on individual plants that possess the greatest number of seed pods. A secondary factor affecting seed-bug density is the nearness of other milkweeds that possess many seed pods. About 60 percent of the seed bugs move between plants each day, so those foraging in a patch that contains many productive milkweeds would be favored over those that lingered in less profitable patches. Interestingly, males tend to stay on individual milkweeds that exhibit relatively few pods if that plant is growing amongst plants with high numbers of pods, whereas females show a greater propensity for abandoning plants with low pod production, regardless of what neighboring plants produce. This asymmetry in plant use may be because the males attempt to secure mates by waiting for females on or near plants with many pods. The seed bugs do significant damage to the milkweeds, so there may be selection pressures on the plants to disperse their seeds widely, thus lowering their density and reducing their attractiveness to seed bugs. If the plants and the bugs are too widely dispersed, however, pollinators (in this case, insects, not the wind) will have difficulty locating individuals, and pollination success will be reduced. Clearly, the trade-offs between the various factors that impinge on the success of the plants generate a complicated pattern of patch dynamics for this system.

Patches of ceanothus, buckbrush, choke cherry, plum, and sumac form some of the most distinct habitat islands on the prairie. They emanate from the surrounding vegetation, and as the seasons change, they display subtle hues that outline their boundaries. Several of the shrub species begin as islets, when a single seed germinates and matures for several years. If such solitary colonizers can survive, they send out underground stems, gradually expanding their boundaries. This creates an island with a domed outline, in which the center stems are the oldest and tallest, while those on the periphery are young and short.

The shrub patches do not constitute an overriding presence on the prairie, but their ecological significance is greater than their size alone would dictate. For tent caterpillars, these patches provide all of the space and food an individual will require. Several species of birds also take advantage of the riches and protection offered by the shrub patches, including black-billed cuckoos, which are among the few birds that will eat the foul-tasting caterpillars. Bell's vireo nests and feeds in the patches, gleaning the leaves in search of cryptic insects. Brown thrashers build nests in shrubs, harvest the fruits of cherry, dogwood, and mulberry bushes in season, and root around on the ground near the shrubs for seeds and beetles. Rufous-sided towhees exhibit a similar pattern of shrub use. The towhee populations, however, are composed of two subspecies; the western form is a winter resident in the shrubs but moves west to breed, while the other subspecies breeds in the shrubs of Konza but winters farther south. Both forms utilize the same shrubs but at different times of the year. For animals that move over large areas, such as lizards or rabbits, the islands of habitat offer either a refuge from predators or shade from a hot sun.

Lichens form some of the most conspicuous patches in the prairie, where they exhibit growth forms that resemble splotches of paint or leafy lettuce. Their basic color is frequently a gray-green, but lichens are often topped with reds and yellows, especially when the colony is reproducing. Lichens are a strategic alliance between a fungus and either algae or bacteria. The fungi require an organic food source, and the algae or bacteria require constant moisture, resources that would be difficult to secure if the organisms were solitary. As a team, however, they can meet their requirements, resisting environmental extremes while gaining sustenance from minerals in the substrate that they inhabit and from nutrients in falling rain water. Thousands of combinations of lichen symbionts are known to exist, but those on Konza have not been identified.

Most of the obvious patches on Konza are characterized by the dominant plant form in the patch, though some patches center around physical features, such as the limestone outcrops that rim the uplands. Whereas most patches are circular or elliptical, the ledges run as long, linear patches that may extend hundreds of yards. Several rodent species take these as their homes, traveling their length in search of food. The contiguous territories of obligate ledge-dwelling lizards frequently abut, thus leading to exaggerated territorial displays in the dispute for space. Under the ledges, in the fine eolian (wind-borne sand or rock) deposits, the larvae of antlions excavate cone-shaped traps. Adult antlions look deceptively like damselflies, but the antlion larvae, called doodlebugs, are queer-looking assassins with monstrous sicklelike jaws. The larvae orient vertically at the bottom of conical pits. Unsuspecting prey that fall into the pit find the steep, loose walls impossible to ascend, so they eventually slide backward into the waiting jaws of the doodlebug.

Whereas the ledges persist for eons, small pools of water that appear in the pits of the rock face or in the crotches of trees are ephemeral. The water may last for several days or weeks, providing

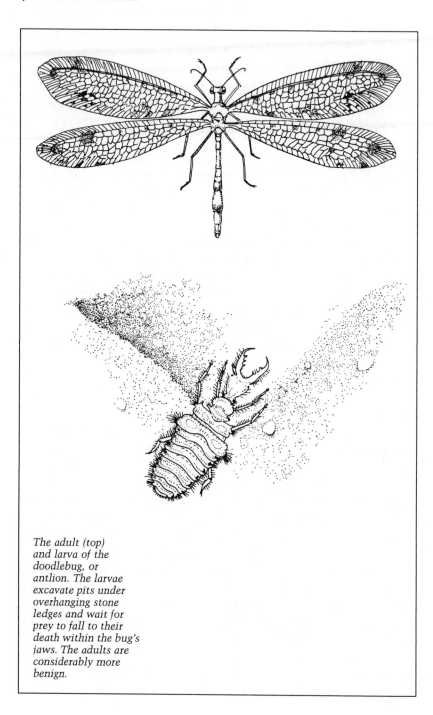

The adult (top) and larva of the doodlebug, or antlion. The larvae excavate pits under overhanging stone ledges and wait for prey to fall to their death within the bug's jaws. The adults are considerably more benign.

just enough time for the water pocket to develop a community of its own. Mosquitoes lay their eggs in the water, singly, in small rafts, or just above the water's edge, where they hatch after heavy rains. The wormlike larvae float upside down at the surface, breathing though tubes protruding from their posteriors. Unlike the quiescent pupae of most insects, mosquito pupae are quite active, hence their name, tumblers. The pupae metamorphose into adults, the females of which must obtain a meal of blood before she can reproduce. Other ephemera, such as tiny crustaceans and insects, also respond to the short-lived habitat and mobilize to take advantage of a burst of productivity.

DISTURBANCE

Various perturbations contribute to the patchiness on Konza Prairie. Until recently, such phenomena were termed disturbances *by ecologists, either because they appeared to be changes in the status quo or because they were extraordinary in their scope or frequency. Over the last two decades, however, ecologists have been forced to reconsider this notion, and most now view disturbances as important integral processes in many ecosystems. For example, fire, which at first certainly appears to be destructive, is currently viewed as a prominent force responsible for maintaining the integrity of the prairie habitat. The same is true in other habitats in which the Smokey-the-Bear mentality of extinguishing every natural fire has led to forests choked with fuel, ready to support a conflagration at the spark of a lightning bolt. Investigators now realize that an unnatural habitat is one in which disturbances have been reduced, altered, or eliminated. That is, disturbance—in its common usage as an alteration with a detrimental effect—may in fact be the absence of such perturbations while regular disruption of the status quo may be the norm.*

Natural habitats are subject to many disturbances by physical and biological forces. Some of the natural disturbances in habitats happen frequently enough to be experienced by plants and animals during their individual lifetimes (such as fires, which probably occurred every few years in the tallgrass prairie). Decades or centuries pass be-

tween other types of disturbances, such as earthquakes and glacial advances, but even these events are inevitable given enough time. If the disturbances are frequent or severe, organisms will either adapt to their effects, move, or become extinct, and some may even take advantage of the circumstance, as grasses have with fire.

For every trauma that visits the prairie, there is an opportunist to take advantage of the circumstance. Fire destroys many organisms in its path, but others survive and flourish in the wake of the inferno. Mounds of dirt piled up by the excavations of rodents smother underlying plants, leaving a barren sere. This seemingly bleak patch is seized by colonizers, because open space is a rare commodity on Konza, and such a disturbance presents some organisms with new opportunities. The pioneer species are frequently weedy plants that share several common traits, such as seeds that disperse widely and have rapid growth rates, which enhance their chances of reaching the patch first and establishing a foothold. On Konza, some of the better colonizers include buffalo bur nightshade, prairie ground cherry, and stickleaf mentzelia. The pioneers may be replaced by a succession of species, each adapted to the changes wrought by their predecessor, until eventually a relatively stable big-bluestem community results. While the replacement is going on, however, new disturbances are yielding fresh opportunities for colonists. Thus, we can imagine that this one simple pattern—which involves a series of disturbances of different ages, populated by plants and animals adapted to each particular successional stage—generates the overall features of the prairie. Alas, the prairie is not this simple; different processes probably occur for each disturbance, amplifying the effect and producing a diverse pattern of patches. Biological succession was once thought to be a straight-line, orderly progression, but more recent evidence suggests that there are many forks in the road to a relatively stable community. By reducing the supremacy of the dominant plants, periodic disturbances return parcels of the prairie to an earlier stage of development, perhaps promoting the success of other biological entrepreneurs.

Brief, localized disturbances can also affect the structure of the prairie community. A single hoofprint alters the local soil environment, perhaps by damaging plants growing on that spot or by altering the ability of the soil to absorb water. Heaving caused by frost in winter makes the soil pop back up, resurrecting it and repair-

ing the isolated damage. A single hoofprint may generate a minor impact, but when multiplied by hundreds of animals and tens of thousands of steps daily, the repercussions can be immense. Furthermore, where animals concentrate their movement on trails, creases in the soil surface may persist for a long time. The paths significantly affect the plant community that can develop along them and may affect erosional patterns for decades.

Some ephemeral patches are produced by localized chemical depositions. The deposition of excrement, either liquid or solid, provides a shot of nutrients, promoting the growth of plants that receive the supplemental dose and allowing them to dominate nearby competitors that were not so fortunate. Thousands of animals, millions of plants, and billions of microbes die on Konza each year, and their carcasses also become nutritional hot spots as they decompose and return elements to the soil.

It is clear that periodic disturbances are part of the natural environment on Konza, although the details of the role that disturbances play in generating and maintaining the diversity of patches, and hence plants and animals, are still poorly understood. On Konza, experiments dealing with fire have shown that when fires occur every two to four years, the result is the highest diversity in the grassland community. Conversely, disturbance rates that are too high, or effects that are too severe, can make existence difficult for most species, thus minimizing diversity. On Konza, floods may occasionally be so severe as to wipe the slate clean, initiating a new round of colonization and maturation of the stream community. As humans, we are probably more comfortable maintaining the status quo, which makes the understanding and acceptance of natural periodic perturbations difficult; but it is now clear that such events are more natural than is their absence.

Many disturbances are the natural consequences of common geological forces on the prairie, but some of the most interesting patches are the result of intentional attempts by animals to alter the environment for their benefit—what might be called "behavioral patches." Secondarily, the behaviors create patches that affect other members of the community. Examples include buffalo wallows, the home ranges and territories of individuals, leks (courting grounds) used by prairie chickens, and the nests and dens of numerous prairie residents.

Shallow basins where buffalo may have wallowed in the mud can still be identified on Konza, even though it has been a century since these grazers loitered in the depressions. Buffalo may have taken advantage of preexisting puddles to initiate their wallowing, apparently to rid themselves of pesky flies, and in the process enlarged the depressions into modest ponds; the wallows may also have served as a meeting place for the implementation of various social interactions between individuals. The soil under the wallows became compacted and received various exudates washed from the animals. The deeper a depression became, the more water it held and the longer it took to dry out. Such physical alterations of the wallow generated patches that supported distinct groups of plants. A line running from the center of a wallow into the adjacent prairie would show a gradual change from more mesic-adapted plants to the typical prairie vegetation in the span of a few yards. The impact is dramatic, and also persistent, as evidenced by the residual wallows still visible on Konza.

Many such small foci of activity are located within an animal's home range, the total area used by an animal. The size of a home range is usually correlated to the size of the animal, with the largest species inhabiting the greatest area. On Konza, the home range of a tent caterpillar is the bush on which it matures, while coyotes range over dozens of square miles and several habitats. Furthermore, carnivores tend to have larger home ranges than do herbivores. The ecological explanations for such relationships are fairly simple. Large animals require large home ranges to fulfill their energetic and nutritional requirements. In addition, the prey of carnivores is more widely dispersed and more difficult to obtain than is forage for herbivores, so the former have larger home ranges than the latter.

An example of such relationships occurs among several coexisting species of birds. Dickcissels are small-to-medium-sized birds that feed on insects during their summer residence on Konza (they consume seeds on their winter ranges in South America). During the summer, their home ranges are about half the size of those of the much-larger eastern meadowlarks, which illustrates the relationship between body size and home-range size. The American kestrel, a small carnivorous falcon, is only slightly larger than a seed-eating bobwhite, but the former has a home range as much as ten times larger than that of the latter. There are exceptions, however. Herbivores that live in herds, such as bison, roam over huge areas during the year, covering hundreds of square miles in their search for nutritious and succulent grass.

Home ranges of individuals tend to overlap, and their boundaries are not exact. If the edges could be viewed from above over a period of time, they would separate and coalesce in an interdigitating pattern. Many animals establish areas of exclusive use by actively defending the borders of their home ranges, securing them against intrusion. Such areas of exclusive use are called territories and are usually somewhat smaller than an entire area (home range) that an animal might use. Territories are usually established to defend an essential resource, such as a nest site or rich source of food. For territoriality to be economical, defending the resource must be more profitable than sharing it with others. Thus, widely spaced, diluted food resources are not worth the costs incurred for their defense. Conversely, patches of dense resources, such as a clump of flowers that provide nectar, may be worth investing time, energy, and the chance of injury to defend. In a number of species, especially birds, males arrive in a breeding area before the females and battle to determine the ownership of parcels of land that include appropriate nesting sites and other resources that will support a female (or several females) and her brood. Once the battle has been resolved, the females will arrive and choose among the males. Males that have procured the most favorable nesting sites, based on features such as food availability, safety from predators, and environmental extremes, will probably be the most successful at gaining a mate and contributing their genes to the next generation. The males of eastern meadowlarks, Henslow sparrows, and dickcissels arrive on Konza a week or more ahead of the females of their species. This is apparently enough time to allow for the assessment of the quality of territories and the negotiations for the resource.

The most dramatic territorial defenses are those involving direct aggression. For example, on Konza, male collared lizards may eventually be driven to physical combat if they are of approximately equal size and vigor. Birds will sometimes attack each other, although the results are rarely fatal. Nevertheless, even moderately aggressive encounters carry with them a chance of injury to the participants; therefore, many animals have evolved ritualistic combat that in-

Meadowlarks are among the most common and characteristic birds on Konza Prairie.

volves bluffing and posturing. During such feigned skirmishes, the individuals use all of their wiles to snooker their opponent into backing down. Collared lizards do push-ups, and they rapidly bob their heads while displaying colorful throat patches; prairie chickens fluff up, making themselves look more formidable than they otherwise would. After a period of assessment, the contests are usually resolved without further escalation. Although this does reduce the chance for inadvertent injury, the combatants have invested heavily in the energetic costs of mock battle. Furthermore, while their attentions are directed toward each other, they are especially vulnerable to predation, a "cost" that is the ultimate price to pay.

Birds have taken ritualized combat to a melodious extreme. Males spend significant amounts of time singing and displaying at the edge of their territories to advertise for mates and to let trespassers know that the patch is occupied. The leitmotif is usually rendered more vigorously when the territories are being set up; then it tapers off to simple reminders broadcast periodically to familiar neighbors. When tape recordings are used on known neighbors to simulate the songs, they attract the attention of a resident as he again attempts to establish his jurisdiction; but recordings of a new intruder incite the territory holder's rage toward the pretender to the patch. If an individual departs or dies, adjacent landlords know almost immediately by the unnatural silence, and they move in to annex the vacated real estate. For breeding territories, as with feeding territories, defense must still be profitable to promote territoriality. In the case of breeding territories, however, profit is measured in opportunities to mate, rather than in caloric or nutritional reward. A male that secures a larger territory might acquire a better mate or more mates, but if the territory is too large, he will not be able to cover the entire area, and he will lose those portions that he cannot defend.

In some cases, the traits possessed by the territorial winner are obvious, even to a human observer. For example, the largest or oldest individuals frequently acquire the best territories, even though it may be very difficult to detect what criteria determine the "best" territory. For example, crayfish that are only fractions of an inch larger than their opponents usually win in brief battles and secure territories on the bottom of ponds and pools on Konza. An obvious advantage such as size can, however, be outweighed by a resident effect; therefore, a small individual that obtains a territory first may be able to hold it against larger interlopers. A territorial crayfish that is 10 to 15 percent smaller than an intruder will usually retain its territories, even though the same intruder would win if the two were placed in a new territory at the same time. In most cases, however, the traits that ensure a male's getting a territory or a mate are not obvious, and we can only guess what a female sees in the victor.

Most territories among birds are maintained by males against other males of the same species. Although the females of a few bird species are known to maintain feeding territories, none do so on Konza. In some cases, males defend territories against other species. This is especially likely when the species compete for the same resources. Spring and summer are the active seasons for territorial formation—when mates are available for courtship and when food resources are dense enough to be economically defended. For most birds, the territories break down in late summer and fall as migration begins and food availabilty decreases below the critical level to make territoriality economically profitable. Some birds of prey, such as owls and hawks, do maintain winter territories on Konza.

The dens and nests that animals construct on Konza are small patches of equable lodging for the residents. They are usually designed to protect the inhabitants from environmental extremes and from predators. Birds build their nests in locations that are relatively safe from predators. The nests are frequently cryptic, or relatively inaccessible. Although the nests are primarily for the birds themselves, many microarthropods inhabit the twig structures, living off the residue of growing nestlings and off of each other. Woodrat dens resemble very large bird nests, being constructed of twigs and sticks hauled back to the nest site. The nest is usually built around some initial support, such as a rock ledge or a tree trunk, and sticks are added to complete the structure. The woven lodge is difficult for a predator to dismantle, and it provides insulation in the winter. Shrews, snakes, and various arthropods are cohabitants with the woodrats in the dens.

Many of the Konza rodents excavate subterranean burrows. The burrows are usually quite simple, with a few tunnels and a nest, located lower than the remaining burrow and insulated with grass, fur, and feathers. Rodents frequently plug up the entrances to their burrows, presumably to keep out predators and chilling breezes. Nevertheless, snakes, lizards, turtles, and frogs sometimes inhabit the burrows with the rodents.

Some animals manufacture their own "dens." Snails along Kings Creek secrete a calcium-carbonate matrix from their skin, which hardens into a shell that they carry with them. When disturbed, they quickly retreat into their shells, making it more difficult for a predator to obtain a meal. Of course, large animals simply ingest the entire animal, shell and all. After the owner dies, the shells may be eaten by a variety of animals as a source of calcium. Several groups of aquatic insects reside in cases that they construct from leaf material or from grains of sand. Their feeding devices extend from the open end, sieving out organic nutrient from the flowing water.

Patches of habitat on Konza are not always immediately obvious, especially where vast expanses of big-bluestem prairie or gallery forest blanket the landscape. Furthermore, the geological and biological processes that are responsible for generating patches are usually quite slow and do not draw the attention of the casual observer. Nevertheless, the formation and the disappearance of patches constitute a vigorous, perpetual process that is responsible for much of the diversity on Konza. Although a major surprise for someone who first peers into the prairie is how diverse and dynamic it is, cognoscenti of the tallgrass prairie seek to understand these patches and the forces that generate them.

4 / Grasslands

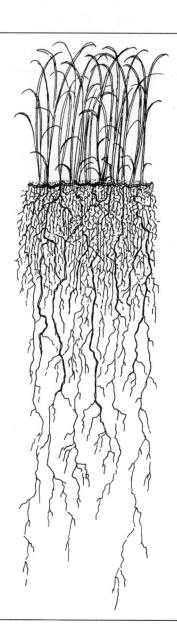

The roots of the
dominant grasses
on Konza form a
dense mat of sod
within a few inches
of the surface. Thick
rhizomes, near the
surface, branch and
spread annually,
while longer roots
extend several feet
below the surface in
quest of nutrients and
moisture.

THE BIOLOGY OF KONZA IS ESSENTIALLY THE BIOLOGY OF grasses. Grasses belong to a major subdivision of the flowering plants called monocots. Monocots have a single cotyledon (the leaf that first emerges from the seed), long leaves with parallel veination, and flower parts in threes or sixes. Most monocots, including the grasses, have no secondary growth to produce woody tissue and to enlarge stem diameters. Furthermore, most of the critical growth tissues (meristems) of grasses are at or below the ground surface, where they are protected from the ravages of the aboveground environment. Dicots (two cotyledons) have leaves with branched veination and flower parts in fours and fives; they can produce woody secondary growth that enlarges the diameter of stems (or trunks). The meristems of most dicots are located at the end of growing shoots, where they are more vulnerable to damage by animals and other environmental factors, although some have adapted to environmental extremes by protecting their meristems. Dicots produce the showy inflorescences that we think of as flowers, although many dicot flowers are inconspicuous; whereas most monocots produce less spectacular flowers (except for such monocots as irises, lilies, and orchids) but are responsible for much of the world's grain production. Wheat, corn, and rice are all members of the grass family.

Grasses are considered to be a very advanced group; they had a long and impressive pedigree prior to their arrival on Konza. There are about seven thousand extant species of grasses, and they occur in virtually every habitat in which plants grow. Some exhibit exotic growth forms, such as bamboo; but most grasses are easily recognized, having the typical narrow leaf with parallel veins and a central flowering stalk, or culm.

Three main forces are associated with the evolution of grasses and the maintenance of grasslands—drought, fire, and grazing by large mammals. Because each of these factors primarily affects the aboveground parts of plants, characteristics that are effective against one should also be helpful in coping with the others. For example, many grasses possess underground stems that can survive fires and that at the same time are protected from drought and grazing. Unfortunately, evidence of all three factors occurs almost concurrently with the origin of grasses, making it impossible to determine if one of these was more important than the others in the evolution of grasses. Regardless, the advantage gained was applicable to each of the environmental conditions.

Most of the evidence suggests that grasses evolved prior to the spread of large grazing mammals, though there were probably grazing dinosaurs around. There are conflicting theories about the habitat in which grasses originated, but the most commonly held supposition is that they evolved in tropical forests more than sixty million years ago, in the late Cretaceous. Their future was in savannas, however, and grasses spread into open parklands as broad regions of the Southern Hemisphere entered a long drying period that may have favored widespread fires. While the origin of grasses was probably on the continent of Africa, South America was only a few hundred miles away, rather than the thousands of miles it has drifted away today, perhaps close enough to allow the ancestors of modern grasses to disperse onto the adjacent continent across land bridges or open water.

The first evidence of grasses in North America is from the early Miocene, about 20 million years ago. Fossils of grasses and grazing mammals appeared concurrently in North America during this epoch, although grasses may antedate grazing mammals on other continents. Most grasses contain silica—essentially, sand—which gradually erodes the hard surfaces of teeth. The grazers that are found in conjunction with grasses have high-crowned (hypsodont) teeth, which are thought to be an evolutionary response to the grinding effect of the silica in grasses. The initial advantage of having silica in the cells is thought to be for the structural support of the long leaves produced by grasses. As grazers evolved in concert with grasses, the silica may have taken on its secondary role of deterring grazing by making it costly to the consumer, in terms both of worn teeth and of reduced digestibility in the gut. Many forbs (succulent green plants that are not grasses) defend themselves with exotic chemicals that poison their consumers or make it so costly to digest or to detoxify the chemicals that the consumption of the plant is a net loss to the herbivore. Very few grasses possess defensive chemicals, so it appears that silica is an adequate defense against most grazers.

One curious phenomenon associated with the interaction between grazers and grasses opens the door for an interesting and controversial hypothesis. Most grasses that are subjected to moderate amounts of grazing exhibit increased growth, so that the total amount of herbage produced in a year is greater in grazed than in ungrazed populations. This would be understandable if the "goal" of a grass were to feed

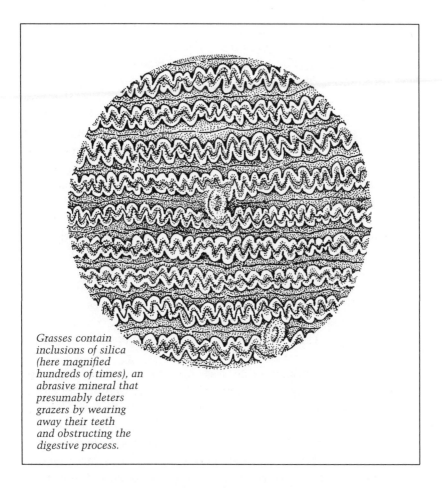

Grasses contain inclusions of silica (here magnified hundreds of times), an abrasive mineral that presumably deters grazers by wearing away their teeth and obstructing the digestive process.

grazers. However, a plant that used its reserves to reproduce more of its own kind, rather than to feed the grazers, would leave more offspring than an altruistic plant and would eventually take over the population. Grazing, however, also promotes clonal growth by stimulating the production of lateral shoots. Thus, it is possible that mild grazing will actually increase the size of individual plants (via cloning) and, hence, evolutionary success. Fires, which exhibit similar effects on plants, may produce the same result.

If this is so, we must still ask why the plant doesn't stimulate itself to reproduce rather than sharing a portion of its tissues with grazers. The answer may be related to the competitive environment in which grasses occur. Because grasses have protected meristems, they can recover from having their leaves and stems cropped by fire and grazing, whereas dicots cannot (this explains why you can mow your lawn regularly but not your roses). Grasses provide abundant food for grazers, thus attracting them to the nearby dicots, which are sensitive to damage by clipping and trampling; they also provide ample fuel for prairie fires. Thus, some scientists hypothesize that grasses may use grazing and fire as a form of pest management by inviting down upon themselves seemingly disastrous events that they can survive but that are devastating to their dicot competitors. It seems like a desperate evolutionary gambit by grasses, but with their elaborate modifications for tolerating drought, fire, and grazing, grasses appear to be able to flourish in an environment that is hostile to dicots. Of course, this is not a conscious effort on the part of grasses; it is just the outcome of natural selection working on the suite of characteristic that the grasses possess. Again, it is not clear what the driving force was in the initiation of these adaptive traits, but the net result is clearly beneficial to grasses. Alas, the struggle would not be over even if the dicots were taken care of; the grasses would still have to compete among themselves for the prairie resources.

Among the array of traits possessed by prairie grasses that protect them from drought, fire, and grazing is the maintenance of a substantial portion of their biomass belowground. Even during the growing season, when they send up several long leaves and one or more flowering stalks, as much as 60 percent of the weight of some grass species on Konza are underground. Of course, many plants other than grasses retain tissue (i.e., roots) underground, but most of their stems are aboveground. Most grasses maintain significant underground horizontal stems (called rhizomes) that extend in several directions from the previous year's flowering stalk. During the subsequent growing season, each rhizome can send up a shoot that will develop leaves and, if conditions are appropriate, a flowering stalk. This is very effective in protecting critical tissues and stored resources from being trampled down and consumed by grazers, from being burned, and from being desiccated during unpredictable droughts.

All but a few plant species (those that are parasitic) get their energy from sunlight and therefore must expose a substantial portion of their tissue aboveground. Most dicots grow aboveground by extending the tips of their growing shoots, much like increasing the height of a building by adding floors on top. Grasses, however, have their critical growth areas (called meristems) all along their stems, just below each node (the juncture of a leaf with the stem). Thus, a growing grass stem telescopes outward (as though a building were getting taller by expanding the height of each floor). This peculiar difference is critical, for when most dicots are damaged, their meristems at the shoot tips are what tend to be destroyed, thus diminishing further growth. In grasses, some meristems along the shoot are destroyed, but others remain intact near the base of the plant; as long as sufficient resources are available in the soil, grasses can rely on their remaining protected rhizomes and on their telescoping meristems for regrowth. Most dicots, when they lose their meristems to fire or consumers, redirect their growth hormones and send out lateral shoots; but their meristems can be damaged only a finite number of times before the plant will suffer mortal consequences.

The tissues that are protected belowground are important to grasses, but their value increases significantly during seasons when substantial portions of the resources that are produced aboveground are siphoned belowground for storage. Energy- and nutrient-rich compounds produced in the leaves are regularly shuttled belowground, both daily and seasonally, into the rhizomes and roots, where they are kept in reserve for times when fresh resources are not available. The redirection of resources occurs regularly at the end of the growing and flowering season as the plants withdraw aboveground nutrients and deposit them in underground reservoirs for protection during the winter. At the beginning of the next growing season, the resources are remobilized to serve as the capital investment for future gains.

If conditions are not optimal for growth and flowering (usually because of insufficient moisture), many prairie grasses save their resources rather than squandering them in a futile attempt to produce seed. In all but the very worst years, however, some investments are made in growth, by yielding leaves that produce additional resources to be stored away underground, literally for a rainy day. When a good (that is, moist) growing season finally occurs, the plants have one or more years worth of resources saved up and can take advantage of the bonanza by allocating their resources aboveground, by flowering, and by producing seed. Sexual reproduction could be very important if the seeds are to reach a suitable germination site and initiate a successful new clone. This is extremely unlikely, however, as most of the space in the prairie is already occupied, prohibiting seedlings from getting started. In one ten-year study near Konza, an average of less than 5 percent of the big bluestem produced seeds in any one year, although in the best year, approximately 30 percent of the individuals flowered.

Seeds are expensive in terms of energy and nutrients, and their chances for success are very low. This may increase the advantages associated with reproducing clonally by sending out underground rhizomes. This begins with the formation of rhizome buds in the fall and is followed by growth in the spring. This pattern can be shifted in time if aboveground foliage is damaged. Segments are added to the previous year's growth as the stems snake their way along underground, spreading out from the parent stock. When tillers (plant shoots) emerge to produce fresh leaves, they can rely on an umbilicus to their siblings from previous generations and to their parents for support while shooting up in a race for the sky with competing tillers. A seed, on the other hand, is sent packing with a finite amount of resources in its possession. If the seedling cannot manufacture its own food through photosynthesis by the time its provisions are depleted, it will die. Death would be the outcome for a similarly depleted rhizome, but most have vast underground connections that minimize the chances of having this occur.

The mass of underground roots and stems produced by many prairie grasses generates an extensive, dense sod. Some grasses on the tallgrass prairie (e.g., the dropseeds) are known as bunch grasses; they form less extensive sods. To the west, in the drier shortgrass prairies, bunch grasses dominate, and so the sods are not widespread. The sods on Konza are so crowded that they are extremely difficult for immigrating plants to penetrate and secure enough resources to survive, further limiting the competitors of grasses. In addition, the sod functions as an anchor, keeping grazers from yanking the entire plant out of the soil while feeding on the aboveground parts. It would be difficult to imagine a more advantageous set of traits for plants living in prairies than those possessed by grasses. The traits are not only successful adaptations to the rigors of the physical environment; they also inhibit invasion and competition from nongrasses.

Just as grasses dominate Konza Prairie, big bluestem dominates the grasses. Big bluestem is *Grass* with a capital *G*; it serves as the namesake and the sentinel for the tallgrass prairie. Big bluestem is widespread, occurring in all but a few states in the continental United States. It reaches its zenith, however, in the tallgrass prairie, especially on Konza Prairie. To the west, in the mixed-grass and shortgrass prairies, it occurs in sloughs, where moisture accumulates and remains throughout the dry season. To the east, trees, shrubs, and other more mesic grasses make it difficult for big bluestem to flourish, though broad tracts of the species do occur where conditions are especially favorable. But in the central corridor of the Great Plains, environmental conditions are just right, and big bluestem dominates as a lush carpet spreading over the landscape.

As spring matures, big bluestem develops a dozen or more leaves that may rise several feet above the surface from a central tiller. Its flowering stalk, however, may extend over ten feet (3 meters) in height in the best of years (perhaps one in ten), thereby defining the tallgrass prairie. Spectacular as this can be, stories of men becoming lost on horseback amidst the flowering stalks of big bluestem are probably exaggerations. At a glance, the stems appear to be packed tightly together, but they are actually an inch or two apart at the soil surface. The vegetation and flowering stalks are so tall and dense, except after long, severe droughts, that only a negligible amount of light reaches the soil surface, thus reducing the opportunity for competitors, including seedlings of big bluestem, to secure a foothold. Periodic droughts may foreclose on the opportunities of plants to reproduce or even survive. The most severe droughts in this century took place in the mid thirties and extended for up to seven years in some locations. During that time, all prairie plant species contracted, and large barren gaps developed on the soil surface. Some relatively minor spatial rearrangements occurred, with one species advancing when another retreated. The dust-bowl droughts were so severe that virtually every plant on the prairie eventually suffered. Even big bluestem, which is protected from moderate droughts, was reduced to one-quarter of its former self by weight in most areas of the tallgrass prairie. When rains finally did come, big bluestem quickly recovered the lost ground and prospered, again dominating before other species had a chance to respond.

Seeds of big bluestem have a very slight chance of successfully germinating. After maturing on a seed head, they may be eaten by birds, mammals, and insects while still on the plant or after falling to the ground. If the season is wet, they may also rot under the attack

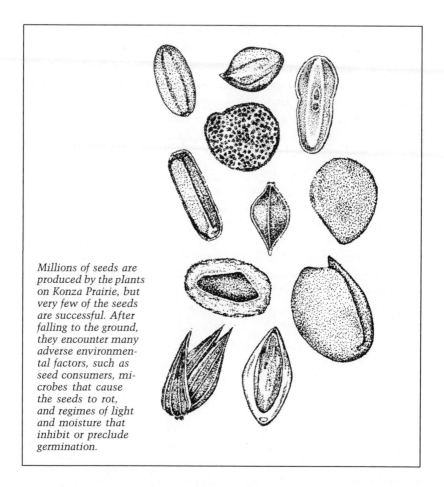

Millions of seeds are produced by the plants on Konza Prairie, but very few of the seeds are successful. After falling to the ground, they encounter many adverse environmental factors, such as seed consumers, microbes that cause the seeds to rot, and regimes of light and moisture that inhibit or preclude germination.

of bacteria and fungi. Even if they survive these rigors, the chance that they will germinate is only slight. Open space for germination is extremely rare on Konza. Sunlight is a major resource, and all of the plants on the prairie are fighting to acquire enough sunlight to survive and reproduce. Seedlings of all species have a terrible time securing their share of sunlight in the shadow of the adults that are already towering overhead. Some seeds may make it to a clearing caused by fire or by surface disturbances and have a chance to start a new life, but very few ever do. Many scientists who have worked for years on the tallgrass prairie have never seen a big-bluestem seedling.

As a seed germinates, root tissue in the seed embryo responds positively to gravity and plunges down into the soil in quest of nutrients and moisture. At the same time, shoots respond negatively to gravity and head upward, seeking sunlight. Under proper conditions, a young big bluestem may reach a foot (30 centimeters) in height and have seminal roots over two feet long in a little over two months. At the end of a single growing season, the plant may reach a foot and half (about 45 centimeters) in height, with roots extending 2 to 4 feet into the soil. The roots usually have one or two major shoots, with hundreds or thousands of tiny sprouts probing the interstices of the soil. These provide an enormous surface area to capture the resources available underground. As the roots mature over the next two or three growing seasons, they may reach a depth of 12 feet (4 meters) or more, spreading netlike in a cylindrical pattern beneath the plant. Where big bluestem overlies beds of limestone, the roots grow through cracks and along seams, yielding a geometric root pattern that outlines the fractures in the limestone. Even though the aboveground foliage and flowering stalks are the most spectacularly obvious, the majority of the tissue of big bluestem lies hidden and protected belowground.

All flowering plants can reproduce sexually by producing seeds from fertilized cells in the ovaries. As noted, however, this can be a tenuous proposition on the prairie, because there are so few places for seeds to germinate and grow. Therefore, it may be an advantage for plants on the prairie to reproduce vegetatively, thereby spreading and occupying more space. Big bluestem sends out rhizomes from the base of the parent stalk; as a rhizome grows, it branches, sending up aerial shoots, called tillers, which become the aboveground stems and producing a new underground rhizome. Roots are also produced near where the tillers arise. Tillers and roots emerge from nodes, the characteristic "joints" along the rhizomes. Virtually all of the rhizomes lie within the upper two or three inches of the soil. Roots extend below this level, but they decrease in number and size at greater depths.

Next to the nodes lie the intercalary meristems. In vertical stems, each meristem can add to the stem's height; but in underground rhizomes, only the last few intercalary meristems add to the horizontal growth. Once a clone is established, it may live and reproduce for an unknown number of years, perhaps centuries, by spreading clonally over the prairie. It is very difficult to analyze clonal growth, because it occurs over long periods of time and takes place underground, where any attempt to observe the process alters the response of the plants. It is thought, however, that as new rhizomes are produced, older ones die, so that as much as 50 percent (but usually no more than 30 percent) of the rhizomes at any one time are from the current year. This eventually leads to a complicated, fragmented pattern, with pieces of the original clone being scattered around the prairie as they shift over the surface.

Another major function of rhizomes, in addition to reproduction, is the storage of photosynthate, or products of photosynthesis. Some photosynthate is used to build plant tissue and to maintain basic processes within the plant, but any excess can be shunted down into the rhizome for storage. Some of the larger roots also serve as storage vessels, but the majority of storage is in the rhizomes.

Rhizome buds begin to swell and break open in late March. By the beginning of April, the growth of tillers and the elongation of the rhizomes occur, processes that continue throughout the summer until mid August. The aboveground stalks develop simple tiny leaves when they first break the surface; but as the stalk extends, a single long leaf is produced at each node. The base of the leaf wraps around the culm in the form of a sheath, and the more distal portion of the leaf folds out and back, orienting to the incoming rays of the sun. Belowground, the rhizomes are also extending, occasionally sending down roots from the nodes. Even though rhizomes are stems, they produce no leaves, which would be useless in the dark, subterranean environment. The amount of growth throughout the summer is affected by a variety of resources, especially water. There is usually a dry period in midsummer (July) on Konza, and growth may be significantly curtailed or even cease if conditions are especially harsh.

In late August, if there has been enough rainfall, the flowering stalk will begin its ascent from within the basal leaves of a big-bluestem axis. The plant shifts its attention to the production of the stalk, which is crowned with a flowering head in which pollen and seeds are produced. Sexual reproduction is costly, so the plant must divert resources, including some of its stored reserves, into building the flowering stalk and into provisioning the propagules (seeds). Flowering does not occur if the season is poor. If a stalk is initiated in the midst of an extended dry period, the plant may cut its losses and cease to make any further investment in a losing proposition.

The flowers of big bluestem are relatively unspectacular, compared to those of dicots, but they are rather intricate. The flowering stalk, which may rise 10 feet above the surface, gives the tallgrass prairie its name.

The flower of big bluestem is tiny, delicate, and complicated. The flowering head itself occurs as three spikes, giving the plant one of its common names, turkey foot. Each spike possesses rows of spikelets, which are arrayed like teeth on a comb. Each spikelet is composed of tiny florets, which contain the essential reproductive parts, as well as several accessory organs of minor or unknown function. Pollen is produced in anthers on protruding stamens, where it is picked up by the wind and passed among neighboring plants near and far. Incoming pollen lands on receptive surfaces of the female reproductive organs (stigmas) where it germinates and sends pollen tubes down into the ovary of the flower. Here, conception takes place, leading to the production of seeds, which are covered by a hard coat; these encapsulated embryos serve as dispersal units for the parent plant, carrying the next generation to its final destination. As noted, very few plants flower in any one year, and the success rate of seedlings is very low.

As the growing season winds down, big bluestem, like many perennial plants, prepares for its winter senescence. Premature freezes could kill the aboveground parts of the plant, trapping costly nutrients in the tissues; those individuals that by early October have begun to translocate material out of the leaves and stems back into the protected rhizomes and roots belowground will usually be protected from early freezes. Almost two-thirds of the nitrogen in aboveground tissues can be translocated down into the storage organs, where it is saved for the subsequent growing season. This represents a substantial savings, obviating the need to replenish the entire supply of nutrients each year.

Big bluestem is a hardy plant that can sustain all manner of environmental ravages. It has its origins in eastern North America, along the inland valleys of the Appalachians, but clearly it was primed to move into the midwestern prairies as the glaciers retreated several millenniums ago. The combination of traits possessed by big bluestem has allowed it to dominate in regions of good soil and moderate moisture regimes, even to the exclusion of most other species, across broad swatches of tallgrass prairie.

Successful as big bluestem is, however, it is by no means the sole inhabitant on the tallgrass prairie. Over one thousand plant species are known to reside in the Flint Hills, and approximately 440 of these form a diverse mixture on Konza Prairie. The physical features of various soils on Konza and their ability to hold moisture have a significant effect on the nature of the plant residents. Where the soil is shallow and rocky, the diversity of species is high, indicating that many microsites exist where specialists can ply their trade. In the deep, more uniform soils of the lowlands, monotypic stands tend to develop as one or a few species dominate and resist invasion. Although the lowlands are less diverse in terms of species, they have higher plant production than the uplands, because the deeper soils are more favorable for plant growth.

Mixed in with big bluestem, or occurring in isolated patches of their own, are populations of Indian grass, switchgrass, and little bluestem, a relative of big bluestem that can tolerate drier conditions. Clay soils support small populations of western wheatgrass, while the moist lowlands host eastern gammagrass. Prairie cordgrass inhabits the wettest of the lowlands and areas around springs that are subject to periodic standing water. Several species of grama grass, which is more characteristic of mixed-grass and shortgrass prairies further west, can be found in dry microsites.

These grasses, however, have little chance against big bluestem except in scattered microsites that favor one or more specialists. Big bluestem simply crowds out competitors by expropriating underground space, and hence the moisture and nutrients that occur there, and by shading young and adult plants alike with its erect posture. In order to succeed on the prairie, plants must be specialists that can take advantage of small opportunities that the generalist big bluestem might overlook. There are large patches of vegetation other than big bluestem on Konza, but they are usually associated with specific environmental conditions. For example, at least two races of switchgrass occur on Konza. One is adapted to the more arid upland soils; the other, to lower and more moist sites. These forms have diverged significantly in their physiological traits; they even have different numbers of chromosomes, suggesting that they are genetically distinct as well. In addition to spatial specialists, some plant species take advantage of certain times of the year when dominant plants are not at their height. For example, Kentucky bluegrass and prairie Junegrass grow and flower early in the spring before big bluestem begins its run.

Prairies are characterized by a predominance of grasses, and tall-grass prairies by a predominance of big bluestem; nevertheless, more than 80 percent of the plant species on Konza are nongrasses. Even out on the true prairie, away from the woods, over 70 percent of the plant species are not grasses. Virtually all of these nongrasses exhibit low abundance, however, and many are rare. Surprisingly, grasses are not the largest family on Konza; that honor goes to the aster family, which is represented by sixty-five species, including several representatives of sunflowers, although the grass family is second, with fifty-five representatives. The sedge family and the knotweed family are underrepresented on Konza, occurring much less frequently than would be predicted from their range on the Flint Hills.

None of the nongrasses is truly common or abundant, although the small, white heath aster is widespread. Dotted gay-feather, inland ceanothus, and catclaw sensitive brier may be locally abundant on shallow soils or rocky outcrops.

What the forbs and shrubs lack in abundance they make up for in diversity and bright colors. Most of them occur in relatively iso-lated patches, which gives the prairie the appearance of having been splattered with splotches of paint. When conditions are right, a num-ber of species may bloom synchronously, their eye-catching appeal belying their low abundance in absolute terms. A few of the forbs are annuals, which must grow from seed each year, but this is usu-ally as unsuccessful for them as it is for grasses. The vast majority of perennial plants do just what grasses do: they shut down for a long, quiescent winter before beginning a new year. Some species, especially perennial forbs and woody shrubs, "pay" animals to help disperse their seeds by packaging them in attractive fruits that are colorful and tasty. Birds and mammals are drawn to the fruits, ingest them, and pass the seeds through their digestive system, to be de-posited at some location distant from the parent plant. Furthermore, the seeds are deposited in excrement, where they will have sufficient moisture and fertilizer. Red cedars often occur as hedges of foliage along fence rows where birds have perched and defecated cedar seeds from berries consumed in earlier stints of foraging. Grasses that do not have showy fruits may utilize a similar strategy to disperse seeds into appropriate microsites by using their leaves as an attraction to herbivores, which incidentally consume the seeds and pass them through their digestive systems.

The flowering season for forbs stretches from early spring to late fall, with two or three peak periods. The major one occurs in early fall, primarily because asters bloom then. Other forbs—such as field pussy-toes, plains wild indigo, wild parsley, and ground-plum milk vetch—also grow and bloom early in the spring, presumably to take advantage of the available sunlight before grasses emerge and intercept the rays. Some plants, such as the redbud trees that occur on rocky breaks in the grassland, flower before their own leaves emerge. The islands of brilliant magenta produced by the redbuds provide an early clue that spring is on the way. Wild roses, with their delicate pink blossoms, also take advantage of early warm weather; and penstemons, with their irregular lavender flowers arrayed on a vertical stalk, pop up in spring. Smooth sumac, whose angular gnarled stalks protrude from the snow all winter, produce leaves and simple inconspicuous bouquets of flowers in midsummer.

By late spring and summer the air and the soil have warmed, and the spring moisture is still available to nurture white and purple prairie-clover. Along rocky slopes, butterfly milkweed makes its appearance with showy orange flowers and broad succulent leaves that drip white latex when damaged. Shrubs such as buckbrush, rough-leaved dogwood, and Illinois bundleflower present their blossoms to bees and other pollinators. Many of the warm-season grasses are also greening up and beginning to exert their influence over the plant community.

Some plants wait until late in the growing season to emerge and flower. Several species of goldenrod flower in late summer, generating wide swaths of yellow. White-flowered yarrow springs up, as does the sagewort, with its inconspicuous flowers. Two distinct forbs dominate the late summer and fall. Heath aster, with its quarter-sized white flowers, is the most common forb on Konza—indeed, in the entire state of Kansas. It seems to peek out from behind every stalk of grass. Buffalo-gourd, which is sometimes called coyote melon, spreads like a giant octopus, with tentacles dozens of feet long. Like many of the melons, it produces large yellow trumpet-shaped flowers that invite many insects to enter. After fertilization, the flowers produce a baseball-sized fruit that contains fibrous strands and scores of seeds. The meat of the melons is bitter, and animals seem reluctant to eat it, as evidenced by the half-eaten fruits in late fall and winter.

Some of the nongrasses on Konza deserve mention, not because of their abundance or ecological importance, but because of their

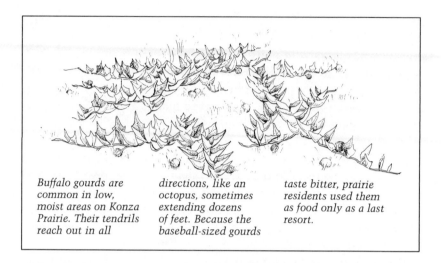

Buffalo gourds are common in low, moist areas on Konza Prairie. Their tendrils reach out in all directions, like an octopus, sometimes extending dozens of feet. Because the baseball-sized gourds taste bitter, prairie residents used them as food only as a last resort.

unusual habits. For example, several species of tiny forbs, such as cancer-root, produce no photosynthetically active leaves of their own; rather, the plants are parasitic on the roots of neighbors, absconding with resources that were intended for the host plant. Cluster dodder, a rare plant on the upland prairies, is another parasitic form that utilizes the resources of one of the dominant goldenrods.

Many plants on Konza use brightly colored flowers to attract pollinators, primarily insects, to dispense their pollen. The plants often pay a fee to the pollinator in the form of nectar. While most nectar is associated with the flower of a plant and pollination, a few species on Konza (two sunflowers, wild licorice, three species of plums, meadow rose, and three willows) are known to possess extrafloral nectaries—that is, nectar-producing glands that are not associated with pollination. In cases in which extrafloral nectaries have been studied, the nectar appears to attract a host of aggressive insects, such as ants and wasps, which help to protect the plant from herbivores. While no studies of such relationships have been undertaken on Konza, it is reasonable to assume that the insect guardians exist in conjunction with plant species that possess extrafloral nectaries. This is a widespread phenomenon in other habitats, especially the tropics; but it is rare on prairies. Legumes—members of several plant groups that collectively are known as the pea family—are abundant on Konza and have many interesting representatives. Catclaw sensitive brier has an exquisitely descriptive name. *Catclaw* refers to its tiny sharp recurved thorns, resembling cat's claws, which grab and hold everything they contact. Its sensitivity refers to the quick folding response of its tiny leaves when they are lightly brushed. Lead plant, so called because of its dull grayish leaves, is also known as prairie shoestring. When the pioneers first plowed the prairie, the plant's tough roots briefly held up the plow before they popped, like worn shoestrings, when given a strong tug.

Recent studies of blue false indigo—another legume on Konza—have discovered several opposing forces that may have determined the time of year that the species flowers. Three types of insects—weevil larvae, moth larvae, and adult blister beetles—feed on the flowers, fruits, and seeds, potentially destroying the plant's reproductive output. Blister beetles—which are named for their propensity to cause blisters on most animals that contact them, as a result of the chemical cantharadin—ravage the plants late in the growing season, making early flowering advantageous. The weevil and moth larvae, which are under pressure to get to the flowers before the beetles do, affect the plant early in its growing and flowering season. Furthermore, plants that flower too early are sometimes caught by late frosts, which may also have serious consequences. Thus, the plants are caught in the middle, with those that can most effectively balance the opposing forces being the most successful.

Several species of plants that are frequently associated with deserts occur on Konza, usually in the driest habitats of the tallgrass prairie. Two species of cactus—a small, lumpy mammillaria and a larger prickly pear—are occasionally found on shallow, dry upland soils. Yuccas, with their green swords protecting an emergent flowering stalk, are common in some localities. Yuccas have formed a mutually beneficial alliance with small, white nocturnal moths that serve as pollinators. The moths must lay their eggs in the yucca flower, where the caterpillars develop in the incipient fruit. Similarly, the yucca relies on the moth as the sole carrier of its pollen.

Dozens of plants that occur on Konza were used by Native Americans, and some continue in use. The most obvious of these have names that ring familiarly in our ears—wild onion, wild strawberry, wild plum, sunflower (seeds), prairie turnip, prairie parsley, and Jerusalem artichoke. Various portions of the plants were used, from cooked and macerated roots to teas brewed with leaves. Fruits of numerous plants, such as prickly pear cactus, currants, and sumac, were consumed directly. More astringent fruits, such as ground cherries, were cooked and made into pemmican. Ground cherries also served as toys for Indian children, giving rise to their common name of pop weed, because they popped as they were squeezed. Beverages and medicinal poultices were prepared from a variety of forbs, and salves were made from shredded root tissues. For example, wild licorice is known to soothe coughs and to reduce the loss of water when it is imbibed as a hot tea. No doubt some herbs were medically effective, while others were simply placebos; it is just as likely that some actually exacerbated any medical problem, for many plants are toxic unless treated according to specific formulas.

The seeds (called grains) of virtually all of the grass species are edible. Many, however, have coverings that are difficult to remove, making the cost of harvesting and processing too high to be economical. Those from which the chaff can be winnowed from the grain served as important food sources for early natives, as camp debris and coprolites reveal. Grasses and a few of the forbs continue to be important for domestic livestock, giving the Flint Hills the epithet "tallgrass pasture," while domesticated grasses such as wheat, corn, and sorghum have replaced their wild-grown predecessors.

More than 10 percent of the plant species that have been recorded on Konza have been introduced by human activity, usually by actual plantings or by accidentally arriving in loads of feed or other agricultural products. Some—such as curly dock, morning glory, and goat's beard—are pernicious weeds that are widespread around the world and have become common locally on Konza. Further human influence occurs around such man-made disturbances as stock tanks, roads, and dwellings.

PHOTOSYNTHESIS

The earth receives huge amounts of energy in the form of sunlight each day. For example, it has been calculated that the earth receives enough radiant solar energy every three days to match the known reserves of oil, gas, and uranium on earth. Much of the energy that the sun broadcasts is absorbed by the atmosphere before it reaches the earth. Some that does reach the earth is reflected back, as evi-

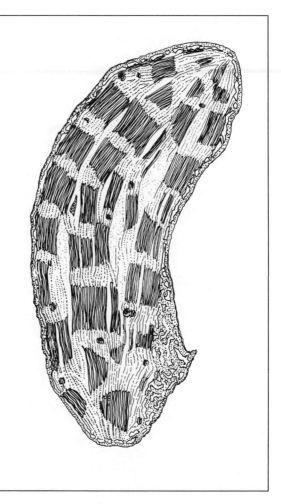

Chloroplasts are small organelles (this one is magnified approximately five thousand times) within the surface cells of most plants. Within the chloroplasts the sun's energy is converted to biological energy, which can be used by the plant or animals that consume the plant tissue.

denced by photographs from space showing the earth as a brilliantly shining sphere. A portion of the reflected light is trapped within the atmosphere, causing the envelope of air around the earth to warm. A substantial amount of sunlight that strikes the earth is absorbed by the surface, heating the soil, the rocks, and the seas. Differential heating of the earth's surface is the principle driving force behind the winds and the ocean currents that flow over the surface of the globe. The winds and currents, in turn, significantly influence much of the planet's weather.

Approximately 1 percent of the sun's energy that reaches the sur-

face of the earth is converted into biological energy by living organisms. This minuscule fraction is responsible for driving virtually every biological process on the planet, from the production of high-energy molecules to the construction of carbon building blocks within plants. In turn, animals consume plants to obtain energy and nutrition, and other animals eat those animals, and so on through the food chain. During the conversion of energy from one trophic (energy) level to another, approximately 90 percent of the energy is lost as heat. With only a 1:9 efficiency ratio between trophic levels, it takes one hundred pounds of grass to feed ten pounds of mice to feed one pound of hawk.

The process by which the sun's energy is converted into biological energy is called photosynthesis, or synthesis powered by light. In its simplest form, photosynthesis can be expressed as

$$CO_2 + H_2O + Light \longrightarrow CH_2O + O_2$$

That is, carbon dioxide plus water, in the presence of light, yields carbohydrates and oxygen. The oxygen is released into the atmosphere, where it is subsequently consumed in the metabolism of most organisms, including the metabolism within plant cells. The basic carbohydrate molecule is further manipulated to become carbon-based fuel molecules, or carbon building blocks. This relationship consists of some of the simplest and most abundant chemicals known, and yet when combined with light, the chemicals produce the most complex and essential reactions in the living world.

The early atmosphere of earth contained no oxygen; organisms that were then alive metabolized energy from organic molecules floating in the primeval soup. These primitive organisms gave off carbon dioxide as a waste gas, which eventually accumulated to high-enough levels in the atmosphere to become a significant source of energy in itself. Once enough carbon dioxide had accumulated, organisms (probably primitive algae) evolved that used the gas as a carbon source while giving off oxygen as a waste gas. This led not only to a reversal of the oxygen:carbon dioxide ratio but also to the atmosphere that we have today, in which oxygen is a predominant metabolic gas and carbon dioxide occurs in low quantities (nitrogen is actually the most abundant gas in today's atmosphere, but it is not directly involved in metabolic processes).

Oxygen was a powerful poison to the earliest forms of life on the planet, causing them to self-incinerate. As oxygen accumulated, anaerobic organisms—those that live in the absence of oxygen—were replaced by aerobic forms, which utilize oxygen as a metabolic gas. The aerobic forms were significantly more efficient at extracting energy from organic molecules; they have come to dominate virtually every habitat on earth. The result is the system we now see on earth, in which plants use carbon dioxide with sunlight to generate biological energy, while giving off oxygen as a waste gas. Animals, in turn, use oxygen to metabolize the plant and animal tissue that they consume, giving off carbon dioxide as a waste gas (again, plants use some oxygen in their own metabolic processes). The relationship between these processes and products is currently in balance, but slight alterations, caused by changing cosmic events or pollution from the earth's inhabitants, could alter the arrangement, sending the balance toward a new equilibrium.

Another major component of photosynthesis is light. Visible light is just a small portion of the electromagnetic spectrum, an array of wave lengths of radiant energy from extremely short gamma rays to very long radio waves. The visible spectrum encompasses the portion that we can detect with our own eyes; it is also the portion used most efficiently by plants for photosynthesis.

Different wave lengths of visible light generate different colors—an effect that can be produced by a prism or by a rainbow in which billions of raindrops function as simple prisms. An object that appears black absorbs all of the incident light, reflecting none, whereas white objects reflect almost all visible light rays. This explains why dark objects heat up in sunlight while light objects stay cool. Pigments in various materials are responsible for the colors that we see; if a piece of cloth is red, the pigment that it contains absorbs all of the light waves except red ones, which are reflected to our eyes, giving the image of the color red.

This should give a clue as to what colors of light are used in photosynthesis. If leaves are primarily green, then we can imagine that green is reflected, while other colors are absorbed and used in photosynthesis. It could be accidental that life has evolved to use this particular tiny segment of the electromagnetic spectrum, but there are reasons to suspect that this is not the case. Most of life is built on large molecules that are held together by relatively weak bonds *between hydrogen, carbon, and oxygen atoms. The shorter a wave length of light, the more energy it packs. The amount of energy that is produced by ultraviolet wave lengths—which are just shorter than the shortest visible light wave lengths—is great enough to break these weak chemical bonds, plunging most biological molecules into chaos. At the opposite end of the energy spectrum, the long wave lengths of infrared are too weak to pass through water, making it impossible for them to penetrate into aqueous environments, or even cells. Thus it would appear that the small range of visible light was the one most suitable for adoption as an energy source during the evolution of the photosynthetic process, because this narrow range of wave lengths possessed just enough energy to power the process, but not enough to wreck the fragile molecules.*

The absorption of light energy and its conversion to biological energy take place in small organelles called chloroplasts, which are scattered throughout photosynthetically active plant tissues (usually leaves). The chloroplasts contain a number of pigments, with chlorophyll a being the most important. Other pigments, such as chlorophyll b and the carotenoids (which give carrots their orange color), also assist in the process by passing energy on to chlorophyll a. When pigments absorb light, atomic subunits called electrons are boosted to a higher energy level, as though a wheel had been rolled uphill and was perched in preparation for rolling back down the hill. After the absorption of energy, three events are possible. First, the energy may be dissipated as heat, which occurs with any object that is placed in sunlight. Second, the electrons may immediately fall back to the lower energy level (the wheel may roll back down the hill); in the process, they will give up the energy in the form of fluorescent light. The third possibility is the important one for photosynthesis: the light energy can cause a chemical reaction within the leaf. When chlorophyll pigments are isolated in a test tube, they fluoresce as they receive sunlight. When the pigment is illuminated in its normal setting, surrounded by specific proteins and embedded in a specialized membrane, the captured light energy is harvested and stored in a chemical form as part of the photosynthetic process.

Photosynthesis is composed of two reactions, one of which depends on light, while the other depends upon the availability of carbon dioxide. The first reaction can be stimulated by increasing light up to a certain level, after which the rate of photosynthesis does not increase. This suggests that at the point of leveling off, a resource other than light is limiting the process. The rate of the second reaction increases with the concentration of carbon dioxide, up to a temperature at which proteins are destroyed, which suggests that this reaction is driven by temperature-sensitive enzymes.

The first reaction, known as the light reaction, involves changing the sun's energy into biological energy by adding a phosphorus molecule to ADP (adenosine diphosphate) so as to make it ATP (adenosine triphosphate). Molecules of ATP are then stored and used for energy in the future, when they are enzymatically reduced to ADP again. Likewise, high-energy electrons are stored for future use in other complex molecules. This process is incredibly complex, and much remains to be learned about its features. One difficulty in working on this aspect of photosynthesis is that most of the molecules are very unstable and therefore pass quickly from one state to another, leaving little trace of their activity.

The second reaction is known as the carbon-fixing reaction, because it is responsible for combining carbon atoms to each other and to other atoms to form a variety of carbon-based molecules, which are the chemical storage units and foundation molecules of all plants and animals. These more complex carbon chains are produced by escorting molecules around an enzymatic cycle in which they pick up extra carbons on each circuit. The product of these cycles, glyceraldehyde phosphate, is a simple three-carbon molecule that would seem to be an insignificant reward for the complexities of photosynthesis. However, this molecule, as well as those derived from it, provides the energy source for almost all living systems and serves as the basic carbon skeleton for all organisms.

The cycles that are involved with the production of these simple carbon chains are very complex. There are several types of processes in plants that revolve around the ways in which carbon dioxide is delivered to the photosynthetic process. One of the paths, involving the Calvin cycle, begins with the binding of carbon dioxide to an enzyme, which is then split to form two molecules of PGA (phosphoglycerate). Each molecule of PGA contains three carbons, so this is known as the three-carbon pathway, and it relies on the diffusion of carbon dioxide into the plant tissues. Another pathway begins with the binding of carbon dioxide to oxaloacetic acid for a total of four carbon atoms, resulting in a four-carbon pathway. Plants that use this pathway also use the previously mentioned pathway (the Calvin cycle); they also incorporate an energetically efficient but physiologically expensive mechanism to capture carbon dioxide. These two pathways, called C_3 and C_4, have a significant impact on the ecological characteristics of the plants on Konza.

Carbon dioxide is essential for photosynthesis. It enters the leaf through tiny pores called stomata, which open and close in response to the plant's requirements for the gas. The stomata are also important in the regulation of water balance in plants, because water vapor can be lost through them when they are open. On dry days or during the driest part of one day, the stomata might be forced to close to prevent the loss of too much water vapor. This also has the effect of limiting the amount of carbon dioxide that can be taken in, and hence the rate of photosynthesis. Plants that use the C_4 route produce an enzyme that has a greater affinity for carbon dioxide than does the enzyme involved with C_3 metabolism. Thus, plants that are water stressed, and therefore must keep their stomata closed to prevent further water loss, will benefit from the C_4 pathway, which can most efficiently use what carbon dioxide is allowed in. Conversely, when carbon dioxide is not limited by the need for water conservation, C_3 plants are significantly more efficient at photosynthesis than are C_4 plants. Temperature also affects the propensity for one carbon pathway or the other; plants in high-temperature regions usually evolve the C_4 pathway.

From the interactions between conflicting constraints of carbon dioxide and moisture on plants, one could predict that C_3 plants would predominate in relatively cool and moist areas or seasons (where open stomata would yield more carbon dioxide but not promote water stress), while C_4's would be more successful in warm and dry areas or seasons. Studies have shown this to be the case, because there is a strong correlation between the dryness of the region and the ratio of C_3 plants to C_4 plants. In the extreme, C_4 plants can flourish under conditions that would be lethal to most C_3 plants. On Konza, this pattern is reflected in the difference between the cool-season C_4 grasses, which are the first to green up in spring, and the warm-season C_4 grasses, such as big bluestem. Because the summers on Konza are hot and frequently exhibit a dry stretch in midsummer, it is not surprising that C_4 grasses dominate on Konza.

The leaves, stems, roots, fruits, and seeds of many plants on Konza Prairie serve as sustenance for animals in the tallgrass. Although it is grossly improper to think of plants simply as animal food, that is one aspect of the plants' biology that both the biologist and the plants must consider. The tallgrass prairie provides a huge quantity of forage—as much as three thousand pounds per acre per year—for animals, and many have evolved to take advantage of the resources. As is the case with the plants on Konza, most of the major animal groups are immigrants from other areas. Very few endemics occur on the prairie—that is, species that originated on the prairie and retain it as their center of the distribution. For example, of approximately 108 species of grasshoppers on the prairies of the Great Plains, at least 105 are from adjacent regions. Virtually all of the mammals on Konza originated elsewhere and then extended their ranges into the tallgrass prairie. Furthermore, Konza is "missing" a number of species (e.g., chipmunks) that don't quite extend into the tallgrass prairie from the east or west but do exist in nearby regions. It is reasonable to anticipate that over the next score of millenniums, species will evolve as tallgrass-prairie specialists and that others will adopt it as their new home, thus increasing its diversity.

Even though the tallgrass prairie is tall by the standard of most grasslands, it is still short compared to forest and shrub habitats. This reduces the actual amount of vertical space for animals to use and the quantity and kinds of food items that are available for consumption. Nevertheless, the expanse of grasses, interspersed with herbaceous plants, provides a smorgasbord of vegetation for herbivores, which, in turn, provide food for carnivores. Although some animals may find the prairie inhospitable, many species feed, nest, and reproduce within the confines of the grassland, taking advantage of the available resources.

Some of the most characteristic grassland herbivores are the aptly named grasshoppers. During most years, about forty species of these herbivores leap and fly around Konza. Almost all of the species overwinter as eggs laid by the adults during the previous summer and fall. In the late spring and early summer, after spending the winter in the soil, the eggs hatch and yield young nymphs, the developmental predecessors of adults. The nymphs go through several additional stages before attaining adulthood. Like most insects, grasshoppers possess a hard shell (exoskeleton) which limits their growth. To in-

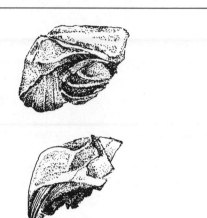

Not all grasshoppers eat grass. These grasshopper mandibles (jaws) are from a species that consumes succulent vegetation (bottom) and another that feeds primarily on grasses. The jaws of the latter are more robust, an adaptation to masticating the tough, silica-laden leaves of grasses.

crease in size, they must shed the old exoskeleton, swell up, and produce a new coat of armor. Grasshoppers molt between nymphal stages before reaching their adult size.

Grasshoppers can be very abundant at times, making them an excellent meal for a variety of consumers, especially birds and small mammals. In response to the pressure of predators, grasshoppers have evolved behavioral and anatomical traits that reduce their vulnerability. They may freeze when a predator approaches, blending in with their mottled background, or spring away and vanish. Grasshoppers also tend to frequent backgrounds that they match in coloration, whether dark soil or green leaves and stems.

Grasshoppers have mandibles that move from side to side, rather than up and down, with the left one overlapping the right. Not all grasshoppers feed on leaves: some consume seeds, whereas others are carnivorous. The ones that do feed on vegetation must process a substantial amount of vegetation to extract sufficient energy and nutrients, as greenery is especially low in the essential elements. Species that feed on the leaves of herbaceous plants have mandibles that are somewhat slender and knife-edged to enable them to slice through the juicy tissue. Those that specialize on grasses, however, encounter the same problems with silica in the leaves that large grazing mammals encounter. Thus, gramnivorous (grass-eating) species tend to have large, bulky mandibles which resist the abrading effect of silica.

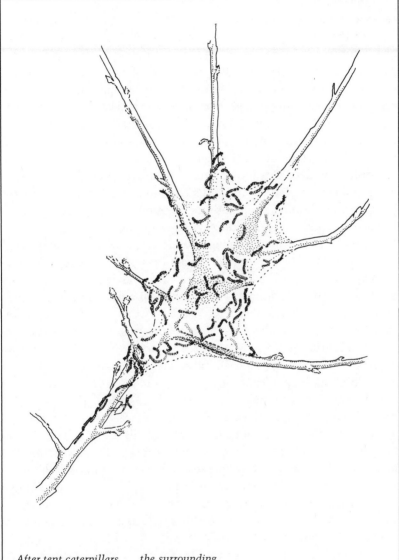

After tent caterpillars hatch from eggs laid the previous fall, they congregate and form large silken bivouacs. Each night they emerge from their camp and plunder the surrounding vegetation, eventually defoliating entire bushes. The surviving larvae ultimately form pupae and metamorphose into adults.

Many insects exhibit outbreaks during which they proliferate, thus severely affecting their environment. This is a common pattern for species that have quite specific requirements for reproductive success. During any one year or sequence of years, conditions may not match their requirements; but when all of the critical elements are present or when detrimental predators or pathogens (disease-producing organisms) are absent, insects can take advantage of the circumstances and explode in abundance. It is usually difficult to determine what combination of factors contributes to the boom-or-bust cycle, because they can interact in very complicated ways. For example, low densities of predators in the fall of one year, coupled with a warm, moist winter and high production of plants in the spring, might induce a population explosion in one species of insect but discourage the population growth of another.

An example of this phenomenon on Konza occurs in tent caterpillars, the larvae of lappet moths. The adults are basically reproductive machines that possess reduced mouth parts, indicating that they may not feed as adults. The moths stay active for a number of days, however, relying on their internal fat reserves as they seek mating opportunities. The males are strong fliers that may travel several miles to locate potential mates, following a pheromone (signaling odor) produced by a receptive female. Females tend to remain near their birth site, which usually offers them a good location for laying their own clutches of eggs. The eggs overwinter in hard cases deposited around a twig. In the following spring, small caterpillars hatch from the eggs and remain together to spin a group tent of silklike material. A phalanx of larvae marches off at night to feed on the newly emerged leaves of their host plant (frequently wild plum on Konza) before returning to their communal tent during the day. The larvae go through several molts as they grow, and the shed skins from previous stages soon clutter the tent. Each of the hundreds of caterpillars is a voracious feeder, which spells trouble for the host plant. Entire shrubs can be defoliated in a day or two by the marauding herbivores. As new leaves become scarce, the caterpillar population declines. The caterpillars are virtually trapped on their shrub islands—they probably don't know how far away or in what directions new, unpopulated islands may lie. Nevertheless, many caterpillars abandon a depleted patch only to find that any new patch they discover has suffered the same fate as the patch from which they had just emigrated.

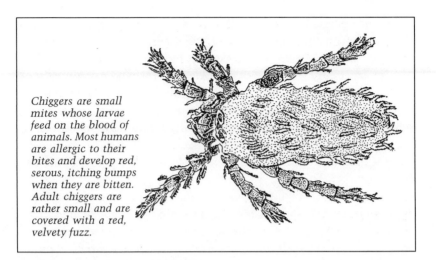

Chiggers are small mites whose larvae feed on the blood of animals. Most humans are allergic to their bites and develop red, serous, itching bumps when they are bitten. Adult chiggers are rather small and are covered with a red, velvety fuzz.

The caterpillars that survive grow through their larval stages (called instars). They eventually reach a little over two inches (5 centimeters) in length. When fully grown, the larvae disperse and find hidden places in which to spin their cocoons. After several weeks of metamorphosis in the cocoon, during which the extreme rearrangement of caterpillar to moth takes place, the youngsters emerge as adults and seek to repeat the life cycle.

Spiders and their relatives are among the most common inhabitants of Konza, where they are often confused with insects. Both groups, along with crustaceans (crayfish, shrimp, etc.) and an array of minor classes, belong to the largest category of animals known, the arthropods, or "joint-legged animals." Closely related to spiders, which have four pairs of legs rather than the three pairs possessed by insects, are mites and ticks, tiny arthropods that have secretive habits. Some of the most irritating of these are chiggers, small mites that feed on a variety of warm-blooded creatures, including humans. In fact, anyone who walks across Konza in midsummer instantly becomes a potential chigger habitat. In the spring, adult chiggers, upholstered in a red-velvet fuzz, arise from winter senescence and lay eggs. These hatch within a week, and the minuscule clear larvae climb up on vegetation to aid them in boarding an unfortunate host that happens to saunter by. On humans, the larvae crawl up, lodging at some tight constriction, such as the cuff of a sock or the beltline. Once situated, they insert a stylet into the skin, thus initiating an allergic response by the host. The protein-destroying enzymes that the chigger injects cause the host tissue to produce copious amounts of body fluids, which are slurped up by the juveniles. Some people are especially sensitive to the invasion, responding immediately with swelling and itching. Others exhibit such a delayed reaction that by the time they detect the presence of the parasite, the larva has departed, eliminating any opportunity for punitive measures. Although chigger populations begin to decline in July, as heat and other environmental pressures increase, they can be pests until the first frost.

Insects make up about 90 percent of all the animals on the planet, so it is not surprising that there is an incredible array of these creatures on Konza. Beetles, which are the largest group of insects, are well represented by a number of forms. June beetles can be common in early summer, arriving with the noise and bulk of miniature low-flying aircraft. A large fauna of dung beetles exists on Konza. These black beetles seek the dung of other animals (usually mammals), chew it into pieces, and roll it away to stash as a source of food for their eggs and larvae. The pieces of dung are sculpted into spheres to facilitate rolling, which is accomplished by doing a headstand and then pushing the ball along the ground with the hind pair of legs. In some cases, a male will do the rolling, and the female will ride either on him or on the ball as a passenger until the deposition site, which may be many yards away, has been reached. The beetle or pair of beetles burrow under the ball; as they excavate soil, the ball slowly disappears into the ground, where it provides room and board for the eggs laid by the female.

Numerous flies occur across Konza, where many are specialized feeders on carrion, dung, or even live animals. On warm nights near still water, mosquitoes buzz about, sending a subliminal message that it is summer. During the day, deer flies can be pests, painfully carving out bits of flesh and driving unsuspecting prey up the windy ridges to avoid further attack. Cicadas and crickets contribute sonorous buzzes and chirps to the prairie, reiterating that it is summer.

Butterflies are among the most attractive and mesmerizing animals on Konza. One never tires of seeing them as they flit about, adding color to the prairie while sipping nectar and pollinating flowers. Perhaps Konza's most recognizable variety is the monarch. Across their vast range these butterflies lay their eggs on a number of species of milkweeds, some of which contain powerful toxins called cardiac glycosides. These chemicals are incorporated into the body tissues of the developing larvae as they feed on the milkweed leaves. The chemicals are carried forth into the adult form after metamorphosis; during development, they protect both the larvae and the adults from potential consumers. Studies show that when birds consume adult butterflies that were raised on toxic milkweeds as larvae, they will regurgitate their meals and will quickly learn to avoid monarchs thereafter. Some monarchs are raised on milkweeds that do not contain toxins, but they also benefit from the toxins possessed by their neighbors because the birds learn to avoid all butterflies that resemble the distasteful ones. For this pattern of protection to persist, of course, most of the butterfly population must be noxious, or the birds may be willing to accept a few foul ones in exchange for many nutritious meals.

Insects are most active at night, when they are obscured by darkness. Lightning bugs, or fireflies, advertise their presence by a persistent dot-and-dash flashing that signals their species, sex, and amorous intentions. The light is "cold" light, produced by the interaction of an energy-rich molecule and an enzyme. Some forms of fireflies have subverted the system by sending bogus signals. A female of one large species flashes the signal of the females of a second species. When a male of the second species approaches, driven by the urge to mate, the duplicitous *femme fatale* nabs and consumes the unwary suitor. Although this phenomenon has not been observed on Konza, relatives of species that are known to exhibit this treachery do occur in the tallgrass.

Vertebrate animals (those with backbones) are not nearly as abundant on Konza as are their invertebrate kin. Only twenty-nine species of amphibians (salamanders, frogs, and toads) and reptiles (lizards, snakes, and turtles) have been recorded on Konza Prairie, which represents approximately 60 percent of what has been recorded for the surrounding counties. Amphibians can spend a significant portion of their lives on land, but they must return to water to reproduce. There are no natural ponds in the grasslands of Konza, but a number of artificial ponds have been constructed through the years. These ponds were built to provide water for livestock, but incidentally they have become focal points for amphibian breeding activity. Shallow ditches alongside the main roads on Konza also become temporary breeding ponds when they fill with seasonal rain water, and a number of species use pools along the streams as breeding sites.

Amphibians are poikilothermic (that is, their body temperature tends to match that of the environment—what has been termed cold-blooded), so they are usually limited in their activity by temperature as well as the availability of water. Once the air begins to warm in the spring, frogs congregate to chirp or bellow their mating calls. Males arrive first and set off choruses that attract females to the soiree. The volume can be painful to the human ear, but these are sweet melodies to female frogs, who must choose among the males seeking their attention. Females invest so much in their nutrient-laden eggs, literally putting all their eggs in one basket, that it is imperative for them to choose the "best" mate to father their offspring. Clues to the quality of a potential mate may be subtle, such as the temperature of the territory a male holds as his domain. By consorting with a male who holds a warm-water territory, the female will give her offspring a developmental head start on eggs laid in cooler water. In addition, her sons will be more likely to inherit those traits of their father that allowed him to secure the preferred breeding site, thus compounding the effects of her decision for generations to come. In some species of frogs the females choose mates based on the deepness of their calls. Frogs do not suddenly attain a maximum size; they continue to grow throughout their lives, and the larger and therefore older frogs have commensurately deeper voices. A young interloper cannot deceive a female with a disproportionately deep voice, so the trait is linked to the age of a male, which, in turn, is related to his success, at least as indicated by longevity.

Male frogs are much less discriminating than are females. The males' investment in reproduction is significantly lower, because sperm cells are less costly than the yolk-filled eggs produced by females. A male's reproductive success is directly related to the number of females he can inseminate, rather than the quality of any one mate. In their ardor to mate, males will mount almost any appropriately sized object, including cobbles, boots, and other male frogs. A male that is mounted by another male will usually respond with a short croak, notifying the intruder of his critical misidentification.

Although frogs are sensitive to temperature, male western chorus frogs on Konza are known to congregate and begin calling as early

Bullfrogs are rather common in the stock ponds on Konza Prairie, where they serve as food for herons, snakes, and fish. Bullfrog eggs hatch in mid to late summer, and the large tadpoles overwinter in the frozen ponds. Those that survive the winter metamorphose into adults the following spring.

as February. Breeding usually takes place in March and April, although it may extend into the summer if standing water persists. Males mount females and fertilize the eggs as they are deposited on surrounding vegetation in the water. A female may lay as many as fifteen hundred eggs in clutches of thirty to three hundred. The eggs hatch in two weeks, and the free-swimming tadpoles feed on algae until they metamorphose into adults two months later. As adults, the chorus frogs eat grubs, beetles, spiders, and ants, and they themselves are consumed by birds, mammals, and larger species of frogs.

Bullfrogs, the largest amphibians on Konza, breed from April through July. The males have a deep "umm-pah" call, which they bellow through the first half of the night in an attempt to secure territories along the shores of ponds and streams. The final negotiations take place with bumping, biting, and kicking between competing males. The eggs (up to forty thousand per female) are fertilized as they are laid, after which they float as a large raft (1–2.5 square feet) for four or five days before hatching. On Konza, the tadpoles usually overwinter in the ponds where they hatched, going into a state of arrested development beneath the ice in winter. The following spring, those that are not consumed by bass, snapping turtles, or herons resume their metamorphosis. Even though a huge number of eggs are laid, very few of the youngsters make it to adulthood. As much as 80 percent of the diet of adults consists of other frogs, although beetles and even a full-grown sparrow have been removed from the guts of bullfrogs.

Unlike amphibians, most reptiles do not lay their eggs in water, yet for many, water is their primary habitat. Snapping turtles spend most of their lives in water, but apparently they cross long distances of open prairie between ponds. The only true terrestrial turtle found on Konza is the western box turtle, which possesses a beautifully ornate carapace (the shell on the top) and plastron (the covering of the belly). Portions of the carapace and the plastron are hinged, allowing the turtle to withdraw into its shell and close the gates, thus stymieing any attempts by a predator to enter. During the summer, box turtles plow through the grass in search of food—primarily beetles, grasshoppers, caterpillars, earthworms, and dead vertebrates, although berries and other fruits are also favored—and mates. Mating appears awkward and cumbersome as the shells of the participants clank against each other. After copulating, the male frequently falls off the female and rolls over on his back, but is usually able to right himself. Each female lays two to eight oblong leathery eggs, which hatch in a couple of months; some females lay a second clutch in the same season. The young take seven or eight years to reach puberty, and the adults may live longer than thirty-five years.

Only four species of lizards have been recorded on Konza, usually in association with rocky outcrops. The most common is the Great Plains skink, a slick, shiny lizard that has a propensity for disengaging its tail at the slightest provocation. The tail contains energy reserves that cause it to twitch on its own for several minutes, usually distracting a predator long enough to allow the lizard itself to escape. The tail can be regrown, although without its vertebrae, in several weeks, to be sacrificed again during a subsequent encounter with a predator. Skinks are aggressive foragers, stalking insects, spiders, and snails. Predation on skinks appears to be slight, probably because they spend much of their time under ledges and rocks, although they may also discourage predation with their foul taste.

The collared lizard can be found along rocky outcrops across Konza. It is a large lizard—up to 1 foot (30 centimeters) long—with a fearsome aspect that matches its malevolent personality. The males develop bright green coloration at the beginning of the breeding sea-

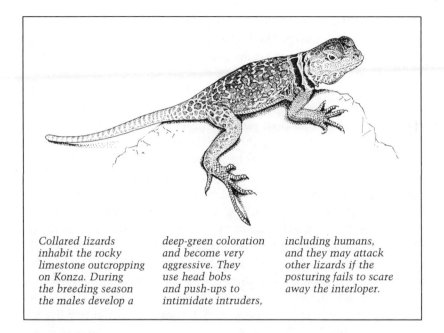

Collared lizards inhabit the rocky limestone outcropping on Konza. During the breeding season the males develop a deep-green coloration and become very aggressive. They use head bobs and push-ups to intimidate intruders, including humans, and they may attack other lizards if the posturing fails to scare away the interloper.

son, during which they are very aggressive and territorial, especially when they are warmed by the sun. They may defend several thousand square feet of territory by performing head bobs and push-ups for intruders, or by chasing other males away. Males actively court females by displaying their bright colors and by slithering around and over potential mates. If the female is receptive, mating takes place, and from two to twenty-one eggs are laid within three weeks. The eggs hatch in about three months, and the females may lay more than one clutch a year.

Texas horned lizards, which are sometimes mistakenly called horned toads, are occasionally spotted on Konza. These lizards, which have an array of spines over their backs and along their sides, look like miniature dinosaurs. The lizards feed primarily on ants but are only rarely preyed upon themselves, presumably because of the ominous spines. Records from other areas indicate that snakes that ingest horned lizards may suffer punctured intestines and may eventually die from a subsequent infection.

A variety of snakes slither through Konza's grass and along the rocky breaks. Thirteen species have been seen on Konza, with nine of these occurring at least occasionally in the grasslands. Several are small, almost wormlike species, including the flathead snake and the ringneck snake. The latter species has a beautiful pearl-gray dorsum, but it flashes a bright gold-and-red underside when it is accosted, apparently in an attempt to scare off potential predators. Larger snakes cruise through the prairie in search of meals of rodents, birds, and their nestlings. Rat snakes, king snakes, gopher snakes, and racers usually bite their prey and immediately coil around them, constricting and suffocating them before swallowing them head first.

Although the tallgrass prairie is not the ideal habitat for many birds, the diverse environment of Konza provides an array of conditions that attract many of them. More than two hundred species have been observed on Konza, a number that is indicative of the mobility of birds and the diversity of available habitats. The range of habitats, from open grasslands to gallery forests, provides a variety of feeding and nesting sites for both visitors and resident birds. Furthermore, Konza is near the Mississippi flyway, a major north-south route for migration, so approximately forty species stop by on their way through in the spring and autumn. About thirty-five of the species that have been identified from Konza are so rare as to be considered accidental visitors, which are either lost or have been blown off course in their travels. These include golden eagles, lazuli buntings, rock wrens, and Mississippi kites. Such birds as hooded mergansers and egrets occur nearby on open bodies of water but are rare on Konza because of scant habitat. Only sixteen species are considered abundant, but approximately thirty-five species live on Konza the year around, and almost sixty species are known to nest there, either in the grassland or within the gallery forest.

Grasslands tend to possess similar guilds of birds, including a grouselike species (a large seed-eating bird—the prairie chicken on Konza), a medium-sized seed-eater (the mourning dove on the tallgrass prairie), and one each of a large, medium, and small insectivores—the meadowlark, the dickcissel, and the grasshopper sparrow. These species, plus the brown-headed cowbird, make up over 70 percent of all the birds in the grasslands.

For the most part, the open grasslands are inhospitable to a great number of birds. The reason is obvious: most birds are associated with trees, and one of the distinguishing features of prairies is the lack of trees. Therefore, the forests along the creeks house many more species of birds, although these species may fly into the tallgrass prairie to forage. Those that do live out on the prairie itself usually specialize on particular types of food (e.g., grasshoppers) and may nest on the ground. Meadowlarks make well-defined nests that are usually covered with a dome of litter, producing a tunnel within which the eggs are laid. Mourning doves and upland sandpipers take advantage of natural depressions or make minor scrapes in the soil and pull a little vegetation in to make a nest. The common nighthawk is even less fastidious, sometimes laying its eggs right on the barren surface of a rock; the mottled eggs blend in perfectly with the rock's surface, making them almost impossible to see. Sedge wrens may be the only species that actually nests up in the stems of the tallgrass prairie, although red-winged blackbirds occasionally nest in wet grasslands. The wrens infuse gathered material into a woven superstructure of big-bluestem stalks.

Most of the ground-nesting species face tremendous pressure from predators that are seeking eggs or nestlings to consume. When predators approach a nest, female upland sandpipers, mourning doves, and common nighthawks (among others) will appear lame, while calling woefully to attract the predator's attention. Many predators fall for the ruse and follow the seemingly wounded parent away from the nest, anticipating an easy meal. When far enough away for the safety of the nest, the female miraculously recovers, eventually returning to the nest once the predator has moved on.

Because of their bright colors, interesting antics, and diurnal habits, birds have always caught the fancy of human observers. Several species on Konza exhibit especially intriguing behaviors. One elaborate scam is perpetrated by the brown-headed cowbird, which lays its eggs in the nests of over two hundred species of birds throughout its range, relying on the foster parents to adopt the abandoned offspring. On Konza, the meadowlark, the dickcissel, and the grasshopper sparrow are victimized by the parasitic cowbird. Some of the parasitized species can recognize eggs that are not theirs, especially if the cowbird deposits them before the host has laid any of its own. If the eggs are detected as foreign, they are ejected from the nest, or the nest is abandoned and a new one is constructed. Other host species are less vigilant and therefore find themselves raising someone else's offspring. Frequently, the cowbird eggs are the largest in the clutch and hatch earlier than the host's eggs, so the foster nestlings end up getting more food, growing faster, and having a greater chance

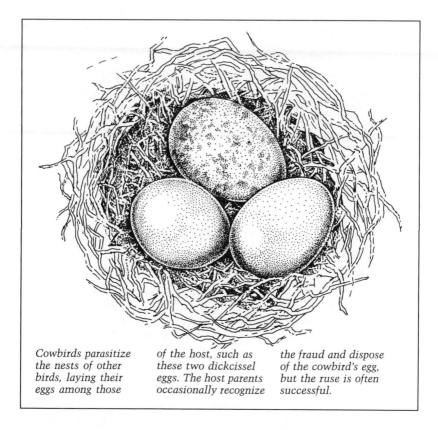

Cowbirds parasitize the nests of other birds, laying their eggs among those of the host, such as these two dickcissel eggs. The host parents occasionally recognize the fraud and dispose of the cowbird's egg, but the ruse is often successful.

for survival than do the host's own offspring. In the most extreme cases, cowbird females carry away the host's eggs as they depart, or newly hatched cowbird nestlings will toss the host's eggs or nestlings out of the nest, thus expropriating the entire parental investment. On Konza, about 10 percent of dickcissel nests that have been parasitized by cowbirds are abandoned. Furthermore, there is a major reduction in the breeding success of the parasitized nests, primarily because of the cowbird's carrying off the dickcissel's eggs after depositing its own. Interestingly, about the same number of nestlings are raised from the parasitized as from the nonparasitized nests—they just happen to be of the wrong species, from the host's point of view.

The behavior of the cowbirds and the responses of their hosts present an interesting example of the countering evolutionary pressures on the participants. Because losing an entire brood is so dam-

Prairie chickens are among the most characteristic animals of the tallgrass prairie. The males congregate on leks (small breeding grounds), where they strut their stuff to females. The performance includes dancing, posturing, foot stomping, and a low gobble, or boom, which gives these booming grounds their name.

aging to a host, there should be strong selective pressure on them to recognize cowbird eggs and to eliminate them from the nest. Conversely, cowbirds that have laid eggs that look similar to those of the foster parents would be more successful than eggs that did not match. Indeed, cowbirds frequently lay their eggs in the nests of birds whose eggs closely resemble their own. The one notable mismatch on Konza is the dickcissel, which lays blue eggs, whereas the cowbird lays tan or speckled eggs.

The epitome of tallgrass-prairie birds is the greater prairie chicken, a large, ground-dwelling seed-eater. These birds spend the entire year on Konza, along with their smaller relatives, the northern bobwhite and the ring-necked pheasant, a nonnative species. Prairie chickens have evolved a spectacular courtship behavior, which takes place on specific sites that are used year after year. These sites offer nothing but open space in which the males can strut their stuff in an attempt to attract a mate. The courting grounds, called leks, are divided up among the cocks into small (approximately 15 feet, or 4.5 meters, in diameter) exclusive areas. The dominant male secures the site of his choice, with each successively subordinate male taking a less desirable location until the lek is filled. The males fight among themselves and display to the females, which are shopping amongst the hyperactive males in a scene analogous to "cruising Main Street."

The leks are also called booming grounds, because the males inflate large air sacs around their throats, exposing brilliant orange swatches of skin, and give a muffled call, or "boom," resembling a resonant gobble. They raise elongated neck feathers called pinnae, stomp their feet, bow their heads, and call to the hens, who coyly strut through the lek, evaluating the males. The scene is one of constant movement and sound; at the peak of the breeding season, dozens of prairie chickens in all stages of their displays will be milling around the lek. The booms of one male seem to excite the others, and the calls reach a crescendo as the participants attempt to surpass each other.

Under normal conditions, the top one or two males will account for 90 percent of the successful mating that take place on a lek in any one season. Satellite males possess either peripheral territories or none at all and must remain celibate until they get older and more aggressive. If the dominant males are removed (experimentally or by a predator), the lek is thrown into chaos, as the top spots are up for grabs. Subordinate males spend all of their time fighting to gain the top positions, and in doing so, they reduce the overall mating success of the lek by as much as 90 percent. Eventually, although perhaps not until the next breeding season, the negotiations are completed, and the group can get back to the business of the lek. Like the frogs discussed earlier, the males are less discriminating than the females, simply attempting to mate with as many hens as possible. The females, however, are very choosy, circulating among the males before settling on a mate. If a female chooses a dominant male, her sons are likely to inherit the traits that made the father successful in the internecine battles at the lek.

While the prairie chickens are on the lek, they are especially wary of predators. If they are too distracted by their amorous interests, they could be surprised by coyotes, foxes, bobcats, or by aerial raptors such as red-tailed hawks, northern harriers, and prairie and peregrine falcons. Every lek will probably lose one or more of its members each year to predators. After an attack by a predator, the lek congregation is more subdued than normal, acting especially cautious as the sun rises, exposing them to potential danger.

After courting from just before dawn until midmorning, the birds fly off to feed and rest for the day. Some may return in early evening, just before dusk, for a few more bouts, but the evening events are less intense. If a female successfully mates, she will fly away from the lek and construct a nest within or near a patch of shrubbery that will offer some protection from cold spring winds and hungry predators. The nest is simple, usually composed of local material rearranged into a bowl, with some added extraneous items. As many as twelve to fifteen buff- to olive-colored eggs are laid in a clutch, which is incubated for slightly over three weeks. Although the nestlings must be incubated for about a week after hatching, they are quite precocial, taking to the air within two weeks of hatching and then disbanding when they are six to eight weeks old. A female whose first nest has failed may attempt a second clutch if the failure has occurred early in the breeding season, which runs from mid March to late May on Konza.

Very few bird species can tolerate the severe Konza winters. Although there can be warm stretches in midwinter and weeks without snow cover, just a few days of extreme cold, wind, snow, or cloud cover can send bird populations reeling. Unlike many other animals, most birds do not construct elaborate shelters for protection, such as the burrows used by many mammals. Instead, they take advantage of existing windbreaks, and they hunker down for the duration of any severe weather. Of course, the strategy most commonly used by birds is to avoid winter altogether by migrating to more equable southern climes. The populations that do stay around Konza for the winter can suffer enormous losses in the worst of years.

Approximately twenty species of birds are known to have spent an entire year on Konza, staying through the winter and breeding in the following season. Black-capped chickadees, northern flickers, and northern harriers (marsh hawks) are likely to be seen every winter, while the remaining species are more fickle, staying on Konza some winters but not others. Birds of another group make Konza the southern terminus of their winter migration, then move back north in spring to breed. This group includes rough-legged hawks, dark-eyed juncos, pine siskins, and American tree sparrows, with the last making up over 50 percent of Konza's wintertime bird population.

Whereas most of the birds on the prairie are active during the day, almost all of the mammals are nocturnal. Among the few exceptions is the great symbol of the prairies, the North American bison. Bison evolved with the prairies and probably were a dominant factor in shaping the prairie community. Although several species are known to have roamed over the tallgrass prairie during the last fifteen thousand years, only one remained when white settlers arrived. Bison quickly succumbed to human greed and the progress of the railroad across the Great Plains. In 1871 a herd of more than four million was recorded in the southwestern portion of Kansas; eight years later, bison reportedly had entirely vanished from the state. Virtually all travelers who crossed the prairie and recorded their observations mention the herds of these massive beasts. Still, it is impossible to reconstruct the bisons' exact habits from these fragmentary reports. Some scientists believe that the bison existed as monolithic herds, migrating across huge areas of the prairie in search of food, whereas others think that relatively small herds separated and reunited over time. Regardless of their particular habits, bison once numbered in the millions, with herds in the Flint Hills and the Smoky Hill River drainages exceeding several hundred thousand head.

Most of what is known about bison today has been garnered from a few isolated managed herds around North America. Individuals are gregarious, forming herds that remain on the hoof while restlessly foraging over the landscape. The groups are not rigidly maintained; rather, they fragment and coalesce every few days. During the summer the tallgrass prairie would have provided ample forage for the large herds, but because big bluestem withdraws so much of its nutrients from its leaves and stems during the winter, what is left behind makes for slim pickings. Thus, in fall and winter, bison may have migrated west from Konza in search of the middle-sized and short grasses that retain more of their nutrients above ground than does big bluestem. Even today the winter diet of cattle on tallgrass pastures must be augmented with feed or hay if the animals are to prosper in the following spring. Pronghorn and elk also roamed over Konza, but they, too, fell prey to Manifest Destiny.

Except for deer, which occasionally appear in small bands, the remaining mammalian herbivores on Konza are small and inconspicuous. Seventeen species of rodents have been recorded on Konza, and several more probably occur in very low numbers. The deer mouse is by far the most abundant rodent on the prairie. It is an opportunistic feeder, consuming vegetation, seeds, and animal matter, especially insects. Deer mice can be trapped all across the tallgrass prairie of Konza, but there are significant differences in densities from the least preferred habitats (unburned lowlands) to the most preferred ones (recently burned rocky breaks).

Deer mice breed two or more times a year, producing litters of two

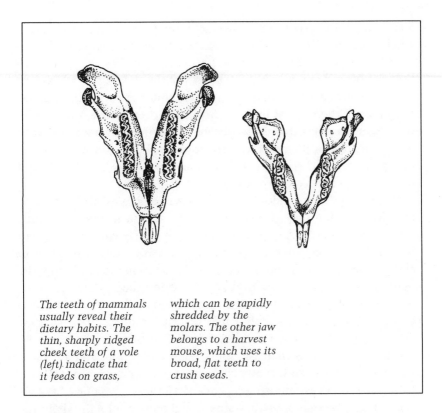

The teeth of mammals usually reveal their dietary habits. The thin, sharply ridged cheek teeth of a vole (left) indicate that it feeds on grass, which can be rapidly shredded by the molars. The other jaw belongs to a harvest mouse, which uses its broad, flat teeth to crush seeds.

to nine nurslings (usually four) after a gestation period of twenty-three to twenty-seven days. The young are virtually helpless at birth, with closed eyes and folded ears and without fur. By two weeks of age they are fully haired and have functional sight and hearing; two weeks later they have been weaned; and after two more they are ready to breed. Their nests are usually located on the ground, under some supporting structure, or beneath the ground, in burrows.

Deer mice are constantly vigilant and always seem nervous. They leap in response to the slightest sounds and are quite secretive. Their fears are not unfounded; virtually every carnivore on Konza, including reptiles, birds, and other mammals, enjoys a deer mouse either as an hors d'oeuvre or as a complete meal.

In most years, the harvest mouse is the second-most-abundant rodent on Konza. This mouse and the deer mouse seem to trade places, as the harvest mouse tends to be most abundant in habitats least preferred by the deer mouse. The tiny harvest mouse, which weighs about three-quarters of an ounce (20 grams), eats vegetation, seeds, and insects, usually at night, sometimes using the grass tunnels produced by other prairie dwellers. Its breeding habits are similar to those of the deer mouse, although most of the events of birth, weaning, and maturation occur in slightly less time, reflecting the smaller body size of the harvest mouse. Unlike the deer mouse, the harvest mouse builds a nest that is usually above ground. They measure three or four inches in diameter and are composed of compacted strands of vegetation; in the winter, several individuals may huddle together in one nest, conserving energy while keeping warm.

Many of the other rodents that live on Konza may be abundant in certain years, but they also experience crashes during which they are rare or even absent. A good example is the prairie vole, a relative of the lemming. Many species of voles exhibit fairly uniform cycles of abundance (usually five to seven years between peaks), although the prairie vole is less regular in its cycles than other species are. The prairie vole has not been studied long enough on Konza to determine if such cycles occur there, but it is reasonable to assume that they do, because cycles have been detected in nearby populations. As population densities increase, individuals fight more and are more susceptible to an array of environmental pressures, from infections to predation. These density-dependent factors—so named because their effects become more extreme as the number of animals in the population increases—eventually cause a decline in the population. Once the numbers are down, the pressures relax, and the cycle begins again as aggression turns to affection.

Voles construct and diligently maintain elaborate runways through the grass. These tunnels are about two inches wide and may be deeply pressed into the litter layer and the soil. The voles keep the runways clear by continuously trimming away grass leaves that dare to enter the tubes; indeed, active tunnels can be identified by the fresh cuttings strewn along the pathway. The runways fan out in all directions from fairly large nests (5 by 10 inches, or 12 by 25 centimeters) about 1 foot (30 centimeters) below the surface of the soil. Females may have several litters a year, each composed of four to as many as seven pups. The youngsters develop rapidly; females are capable of breeding at thirty days of age and males at thirty-five days, when they have attained about 70 percent of their adult size.

Several other species of rodents **are locally ab**undant or are abun-

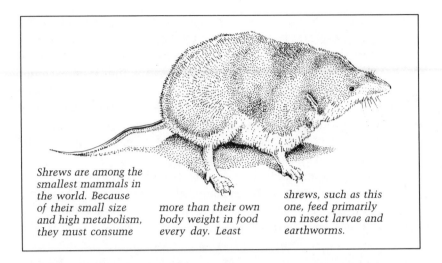

Shrews are among the smallest mammals in the world. Because of their small size and high metabolism, they must consume more than their own body weight in food every day. Least shrews, such as this one, feed primarily on insect larvae and earthworms.

dant in some years. The white-footed mouse, a close relative of the deer mouse, is dominant in the forests, but it also extends into the prairie. Cotton rats and diurnal (active by day) ground squirrels can also be common under certain circumstances. A half dozen other rodents reside in the grasslands, but their contribution is more one of novelty than of ecological significance.

The short-tailed shrew is a small mammal abundant on Konza that is frequently misidentified as a rodent. Actually, it is an insectivore, a member of a primitive group of mammals that fit into the ancestry of humans. Shrews are among the smallest mammals in the world, although the short-tailed shrew is the largest shrew in Kansas. They can be as abundant as deer mice, especially in the fall, after spring and summer reproduction has swelled the populations.

Shrews exhibit a furious pace to their lives, necessitated by their small size and high metabolic rate (their hearts regularly beat at seven hundred times a minute). Being so small makes them vulnerable to low ambient temperatures, so they must continuously stoke their metabolic fires with food to maintain a constant body temperature. Consequently, they eat several times their body weight in food each day. Shrews feed primarily on insects and earthworms, but they may also use a mild salivary poison to paralyze small prey which can then be stored until they are consumed. These fierce little carnivores also tackle vertebrates much larger than themselves, including mice and voles, by biting them at the base of the skull in one lightning-fast movement. Shrews also possess an unappealing fragrance that keeps even some carnivores from returning the favor.

Among the several species of larger mammals that inhabit Konza is the opossum, a primitive pea-brained mammal that is an extreme generalist. Opossums will eat almost anything they can track down, including insects, crayfish, frogs, snakes, birds, birds' eggs, and small mammals. Coyotes are common on Konza, and foxes are spotted occasionally. Raccoons, badgers, skunks, and bobcats can be seen on Konza, but their influence on it is not known.

Of course, humans are the one mammal—indeed, the one organism —that has a constant and overriding effect on Konza. The most extreme impacts are wrought through the few acres of tilled fields, the dwellings, and the other structures on the prairie. Additional impacts are left in simple footprints or other minor disturbances. We can only hope that the most important impact of our species will come from what we learn about the grasslands of Konza Prairie, rather than what we do to them.

FIRE

Fire, a natural component of many habitats, was a primary force in molding grasslands, and it continues to impinge on the limits and boundaries of the tallgrass prairie. Anywhere that high plant production is exposed to a dry season, both the fuel and the opportunity for conflagrations exist. In those habitats where fire is a regular occurrence, plants and animals have adapted to minimize its liabilities and even take advantage of its benefits. The question then becomes, Is fire solely responsible for the origin, structure, and maintenance of the tallgrass prairie? This question is difficult to answer; we have but one planet and one set of grasslands, which we view only in hindsight. We cannot rerun the evolution of grasslands for our edification, nor can we peer back at the past with great accuracy. We can, however, use analogy and observation to seek those similarities between various grasslands that may shed light on the relationship between grasslands and fire. Furthermore, research carried out on Konza and in other habitats is directed toward answering questions associated with the effects that fire has on natural communities.

Grasses probably evolved initially in response to increased aridity in landscapes where trees and shrubs were at a disadvantage because of periodic drought. Because a substantial portion of their critical tissue was underground, early grasses could take advantage of seasonal moisture to grow and reproduce, thus staving off desiccation during the dry seasons. Grazing mammals probably followed on the heels of the geographic radiation of grasses, taking advantage of the huge amounts of readily available forage within their reach. Fire would also follow, a natural consequence of an accumulation of fuel (drying grass) and sparks provided by seasonal lightning. Once the coalition of grasses, grazers, and fires formed on the arid plains of the temperate latitudes, it would be especially difficult for nongrasses to reclaim any lost ground, even when the regions returned to a more mesic condition. If invasions were launched by trees to reclaim their territory, lightning would pick off the isolated insurgents before they could establish a foothold. Thus, it seems likely that while a combination of selective forces, including climate, substrate, and grazers, was responsible for the evolution of grasses, fire has become the guardian of the tallgrass prairie. The domination of grasses in prairies is especially striking in the youthful tallgrass prairie, where nongrasses have not had time to adapt to the special circumstances imposed by drought, grazers, and fire. In some older grasslands—for example, the Serengeti in Africa, which may be over one million years old—some forbs, shrubs, and trees have also adapted to these environmental forces by protecting critical tissues belowground and by relying on fire to stimulate seed dispersal.

The carpetlike growth of grasses ensures that once a fire has started, it can burn for a long time, perhaps until it reaches a natural firebreak, such as a river or an open ridge, or until rainfall from the accompanying lightning storm douses it. Records reveal that in the past, tens of thousands of acres may have burned at one time, and fires have been known to travel 125 miles in one day. The gentle, rolling topography of the tallgrass prairie also promotes the spread of fire, as does a prevailing wind that blows relentlessly in one direction, keeping a wildfire from reversing and stalling. Nothing on Konza is as impressive as a head fire roaring uphill and down wind on a gusty day.

Although fires may cover extensive areas, their effects are not uniform across the entire swath of the blaze. Fires that burn with the wind hop and skip, leaving small patches unburned or lightly singed. Patches of green vegetation may resist burning and may thus remain intact once the fire front has passed. A slow-burning fire that is moving into the wind is much more thorough, having both enough time and enough oxygen to completely burn the fuel that lies in its path. Fires that burn with the wind leave black ash and soot, while those that burn into the wind deposit a light gray ash, which is indicative of their intensive heat. On Konza Prairie, resinous cedar trees burn like torches once the flames have broken through the skirt of low vegetation that surrounds them, and dead, dry tree snags serve as kindling and cordage for curtains of flame. Furthermore, both the frequency of fire and the season in which a fire occurs significantly alter the composition of the tallgrass-prairie community. Through its capricious pattern of consumption, fire contributes to the dynamic mosaic of patterns on the tallgrass prairie.

One of the great values of Konza Prairie is the research that is being conducted there to analyze the effects of various fire regimes on the tallgrass prairie's ecosystem. Although the research has been going on for just a few years in comparison to the age of the prairie, exciting results are already emerging. These results, coupled with those from other tallgrass prairies, reveal almost three dozen known effects of the occurrence, frequency, and timing of fires; many of these effects are related. For example, when fire removes the standing dead grass shoots and underlying litter, the soil is laid bare, allowing it to warm and dry faster than unburned sections. This, in turn, alters the trajectory of future community development.

The natural frequency of fires on the tallgrass prairie is not known. Information from journals of prairie travelers and from a few bio-logical studies suggests that any one area could be expected to burn at least once every ten years, perhaps as frequently as every three or four years. The probability that a piece of prairie is going to burn is dependent on such factors as the frequency of lightning strikes, the seasons in which they occur (strikes during the dry season are more likely to produce a fire than are those in moist seasons), and the amount of available fuel, which is partially dependent on the length of time since the last fire. If the plants and animals on Konza Prairie were statisticians, they could calculate the most common burn frequencies over the centuries and could thereby alter their habits to minimize the liabilities and maximize the benefits of fires. Of course, they are not statisticians, but the evolutionary process may, in effect, have done the calculations for them. Individuals with characteristics that maximized their success over the average frequency of burns would, in the long run, leave more offspring in subsequent generations, leading to a convergence of features that are most compatible with the average frequency of burns. As with other traits, adaptation to fires is a passive process that relies on natural selection to sort among the relative patterns of life history exhibited by the inhabitants of Konza.

The natural frequency of fires is highly variable, because it depends on environmental vagaries. Nevertheless, most of the major plants and animals on the prairie seem most successful, in terms of the amount of biomass produced, when fires occur every two to four years. This roughly coincides with the available historical information about fire frequencies. The research results from Konza indicate that if fires occur more frequently than every other year, the prairie changes character by exhibiting lower biomass production and lower densities of many residents. If fire occurs too infrequently—for example, if there are more than five years between fires—the tallgrass prairie becomes choked with standing dead stems and unusable litter, thus producing a nutritional bottleneck that severely retards critical processes.

What do fires do to the tallgrass prairie, and what does this mean to the prairie inhabitants? The direct physical effects of fire are mediated through the opening up of the canopy and the elimination of standing dead material and accumulated litter near the surface of the soil. Before a fire intrudes onto the tallgrass prairie, the environment near the soil surface is cool and moist. The overlying mat of litter shades out more than 99 percent of the sunlight hitting the canopy; it also restricts the drying flow of air. When fire removes these impediments, the soil is exposed to warming by the sun and to drying by laminar wind flows over the surface. The warming can be especially pronounced right after a fire, when the black ash absorbs the sun's energy and insulates the soil against heat loss at night. In addition to warming the soil, the full sun provides energy for photosynthesis in the emerging leaves in spring, energy that would not reach down to the new shoots if the litter layer remained. Seedlings are especially vulnerable to shading because they are relying on stored provisions as their sole source of nutrients and energy, and they would have almost no chance to wedge their way up through a smothering litter layer and shading stems into the energy-rich sunlight. Even big bluestem, which can call upon the nutritional deposits of previous generations through its network of rhizomes, must, in the absence of fire, struggle for the sky.

When fires occur during the spring, drying is usually not a problem, because the soil is near saturation from snow melt and the soaking rains of the season. This generates ideal conditions for the sprouting and growth of the prairie-adapted plant species. Having been rid of its overlying canopy, the ground warms in response to the sun's rays, and enough moisture is available to promote growth and nutrient intake. Clearing the soil surface of litter can increase water runoff and loss of nutrients, but the underground roots and rhizomes tend to hold the soil in place, and the newly emerging sprouts quickly establish dikes that retain any rain that falls. As spring moves on into summer, the absence of litter and of standing dead material increases air movement around plant leaves, keeping them cool compared to conditions down inside an unburned layer of litter.

A second major effect of fires is also mediated through the incineration of standing dead stems and the litter layers. The aboveground debris retains a small portion of nutrients, such as nitrogen, that are not available to plants and animals in the underlying soil. Most plants have abscission layers (tissues that split apart) at the base of their leaves, which causes the leaves to fall off when their nutrients have been recalled. Many grasses, including big bluestem, do not drop their leaves; the leaves remain erect until they have been beaten down by wind, rain, or the footfalls of animals. Once the leaves have been knocked down near the surface, soil microbes and other organisms can process the detritus, passing it on to the next step in the nutrient cycle, but this may take several years. Fires can accomplish a similar feat in seconds, reducing the miniature forest to a thin layer of ash. Some of the nutrients are consumed by the fire and are thereby lost to the system, but the remainder quickly reenter the system, stimulating subsequent growth. Whereas many ecosystems employ microbial decomposers to reduce the system's trash to usable form, tallgrass seems to rely on fire as the major process in recycling its nutrients.

Perhaps even more important than the sequestering of nutrients by the litter is the effect that dead stems and leaves and their resident microbes have in intercepting water and nutrients bound for the soil. The leaves, with their rough surfaces and tiny hairs, trap rainfall and retain it until it evaporates, thus preventing it from reaching the ground. Water from a slow, gentle rainfall is more likely to be diverted in this manner than is rain from a storm that produces pounding raindrops, which plunge through the overgrowth, and winds that can shake the water droplets off the leaf surfaces and onto the soil. Nevertheless, a significant amount of rainfall may never reach the soil in areas that go unburned; instead, it may evaporate, to become part of a cloud that sheds its moisture on some distant region. Of course, water that does accumulate on leaves and runs down their length will accumulate at the plant base, perhaps spilling over and offering a tiny spring for the plant's own roots and rhizomes.

As much as one-quarter of the nitrogen, a critical nutrient, that is fed into the Konza system comes from rainfall. Lightning causes some of the nitrogen in the atmosphere (which is almost 80 percent nitrogen) to change into a form available to plants as fertilizer. This nitrogen falls out with the rain and enters the nutrient cycle of the prairie. The standing dead stems and litter layer are blanketed with a vast array of microbes that also require nitrogen. From their position on the emergent platforms, the microbes intercept nitrogen before it reaches the ground, thus starving the plants and animals in the soil and erecting another bottleneck in the nutrient cycle. Fire destroys the aboveground habitat for these microbes, thus increasing the amount of nitrogen that reaches the soil in usable form, especially during the critical spring growing season.

Fires also reduce competition in prairies by killing plants that are not specifically adapted to tolerate burning. Small, newly emerged forbs or the seedlings of woody plants can have their critical meristems damaged or destroyed, thus reducing their success and eventually leading to death. Some trees survive fires by making it through the vulnerable seedling and sapling stages, extending their growing tips above the inferno below. This may require a decade or more of growth, however, a period during which the trees may be consumed by fire or damaged beyond repair.

If fire opens up the prairie, if it enhances the rapid cycling of nutrients that would otherwise be trapped in the dead vegetation and the resident microbes, and if it reduces competition from dicots, how are these effects revealed in the responses of the tallgrass prairie? It is difficult to construct a chain of events that leads directly to the differences seen between burned and unburned areas, because these are not simple cause-and-effect relationships. There are many forks in the paths to the communities that result from periodic fires, and the exact track that is taken is governed by specific conditions at the time of the blaze. Even with such complications, there are common routes that generate predictable results of fires.

If fires occur in early spring, the most important effects of burning accrue even before new sprouts emerge above the soil surface. The opening of the vegetational canopy and the deposition of a dark layer of ashes warm the soil by as much as 30 degrees Fahrenheit (17 degrees Celsius) at the surface and 16 degrees Fahrenheit (9 degrees Celsius) four inches below the surface, thus speeding the below-ground development of tillers in big bluestem. The exposed surface is susceptible to drying and excess runoff if a downpour occurs, but in the spring there is usually plenty of residual moisture in the soil to maintain productive plant growth. If the burns occur at least two years apart, the release of nutrients into the soil will also provide a boost: even though some nutrients are lost in the holocaust, the net result is beneficial. Not only are more nutrients available, the roots of big bluestem are more efficient at absorbing what is present in areas that are burned every few years. Nutrient intake is also enhanced by the moist conditions, because most nutrients flow into the roots and root hairs passively while water is being siphoned up by the plant.

The early robust growth of grasses, especially of big bluestem, generates several important features exhibited by the mature plants. The most striking is simply increased biomass—more pounds of plant tissue are produced in areas that are burned every other year than under any other condition. The increases in plant production can be more than 75 percent over what would have been produced had the area not burned. For the major warm-season grasses on Konza (big bluestem, little bluestem, and Indian grass), a spring burn every two years also increases the number of tillers produced per acre, increases the diameter of the basal area of the plants, and increases the biomass of underground rhizomes. Areas that are burned every year show somewhat lower changes in these features,

*and areas that are left without burning gradually decline in produc-
tivity, eventually choking on their own excess litter.*

*In addition to these gross differences in plant production, specific
changes in the anatomy of the grasses are related to fire on the
tallgrass prairie. After the prairie has been burned, the thickness of
individual leaves increases, making them more efficient photosynthetically. Concurrently, leaf weight increases, and the number of
stomata—the tiny valves on the underside of leaves that regulate
the movement of gases and water vapor in and out of the leaf—
increases. The specific types of pigments that are produced in the
leaves also respond to the opening up of the canopy. In response to
fire, all of these features combine to increase the maximum photosynthetic rates of the primary grasses, thus yielding the optimum
condition for the production of grass tissue.*

*Of course, spring fires are not an advantage for all of the plant
residents on Konza. As noted earlier, spring forbs that are sprouting
when a fire arrives are killed or maimed, preventing them from
taking advantage of subsequent beneficial conditions. Even if some
of the forbs were to recover, the warm-season grasses would have
a jump on them, for they would already be crowding the sky and
shading any pretender to that resource. The early-developing cool-
season grasses can also be inhibited by spring fires, because they
will have begun their nutrient mobilization for the incipient growth
and reproduction and may get caught with all of their resources up
in green leaves, where they can be lost to the fire. The overall effect
of frequent fires is to reduce the diversity of the plant community
while increasing the abundance and dominance of a few specialists,
such as big bluestem.*

*When fires increase plant productivity, the quality of life for other
organisms on the prairie, especially the major herbivores, is also
elevated. Consequently, their growth, production, and reproductive
success follow a pattern similar to that of the grasses. Both bacteria
and fungi increase within a few days after a fire, perhaps stimulated
by the warming sun. On areas that have been burned regularly, the
contributions of bacteria and fungi to the biotic process remain high
relative to areas that go unburned for too long. The total biomass
of small subterranean herbivores (mostly insect larvae) in the soil,
which feed on the increased plant productivity of the burned areas,
is also significantly greater in burned than in unburned plots of*

prairie. The increase in the number of herbivores, in turn, makes more food for belowground predators, which multiply in burned plots. As might be expected, even smaller arthropods, which feed on litter rather than on living plant material, are reduced in numbers in burned areas if their food resource goes up in smoke. Native earthworm species also increase in the soil of burned sites, because they take advantage of the increased productivity and the equable soil climate.

Aboveground herbivores are significantly affected by the burning regime they encounter. For example, grasshoppers are directly affected by fires if the burning takes place when early life stages (nymphs) are trapped by the flames. They may also be indirectly affected by changes in microclimate (burned areas are hotter and drier than unburned plots), in the quality and quantity of food, and in susceptibility to predators. Removing the litter layer and other cover may make the climate near the soil surface inhospitable for developing grasshoppers. Changes in the plant community that are wrought by fire may favor one group of grasshoppers over another (e.g., fires that promote grasses would promote the success of species that specialize on grasses). By opening up the prairie, fires make some grasshoppers more conspicuous, thus increasing their chances of being claimed by a predator. Each of these factors affects different grasshopper specialists in different ways, but the overall pattern indicates that maximum grasshopper density and maximum species richness occur in areas that are burned about every other year. Areas that are burned annually show the lowest abundance and diversity, while those that are left unburned for four or more years are intermediate.

Birds are so mobile that they are not likely to be directly affected by fires, except those that might have nests in the path of a blaze. However, brown-headed cowbirds, mourning doves, meadowlarks, upland sandpipers, and such migrating species as rusty and Brewer's blackbirds and water pipits flock to the burned areas to forage. They may be responding to the opening up of the habitat, which uncovers more items of prey, or to subsequent increases in grasshopper densities once the vegetation returns. The upland sandpipers nest in the unburned areas, but they bring their fledglings into recently burned watersheds to feed. Raptors also take advantage of the newly exposed landscape for foraging, but the use gradually declines as grass reappears and obscures the prey.

The number of rodents on Konza is greatest in areas that burn every one to four years. The details vary depending on the species—the dominant deer mice appear to be most abundant in habitats that are burned every two or three years, whereas the greatest number of all rodents combined occurs in areas that are burned annually. The rodents feed on a variety of items (vegetation, seeds, insects) that respond to specific burn frequencies, so it is not surprising that the rodents exhibit different patterns. Changes in the numbers of rodents in the different treatments may reflect variable mortality, differential reproductive output, or migration to and from burned areas. In grasslands other than Konza, investigators have noticed that bison head toward burning, smoking areas, apparently in anticipation of the incipient flush of new growth.

The tallgrass prairie is capable of burning during any month of the year, although snow cover in winter and luxuriant growth in a moist summer inhibit widespread fires. The exact timing of a fire is important in determining its overall effect. Many plants and animals on the tallgrass prairie are synchronized with seasonal variables that serve as cues for such events as growth and reproduction. Thus, important components of entire communities may burst forth in unison when appropriate conditions prevail.

The relationship between the timing of a fire and the onset of concurrent community phenomena will determine the range of effects inflicted by the burning. A number of experimental plots near Konza Prairie have been burned annually at various times of the year for over fifty years. Information from these plots indicates that burns occurring as the warm-season grasses (especially big bluestem) are emerging (that is, early April) promote their success and dominance in the community. Burns that occur in early or mid spring increase the success of little bluestem, whereas winter burns promote the success of forbs and woody species. Unburned plots are susceptible to invading forbs and woody plants, which eventually dominate those plots. The late-spring burns supported the greatest sustained overall plant production of any of the experimental treatments.

The direct and indirect effects of fire are numerous, and they generate an extremely complicated pattern of biotic and abiotic interactions. To the untrained eye, differences may be difficult to spot, but a boot dragged through the litter will reveal which watersheds are choked with litter and which are not. Attempts are being made to tease apart the various influences wrought by fire, but the *overall pattern remains elusive. It is obvious that the intensity, the frequency, and the timing of fires interact with grazing and other impacts of prairie residents to produce a mosaic of patterns on the tallgrass prairie. The occurrence of fire and its influence are determined by a large number of chance events, from the presence of sufficient fuel to the probability that lightning will strike the appropriate kindling. What we do know is that fire is an important determinant of prairie form and function, that it was involved with the origin of prairies, and that it is responsible in large part for their continued success.*

5 / Forests

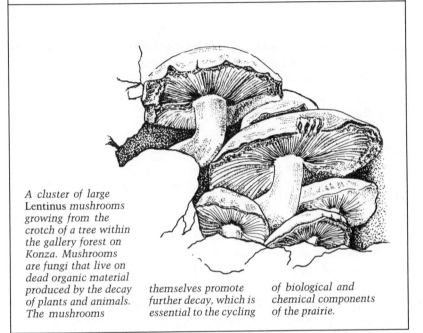

A cluster of large Lentinus *mushrooms growing from the crotch of a tree within the gallery forest on Konza. Mushrooms are fungi that live on dead organic material produced by the decay of plants and animals. The mushrooms* themselves promote *further decay, which is essential to the cycling* of biological and *chemical components of the prairie.*

ALTHOUGH FORESTS CONSTITUTE ONLY 6 PERCENT OF KONZA prairie, the mass of vegetation tied up in woodlands makes a significantly greater contribution to the overall biomass of Konza. The wooded bands, which usually stretch along stream courses, run for several miles in widths that range from 30 to 1,000 feet (9 to 305 meters). The boundary between grasslands and the forest can be quite abrupt, especially where the forests occur down in the eroded flood plain of the supporting stream and where the grass inhabits adjacent uplands. Even without this physiographic barrier, there is usually a distinct boundary (called an ecotone) where grass meets trees. Along these edges, trees launch tentative excursions into the grasslands but are turned back by dry soil and periodic fires, while grasses that invade the forest are deterred by its deep shade under the tall, closed forest canopy.

Shade stratifies the forests, with lower layers composed of plants that can get by on less light or that do their photosynthesizing early in the spring before the overhanging trees leaf out and intercept the sunlight. The forests of Konza Prairie exhibit three basic layers: the tree canopy, an intermediate shrub layer, and an herb layer near the ground. The tree canopies are 45 to 80 feet (14 to 24 meters) high in mature forests, and at their densest, they completely enclose the woodland. The shrub layer may reach 15 feet (4.5 meters) in height, and it tends to occur more patchily, intensifying the shade directly below. The herb layer, which measures a few inches to a few feet high, is composed of a wide variety of plants that compete for what little light and space remain near the ground surface. At any particular site, of course, the actual arrangement is not composed of discrete layers with characteristic heights; there is a gradual transition from one layer into another.

Three prominent species of trees make major contributions to the Konza woodlands; these occur in various combinations at different sites. Chinkapin (or Chinquapin) oak and bur oak frequently occur together, while bur oak and hackberry form another prominent community in other reaches of the forest. In a few areas, chinkapin oaks form almost monotypic stands. The forests also contain a smattering of green ash, American elm, box elder, and black walnut, but these species rarely make a significant contribution to the overall forest community in comparison to the dominant oaks and hackberries. Near the stream banks, cottonwoods, willows, and sycamores make cameo appearances.

Land Office surveys made in 1858 suggest that forests then were mere ribbons along the water courses. Fire, then uncontrolled, was the major factor restricting the spread of young trees. Until the late nineteenth century, when ranchers first began to control fire, wild-fires frequently invaded the margins of these woodlands, limiting their expansion primarily by killing saplings. By 1939, when the first aerial photographs of Konza were taken, the forests had expanded significantly, and aerial photographs taken in 1978, just forty years later, revealed a doubling of forest acreage. The forests on Konza probably cover as much area now as they did when the woodlands followed the retreating glaciers northward more than eight thousand years ago.

Young trees are especially vulnerable to incineration. According to

The prairie larkspur attracts insects to a nectar reward in its upturned corolla tube. A packet of pollen is poised over the entrance to the nectar, where it can be applied to a visitor who will then carry it to another larkspur. (Reichman)

A yellow spider eating a fly on red flowers. Crab spiders are aggressive predators that snare their prey, such as this sweat bee. (Rob Gendron)

Fire line. During the spring of each year the watersheds on Konza come under the torch. Each area is burned in a particular sequence to determine how fire, a natural feature of prairies, affects the inhabitants. (Sharon Gurtz)

Kings Creek is one of the few streams in North America that originates on relatively pristine tallgrass prairie. It serves as a natural laboratory and as a benchmark for comparisons with creeks that have been influenced more significantly by human activity. (Elmer Finck)

A yellow crab spider on a variegated plant.

A milkweed seed pod. As milkweed pods mature and dry in the summer sun, their feathery plumes began to unfurl. Once thoroughly dried, they will be cast free to drift with the breezes. (Rob Gendron)

Grass flowers. Delicate big-bluestem flowers rest at the end of the long stalks that give the tallgrass prairie its name. (Reichman)

Smoke. Once the blaze of a prairie fire has passed, the ashes continue to smolder for hours. Slight breezes can resurrect the blaze, incinerating any remaining vegetation. (Reichman)

Brown prairie. During the fall the prairie rapidly turns brown as the plants withdraw their nutrients into underground parts. The remaining stems are hardy and persist until beaten down by a footfall or heavy snow. (Marty Gurtz)

Green prairie with white flowers. At the height of summer, the prairie is a lush green carpet. While the surface appears to be dominated by grasses, numerous patches of bright forbs form splotches across the landscape. (Reichman)

Close-up of a leaf. The leaves of buffalo melon are thick and fibrous, with coarse veins running through them. This view is approximately 2 inches across (5 centimeters), but without a frame of reference, it could just as easily be a view from outer space. (Reichman)

A limestone ridge. Limestone underlies much of Konza Prairie, forming several major ridges. This emerging ridge will eventually stand above the surrounding prairie when the soil around it erodes downhill. (Marty Gurtz)

Fall colors. Many plants on Konza turn brilliant colors in the fall. The colors are usually a result of the loss of green chlorophyll, which obscures the underlying pigments during the summer. (Sharon Gurtz)

Winter. Many inhabitants of Konza either leave for the winter or retreat into a frigid torpor. Other residents must face the gelid season head-on, securing what food and shelter they can when little is available. (Marty Gurtz)

This tiny long-horned grasshopper stands atop a flowering head of catclaw sensitive briar. (Reichman)

A damselfly. Dam-
selflies are graceful
fliers that hover over
the ponds along the
tributaries of Kings
Creek. After mating,
the males guard their
partners against in-
terlopers until the
females lay their fertil-
ized eggs. (Reichman)

A solitary bee scruti-
nizes its domain from
a moth mullein flower.
(Reichman)

A wave on the inland sea.

one study conducted on Konza, there were twelve hundred saplings in a woodland area prior to burning but none after the fire. Fires also significantly reduce the shrub layer, often causing an 80 percent decline in shrub densities.

The patriarchs of the Konza forests are the oaks. Under full sunlight, oaks grow dozens of feet in height, and their symmetrical canopies form a thick pelt of vegetation. One cohort of large oaks on Konza is about eighty years old, suggesting that around the turn of the century the forests were released from the bonds of fire and the oaks reached for the sky, securing their dominant position. But in those places where fire does not periodically open the forest up to the sun-loving (heliophilous) oaks, shade-tolerant species have encroached and are taking over. Today oaks are not reproducing as they did seventy or eighty years ago, because their seedlings and saplings cannot compete successfully in the shade produced by their own parents. Instead, hackberry, red mulberry, and elms, which are more shade-tolerant, are gradually replacing the oaks when they die. The evidence is clear in the relative numbers of smaller and younger groups of trees. For example, hackberrys average about twenty to forty years of age, and many of their saplings are represented in the undergrowth. Conversely, oaks average over eighty years of age, and they are virtually absent from the understory. Interestingly, a survey of the Konza forests reveals a gap in the ages of the oaks and the more recent replacements, which coincides with the droughts during the 1930s. This suggests that the oaks tolerated the drought and that the other trees invaded when normal moisture patterns reappeared on Konza.

The succession from oak woodlands to forests that are dominated by hackberry will probably proceed over the next decades wherever fire is excluded as a natural component of the environment. Elms would also be a participant in the successional process were it not for Dutch elm disease, a fungal pathogen that has severely limited the distribution of elms all over North America. Where fires are allowed to invade the woodlands, thus ravaging seedlings and saplings, the reproduction of all tree species will be curtailed. Fires are currently being reintroduced into the forests on Konza, and eventually the forests will be reduced to their earlier ranges and be dominated by the oaks.

Even in forests that are not shaped by fire, gradations may favor some tree species over others. For example, oaks are very tolerant of dry conditions and can persist in desiccated soils through drought years that severely restrict hackberry populations. This tolerance is also demonstrated by the success of oaks on slopes, where water tends to run off rather than soak in, and in silty soils, which exhibit poor water-percolation properties. Hackberrys displace oaks on the more mesic sites, while redbuds tend to expropriate the drier sites. Of course, changes in the forest occur very slowly. Trees have evolved multiple sit-and-wait strategies, which allow them to deal with a wide spectrum of environmental extremes. If one year is dry or if another brings a severe attack by insect herbivores, trees can bide their time, waiting for the next year or the one after that, when conditions will be more beneficent. Rather than the quick, tactical invasions that occur on the open prairie, the turnover of species in the forest is sluggish and usually requires the death of individuals from old age before others move in.

After rousing from a winter quiescence, the trees mobilize their resources for the forthcoming growing season. They have two basic circulatory systems, one to carry water and nutrients up from the roots (the xylem) and another to transport photosynthate down from the leaves (the phloem). As water begins to evaporate from the newly formed leaves, a water-pressure deficit is produced, which has the effect of drawing water and elements dissolved in the water into the roots and their tiny root hairs. Some of the water is used in photosynthesis, while the remainder evaporates through the stomata (small apertures) on the underside of the leaves. While the sun is shining, the products of photosynthesis are produced and gathered within each leaf and are shipped through the leaf stem (petiole), where they gather in the twigs, branches, trunks, and roots, to be reorganized for growth, stored for later use, shunted into flower buds and reproduction, or made into defensive chemicals to ward off herbivores.

Both oak species and the hackberry form leaf buds early in the year and leaf out in mid spring. The leaves grow slowly, but for the most part they have no serious competitors for light. The trees add height and spread in canopy volume by growing at the tips of new shoots; several inches of new growth may be added in good years. Woody plants, unlike grasses and forbs, also grow in girth as tissue is added from a secondary meristem called the cambium layer. This thin generative layer lies just under the bark, where it grows both inward

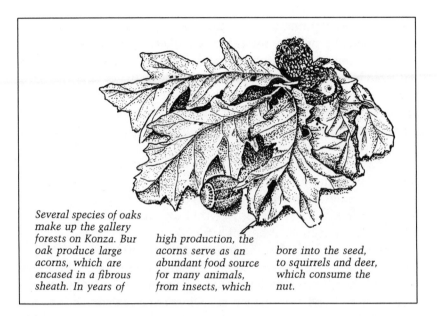

Several species of oaks make up the gallery forests on Konza. Bur oak produce large acorns, which are encased in a fibrous sheath. In years of high production, the acorns serve as an abundant food source for many animals, from insects, which bore into the seed, to squirrels and deer, which consume the nut.

and outward. Its inward growth produces sequential rings that vary in size depending on the quality and quantity of resources during the growing season—thick rings indicate warm, moist growing seasons, while truncated rings suggest less hospitable conditions. Tissue is added to the cork and bark layers by the outward growth of the cambium.

Bur oak and hackberries flower shortly before the leaves develop in late April and early May, and chinkapin oak follows a few weeks later. All three produce both male and female flowers on the same tree. The oaks have long, cylindrical flowers known as catkins, while hackberry flowers look more like typical flowers with petals, although they are small and rather inconspicuous. All three of these trees rely on the wind to carry their pollen—this suggests that the wind is a reliable vehicle for pollination and that insects may be less trustworthy in the face of incapacitating spring storms. Furthermore, the costs of producing—and perhaps losing in spring storms—large, showy flowers to entice insect pollinators may be disadvantageous for the trees.

Oaks produce a nut inside the shell of an acorn, one of the most recognizable forms in the natural world. The nuts are dropped within the year, usually in early to late fall. Under appropriate conditions, the nuts will germinate soon after dropping; if germination is not accomplished promptly, the acorns are likely to be consumed or to rot under the onslaught of microbes. Some of the acorns that are gathered by squirrels and blue jays are stored in the ground for future use. If a few of these are forgotten or if their owner should die before recovering them, the burying of the acorn may have the effect of actually planting the seed. Rather than producing an armored nut, the ovaries of hackberry flowers develop into small cherrylike fruits, one-fourth to two-fifths of an inch (6 to 10 millimeters) in diameter. These purple or dark-red fruits are consumed by many species of birds and mammals, which then disperse the seeds in their feces. Some of the fruits stay on the tree throughout the winter, but most of them are consumed or fall off before spring.

In the fall, at the end of the growing season, the trees extract vital nutrients from their leaves before shedding them. Once the major nutrients have been withdrawn and the green chlorophyll pigments have been reduced, the background colors are revealed, allowing the bright yellow, orange, or gold tints associated with fall foliage to dominate. As much as 50 percent of the nitrogen and 35 percent of the phosphorus in the leaves is resorbed each year before the trees cast off their used leaves. The trees on Konza retrieve much less phosphorus from their leaves than do trees in the eastern deciduous forests. This suggests that phosphorus may not be especially limited on Konza, because otherwise there would be selective pressures to conserve it when the leaves were shed. The size and the age of trees are directly correlated with the percentage of nitrogen and phosphorus that is retained—bigger, older trees recover more of the nutrients than do smaller, younger trees. Elements that occur in trace amounts are also shuttled around when the leaves drop off. For example, zinc appears to be withdrawn from the leaves before they are dropped, especially in oaks. Several species of trees actually increase the levels of copper, iron, and manganese in their leaves just prior to jettisoning them. Although it is obviously advantageous to retain important nutrients such as nitrogen and phosphorus, the ecological significance of increasing the concentration of some trace elements in the leaves before dropping them is unclear, unless this is a way of ridding the plant of excess or potentially toxic chemicals. Leaves become extremely abundant on the forest floor by late autumn, but because most of the nutrients in the leaves have been reclaimed by the trees, only a few organisms, primarily microbes such as fungi and bacteria, can subsist on them.

Although trees possess massive amounts of tissue, much of it is woody and insufficiently nutritious to attract herbivores; only a few insect species carve their way through hardwood, processing huge amounts of wood while leaving twisting bore holes as evidence of their activity. Many long-lived plants, including trees, can afford to—indeed, must—invest in noxious chemicals as a defense against herbivores. For example, oaks contain significant amounts of tannin, the same chemical that colors aged whiskey and tea and that is used in tanning hides. The tannins reduce the ability of a herbivore to digest plant tissues by debilitating the community of microbes in the herbivore's gut. Without the aid of symbiotic microbes, the digestive efficiency of the herbivore drops below a level that is energetically advantageous, thus causing the herbivore to shift to a more profitable diet. As tree species evolve different schemes to deter herbivore attack, herbivores evolve counter strategies to skirt the plant's defenses, and the continual battle between the consumers and the consumed rages on.

While many species of trees invest heavily in defense, the hackberrys seem to stand undefended in the Konza forests—it seems as though everyone in the forest takes a bite from the hackberry trees. Caterpillars either chew holes in the leaves or consume them entirely. If the tree produces another flush of leaves in an attempt to capture some of the season's remaining opportunity, galls form on the leaves, robbing them of their produce. Deer browse on the leaves, and dozens of birds and mammals consume the berries and the seeds. It is not clear why hackberrys are so defenseless, but they seem to bear the brunt of the forest's consumers on Konza.

The shrub layer is poorly developed in the forests of Konza Prairie. Historically this may be the result of the grazing practices of the past century, when livestock were allowed into the woods to feed on the young shoots. Cows have only been excluded from the forests over the last decade, so it is too early to determine if they were responsible for the missing shrub layer; if the shrub layer does recover in the future, it will be strong circumstantial evidence that livestock was a contributing factor.

Recent studies have indicated that saplings of invading tree species, such as hackberry and elm, make up a substantial proportion of the

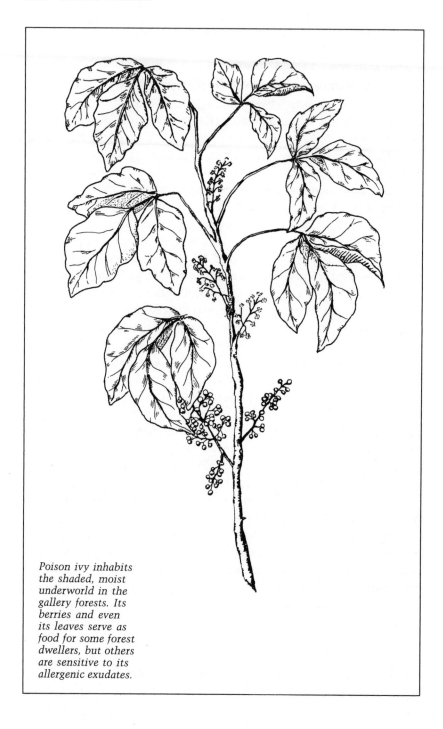

*Poison ivy inhabits
the shaded, moist
underworld in the
gallery forests. Its
berries and even
its leaves serve as
food for some forest
dwellers, but others
are sensitive to its
allergenic exudates.*

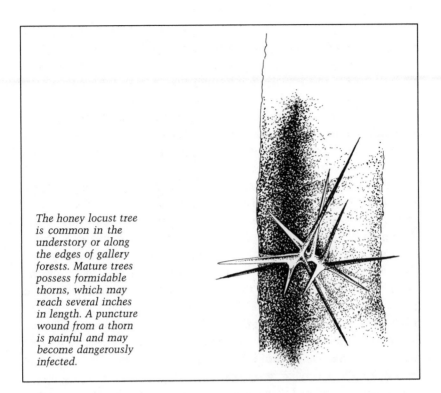

The honey locust tree is common in the understory or along the edges of gallery forests. Mature trees possess formidable thorns, which may reach several inches in length. A puncture wound from a thorn is painful and may become dangerously infected.

plants in the forest's shrub layer, even though they are not considered shrub species. The saplings are waiting their turn, ready to shoot up should a hole in the canopy become available. Buckbrush, ceanothus, and rough-leaved dogwood may grow in the understory of the forests, especially along the forest edge or where the canopy is more open and where some light penetrates to the understory. Prickly ash and two species of wild plum also occur in the shrub layer, but they are quite rare in the gallery forests. Two vines—river-bank grape and Virginia creeper—do not grow like typical shrubs; rather, they climb their way along tree trunks and take up residence among the shrubs.

Poison ivy is a common inhabitant of the gallery forests, where it assumes many forms of growth: it can grow like a vine up tree trunks to a height of 60 feet (18 meters) or as a prostrate herbaceous forb on the forest floor. Poison ivy has evolved an irritating secretion, presumably to inhibit animals from consuming it, although deer eat it with impunity. Even though some people do not react to its allergenic exudates, it has a well-deserved reputation for hostility in the forest. A common misconception is that poison ivy manufactures a toxic substance that causes blisters to develop where the plant touches the skin. The blisters, however, are actually the body's allergic response to the detection of foreign agents from the plant, which may be picked up directly or indirectly from clothing, animals, or any item that has touched a poison-ivy plant. Because the response is an allergic reaction to the plant, the blisters cannot be spread by touching them or their seepage, although smearing the plants toxin around on the skin will spread the damage.

The honey locust is another plant in the understory that protects itself effectively. It frequently grows in patches on the edges of the forest, where it can reach 20 feet (6 meters) in height, but under the forest canopy it rarely grows taller than 6 or 8 feet (1.8 to 2.4 meters) high. The branches have clusters of daggerlike spines that are several inches long. On mature plants, spines even cover the main trunk, leaving no part unprotected. The spines possess a mild protein-digesting enzyme, which causes the skin around a minor prick to discolor and take on the appearance of an old bruise. During the winter the spines tend to stand out on the leafless branches, making them easier to avoid; but when fully sheathed in leaves, the spines are effectively camouflaged.

The forest floor is a Lilliputian environment, with many tiny plants peeking out from under the miscellaneous litter of dead plants. The floor records many dramatic past events: the carcasses of trees that have fallen or been blown down are strewn about in various stages of decomposition. The dead trees rot as microbes and fungi, which invade them to secure resources, flourish in the moist environment. Mosses also grow in dense mats where there is sufficient moisture, adding brilliant green splotches to the forest, especially where flecks of light play on the greenery. The plants that are close to the ground receive very little of the sun's radiant energy, and so their growth forms are modest.

Some grasses invade the forest floor, most commonly near stream beds. Prairie cordgrass is especially prominent in the wettest forest habitats, as well as along wet areas in the grassland, but in addition, wirestem muhly, one species of panicum, and two species of wild ryegrass occur near streams. Bottlebrush grass and several introduced species of brome reside on the forest floor, even in the drier areas.

FORAGING

Photosynthesis provides the basic resources for all but a tiny fraction of the biological processes on earth (a few bacteria get their energy by using sulfur-based chemicals, rather than sunlight, as a resource). Billions of tons of plant tissue are produced every year, and only a small portion of what is produced is consumed by herbivores, nature's vegetarians. Many insects and mammals are herbivorous, and almost every group of animals contains some herbivorous members. A few groups of parasitic plants also live off of their brethren, rather than carrying out their own photosynthesis. The herbivores, in turn, provide food for a large number of carnivorous predators, including certain insects, fish, snakes, predatory birds, and various mammals.

Many small herbivores and carnivores specialize on particular parts of the plants and the animals that they consume. Aphids specialize in sucking nutrients out of the vascular system of plants, and nematodes invade and consume root tissues. Bees and some birds specialize on nectar or pollen, while wood-boring beetles feed on the soft wood under tree bark. Among the specialized carnivores are blood-sucking mosquitos, mites, and ticks and horned lizards and frogs, which feed primarily on ants. The most extreme specialists are parasites, which live in specific sites within their hosts. For example, tapeworms live in a tiny segment of the intestine of their hosts, and follicle mites stack up in the shafts of bird feathers and mammal hair, including the eyebrows of humans. The basic difference between predation and parasitism is death; predators kill and consume their prey, whereas parasites live off of their live hosts for some time. Parasites probably reduce the fitness of their host, perhaps even leading to an early death, but the parasites themselves rarely kill their host directly. In addition to all of the specialists, there are generalist feeders, known as omnivores, which will eat almost anything, plant or animal, dead or alive.

Eventually, all living tissue dies and is passed on to the decomposers. Except for minor physical decomposition and chemical leaching, the generalist feeders are responsible for breaking down all the debris that is left behind when plants and animals die. A leaf may be eaten by a woodrat, which extracts some of the nutrients and passes along its fecal pellets to fungi, which take their cut.

The remainder will eventually fall to microbes, which carry out the final steps of decomposition, freeing the last of the various elements that made up the leaf. Once the components of the original leaf are dispersed, they can be reassembled by plants and recycled through the system.

All animals that are familiar to us are either carnivores (such as dogs and cats) or herbivores (such as cows and horses). But the unseen decomposers arguably constitute the most important component of the ecosystem, keeping it from choking on its own remains. Nevertheless, most ecological studies have concentrated on the processes of herbivory and predation, even though decomposition is extremely important. Herbivory and predation tend to be dramatic and obvious, occurring at a rapid pace in the visible world, and therefore are more easily understood. Decomposition, on the other hand, involves microscopic events in tiny organisms in out-of-the-way places, thus making it difficult to analyze.

Ecologists have developed an intriguing set of rules to describe how animals choose what to eat. The basic premise is that the most successful individuals will be those that maximize the difference between the cost of securing food and the benefit that it will ultimately provide. The rules further suggest specific details about what animals should include in their diets and about how long they should forage in one patch of food before moving on to another. By should, ecologists mean that those individuals that follow the rules will be more successful in passing on their genes to the next generation, the ultimate measure of evolutionary success. Similar types of cost/benefit calculations are familiar to all of us, even if we haven't studied economics. For example, it makes sense to drive one hundred miles to save $150 on a new refrigerator, but not to save fifteen cents on a magazine. Such false economy might cost us a few dollars, but it could cost an imprudent plant or animal its life.

Although the rules of foraging are relatively simple, they generate some nonintuitive predictions. The basic rule suggests that animals are able to rank the array of available food items in the order of some perceived benefit—for example, net, not gross, return in calories. The animals should then choose only the "best" items (i.e., those with the highest benefit/cost ratio) and should eat enough of those to fulfill their caloric requirements. The net gain of any item is a function of its absolute value (benefit) and the cost of obtaining it, *including travel costs (e.g., running, flying, etc.) and handling time (e.g., husking an acorn).*

One nonintuitive prediction that emerges from such calculations is that animals should not eat some items, even if they have to walk right by them to get to a more preferred item. Why would they do this, even if they had already "paid" the cost of getting to the nonpreferred item? The answer lies in the relative worth of other available items. Imagine going from store to store picking up one or two items at each in the hope of securing a good bargain: although you might occasionally stumble onto a special deal, much of your effort would be unproductive, especially if you factor in the time and cost of driving around town. Conversely, if you know of a store that has all the items you need at reduced prices, it would pay to ignore all of the other stores as you drove by and instead to head directly for the "best" store. Many studies have revealed that animals can make similar decisions about where to shop for food.

The foraging rules suggest another interesting behavior—an animal should leave a patch in which it is foraging before the patch is totally depleted. At first this doesn't make sense. If the animal is already there, why not take everything? The answer is that the cost of obtaining the last few items in a patch is usually much higher than the cost of finding a new rich patch. Imagine picking up pennies from abundant piles containing one hundred pennies each in the tallgrass prairie. The first ninety-five pennies might be relatively easy to scoop up, but searching for the remaining five would take longer than finding another pile of one hundred and skimming the cream off it.

Many experiments have been carried out to determine the validity of these and associated ideas, and the general conclusion is that they do provide insight into foraging choices made by consumers. There will always be some errors in the predictions; for example, animals must sample all food available, even the lowest quality items, to be able to make comparisons with the preferred items. In addition, nutritional requirements must be integrated into the procedures regarding choice. Thus, the ranking of items is complicated by the fact that some food may be high in energy but low in other essential nutrients, even some trace nutrients required in minute amounts.

The processes of herbivory and carnivory are ecologically distinct in several important ways. The food value of vegetation is generally quite low. It is primarily composed of indigestible material (e.g., cellulose), and many plants do not provide vital nutrients that animals require, such as sodium. Thus, herbivores must process tremendous amounts of vegetation in order to extract enough energy and nutrients. Most animals do not, however, have the appropriate enzymes to break down plant material; therefore they must rely on symbiotic microbes in their digestive systems to assist in obtaining what few nutrients the vegetation offers. In return, the microbes get a hospitable environment in which to live and a cut of the food taken in by the herbivore. There are classic examples of this relationship. Termites house tiny protozoans (single-celled animal-like creatures) in their intestines, which digest the cellulose in the wood consumed by the termites. Ruminant mammals, such as buffalo, have several stomachs that serve as fermentation vats for the microbial digestion of vegetation.

Because of the poor quality of most vegetation, the amount of nutrition and energy that herbivores can acquire tends to be limited by the rate at which they can consume and process greenery, rather than the time required to locate and "capture" vegetation. The supply is plentiful; in fact, herbivores are usually wading in greenery. Most herbivores must, however, eat almost all day long in order to secure enough energy and nutrients. Herbivores tend to have long digestive tracts, thus increasing the volume for digestion and the surface area for absorption of whatever nutrients do occur in their food. The digestion of vegetation is so inefficient that the feces of herbivores retain enough nutrients to support an array of adult and larval insects that sort through the remains and extract undigested particles.

A constant evolutionary process of thrust and parry occurs between plants and herbivores in the battle over the plant's tissues. For their part, many plants have evolved schemes to invest heavily in chemical and physical defenses against herbivores. The cost of maintaining such a defense may be very high and must be traded off against the benefit of shedding some of the herbivore load. Of course, these are not conscious calculations; they are simply the outcome of all the interactions of plant self-protection and herbivore countermoves that yield the most effective combination of features promoting success for the participants.

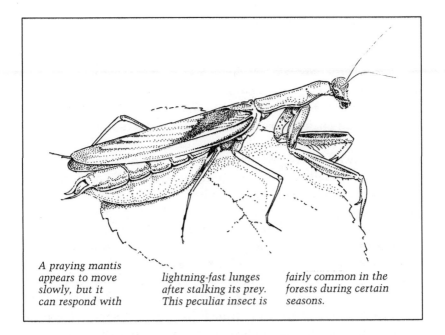

A praying mantis appears to move slowly, but it can respond with lightning-fast lunges after stalking its prey. This peculiar insect is fairly common in the forests during certain seasons.

Predators have different problems. Flesh is generally quite nutritious and can be efficiently digested, but it is difficult to locate and capture. Thus, the success of predators tends to be limited by the rate at which they can capture prey, rather than the processing rate, as is the case with herbivores. Predators have evolved many characteristics that promote success at hunting, including stealth, camouflage, speed, and endurance. Even so, most predators are successful in less than 20 percent of their attempted attacks. They are frequently spotted by wary prey or are outmaneuvered once the chase has begun. Furthermore, predation is a dangerous business; for example, when a hawk dives on its prey, three things can happen—it can miss high, losing a meal; it can miss low, crashing into the ground; or it can capture its prey—and only one outcome is beneficial.

Predators employ a variety of tricks to increase their rate of success, while their prey counter by becoming more difficult to capture. Being a predator is a tough way to make a living, but clearly many specialists have developed the skills to make it a viable life style. Virtually every group of animals on Konza has representatives that are predators, preying either on each other or on some distantly

*related unfortunate creature. Most successful predatory events are
over very quickly, turning an instant into eternity for the victim.*

Myriad insects hide, feed, reproduce, and die in the forests of Konza
Prairie. Some of the most abundant and potentially damaging insects are plant-sucking insects, such as leafhoppers and aphids. The
leafhoppers are a very large group, with over twenty-five hundred
species known from North America alone. On Konza the adults live
on leaves, especially on the trees in the forests. Leafhoppers insert a
piercing stylet into the phloem of a leaf, tapping the nutrient broth
that is being pumped back into the plant from the photosynthetic
operations within the leaf. Leafhoppers damage trees by pirating
some of their nutrients. The probing for resources frequently dams
up the free flow of sap in the phloem, causing the leaves to undergo
abnormal growth in the area of the wound. When the leafhoppers in-
ject their piercing stylets into the plant's vascular system, they may
also inoculate the plant with virulent pathogens, thereby spreading
diseases in trees, much as mosquitoes spread malaria in humans.
Leafhoppers can be extremely prolific, spending the winter either as
adults or as eggs before hatching out in the spring and then pillaging
the forest over several generations.

Aphids are closely related to the leafhoppers and are common pests
of ornamental and agricultural plants, as well as plants in natural
communities. Aphids form a huge group of soft-bodied insects that
also extract resources from leaves. Most have a complex life cycle,
overwintering as eggs that hatch out in the spring. The adult females
are winged; they migrate to a host plant, where they produce several
parthenogenic (asexual) generations of wingless offspring. The offspring then migrate to another host plant, mate, and lay eggs, which
starts the cycle again the following spring. This type of cycle generates enormous numbers of asexually produced aphids in the middle
of summer, when leaves are most abundant.

In many cases, when an aphid pierces a leaf to suck out the juices,
the tissue is stimulated to produce a gall, a hard, tumorlike structure. (Galls produced by other insects are common on hackberrys
and oaks on Konza.) It is not clear whether the plant or the consumer
benefits from the formation of a gall. The insect is protected from
the environment and from predators by the natural casing, while the

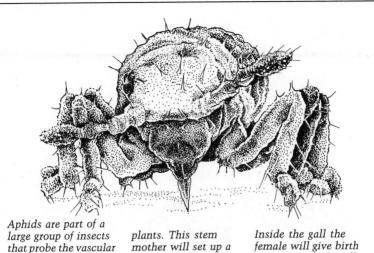

Aphids are part of a large group of insects that probe the vascular systems of plants and suck out the nutrients before they can be assimilated by the plants. This stem mother will set up a home at the base of a cottonwood leaf, thus inducing the tree to form a cancerlike gall. Inside the gall the female will give birth to young, which will eventually migrate to another host plant to spend the winter.

plant effectively corrals the antagonist, perhaps reducing its impact. Aphids on the cottonwoods of Konza attempt to set up shop at the base of the leaf, near where the leaf stem leads to the branch. All of the newly synthesized material from the leaf must funnel through this juncture, making it the most efficient location for pirating resources. It has been shown that individual females that secure this location, especially on the biggest leaves, will produce significantly more offspring than females that are relegated to inferior positions farther out on the leaf or to smaller leaves. In some species, the females will even tussle for the optimum location for several days before settling down to the business at hand. The species of cottonwood that occurs on Konza drops its aphid-infected leaves much earlier than the leaves that have not suffered aphid attack, suggesting that the plant may have evolved an antiaphid strategy of rounding up the pest in galls and discarding the leaf before the aphid can pilfer substantial amounts of nutrients.

As abundant as aphids are, they would be considerably more detrimental were they themselves not heavily parasitized and preyed upon. The principal parasites are tiny members of the wasp family; the major predators include lacewings and the larvae of certain

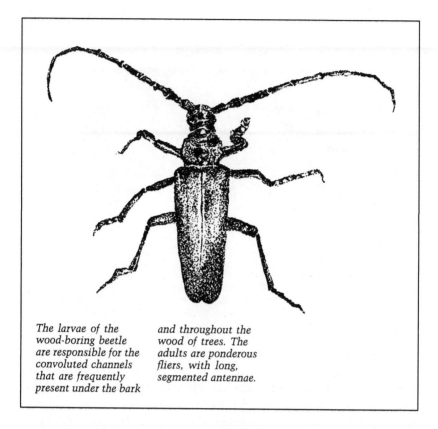

The larvae of the wood-boring beetle are responsible for the convoluted channels that are frequently present under the bark and throughout the wood of trees. The adults are ponderous fliers, with long, segmented antennae.

flies. These insects tend to track the densities of aphids, and they increase in numbers as the aphid populations grow, thereby serving as a natural biological control agent. The females of the parasites drill small apertures in the galls and lay their eggs inside the galls. The eggs hatch, and the developing larvae feed on the helpless aphids inside until sated or until the parasites mature and leave the gall.

Beetles, which constitute the largest group of insects in the world, are well represented in the fauna of the Konza forests. June beetles and rhinoceros beetles, which may have arrived on Konza only within the last few years, spend the majority of their lives as larvae in the soil of the forest floor, but they emerge as adults to drone through the night, looking for mates while haphazardly crashing into trees, buildings, and people. The adults of long-horned beetles feed primarily on flowers during the spring and early summer, but their larvae inhabit the forests, excavating tunnels into the heartwood of trees. They can cause significant damage, because they inoculate the trees with parasitic diseases that cause premature death. Bark beetles do similar damage, both as adults and as larvae. They burrow just under the bark layer of the trees, scraping but not entering the hardwood core. One species has been responsible for spreading Dutch elm disease all across North America.

The larvae of tiny moths can cause tremendous damage to trees, completely defoliating an 80-foot (24-meter) tree in a week or two. In the summer of 1985, large groves of hackberry trees were entirely stripped of their leaves by a phalanx of spring cankerworms, the caterpillars of geometrid moths. Adult females of these caterpillars are flightless, but they attract flying males by secreting a pheromone (a chemical that produces an odor used for signaling). Once having mated, the females lay their eggs on twigs after living just a few days as an adult. The eggs hatch out shortly thereafter, releasing millions of voracious herbivores on the trees. After the cankerworms have gone through several larval stages, they rappel down out of the trees, leaving silken threads dangling in the breeze. Once on the ground, they spin cocoons and subsequently metamorphose into adults. As is the case after most major defoliation events, the trees leaf out again in an attempt to regain some of their lost time and resources before the winter recess, but the cost of losing an entire set of leaves must be extremely high. Herbivorous insects have highly variable life cycles, which are affected by many environmental conditions; therefore it is rare for the same group of herbivores to exact its toll year after year. Large perennial plants such as trees are well buffered against the episodic sieges of insects, recovering sufficiently during the years of low insect attack to survive and reproduce over the long term.

Trees and other plants in the forest are faced with a formidable array of insect herbivores. Many of the insects go through several life cycles in a year and thousands during the life span of a single oak tree, making it difficult for trees to keep up evolutionarily with the abilities of insects to inflict damage. Trees must compensate by having significant reserves and diverse strategies for fighting off attacks. Perennial trees use physical defenses such as tough bark or armored leaves to deter herbivores. Chemical defenses are also employed in an attempt to reduce the damage wrought by insects. In almost all cases, the balance is probably a delicate one, just tottering between a landslide victory either for the choosers or for the chosen.

Even though the forests of Konza are associated with water courses, amphibians are uncommon in the woodlands. The western chorus frog will use wet lowlands, damp meadows, and slow-flowing pools as sites for courting and breeding. This is one of the earliest breeders on Konza, sometimes beginning its choruses in late February or early March, when the temperature is no higher than 35 degrees Fahrenheit (2 degrees Celsius). The first choruses always seem peculiar so early in the year. Females lay up to fifteen hundred eggs in clutches of twenty to three hundred each. The eggs hatch in a fortnight, and the tadpoles mature in less than two months. On warm, moist nights after they metamorphose, young adults can be found hundreds of yards from their birth pond, apparently dispersing to sites where they will overwinter before returning the following spring for their own courtship rituals.

Another tiny amphibian of the woodlands is the Plains narrow-mouth toad, which is less than one and one-half inches (4 centimeters) in length. This species is distinct in that it prefers dry, rocky upland woods rather than the more moist areas that other prairie amphibians prefer. It is also less tolerant of low temperatures, waiting until late May to begin breeding, which lasts until August. Pairs mate within a day or two of arriving at a breeding pond; each female lays approximately six hundred eggs, which take only two days to hatch. Maturation is also quite rapid, occurring in twenty to thirty days. The young adults migrate to their winter sites during the first rainfall after they have metamorphosed. Adults take one to two years to reach sexual maturity, but it is not known where they spend the intervening time. Their diet consists almost entirely of ants.

As its name implies, the gray treefrog inhabits the gallery forests of Konza Prairie. Like all tree frogs, it is a climbing species, aided by expanded gripping pads on the ends of its toes. The males call from perches in low shrubs and trees, which they defend with specific territorial calls or by actual combat. The males intercept females, as the latter pass by, and escort them to the breeding pond. The pairs copulate in the water, after which the females lay as many as four thousand eggs. Hatching and development is quite rapid.

Newly metamorphosed juveniles apparently stay near their birth ponds during the first year after hatching.

The forests are also poorly endowed with reptiles. The primary lizard of note in the woodlands is the slender glass lizard, the largest lizard in Kansas, which reaches a length of almost three feet. Its most distinguishing feature is the absence of limbs, which makes it look like a snake. As a lizard, however, it possesses an ear opening, eyelids that close, and evolutionary remnants of shoulder and pelvic structures, traits that distinguish it from a snake. Very little is known about this secretive species. It is thought to be primarily diurnal, feeding on insects, spiders, snails, and the eggs of other reptiles. As is true with other species of lizards, the slender glass lizard can autotomize its tail when grabbed, escaping while the predator's attention is distracted by the squirming appendage.

Only one species of venomous snake, the copperhead, has been found on Konza Prairie. The oak woodlands are suitable habitat for this species, but Konza lies on the extreme western edge of its natural range. Copperheads usually inhabit rocky hillsides among the oaks, frequently near streams or ponds, where their color pattern blends in well with the mottled background. The snake is long-lived (perhaps as long as fifteen years). The females do not lay eggs; rather, they give birth to as many as fourteen live young and perhaps breed only every other year. Although they consume many insects and vertebrates, especially rodents, their impact on Konza is probably minimal because of their low abundance.

Because the forest is much more complex vertically than is the open prairie, it is not surprising that the woods support the highest diversity and density of birds on Konza. Black-capped chickadees are year-round residents that use the cavities in old snags in open woodlands for nesting sites. Blue jays also nest in the forests, constructing typical baskets of woven twigs and bits of vegetation. They are among the loudest birds in the woods; other animals pay attention to their raucous calls, which frequently reveal an approaching predator. Jays often occur in pairs or small family groups, which may join up to mob intruders such as hawks or owls. In late summer the cacophony continues as young birds of the year follow their mothers around, still begging to be fed while the mother is attempting to ignore them.

Red-bellied woodpeckers frequent the gallery forests, where they nest in tree cavities. Their staccato hammering frequently penetrates the quiet of a summer morning in the forests of Konza Prairie.

A number of owls live on Konza, and three—the great horned owl, the eastern screech owl, and the barred owl—are residents the year round. The great horned owl is an impressive sight when it perches on an oak snag at dusk. The birds are nearly 2 feet (60 centimeters) tall, and their height is amplified by a pair of ear tufts that emanate from their heads. Like many owls, they forage at night, relying on their extremely sensitive hearing to locate prey. Most owls have asymmetrical skulls, with one ear lower than the other. Sound reaches one ear slightly before it enters the other, allowing the birds to use stereophonic hearing for depth perception, much as we use stereoscopic sight. Mated pairs are monogamous and construct nests in many places, including abandoned nests of hawks and squirrels. Female great horned owls average two eggs per year, which they incubate for a month. The scraggly nestlings grow slowly, eventually fledging in nine to ten weeks.

Several species of woodpeckers inhabit the gallery forests during the entire year. Some species use their pointed bills to drill for insect larvae, which they extract with long, sticky tongues. Woodpeckers are tireless workers, pounding away with a staccato beat that resonates through the woods on a still day. Their bills and skulls have built-in shock absorbers to cushion the brain against the thousands of blows struck each day. Other species of woodpeckers forage for acorns and nuts, which they consume immediately or cache for later use. If acorn production is high, the red-headed woodpecker will stay on Konza all year and will exclude the subordinate red-bellied woodpeckers altogether from the forests or will force them into more marginal habitats. When acorn crops are poor, the red-heads are forced to move elsewhere, leaving the forest to the red-bellies, which can apparently exist on a poorer crop of nuts than can the red-heads.

All of the woodpeckers on Konza nest in cavities, acquiring old holes or making new ones in high trees and dead snags. Woodpeckers have two toes that point backwards and two that point forward, rather than the more typical pattern of one backward and three forward. This configuration apparently assists them in clinging vertically on tree trunks while they search for food. Furthermore, the ends of their tail feathers are pointed, so that when they perch vertically, the tips stick into the bark and serve as props for the body.

While the forest is an ideal habitat for birds, it is less hospitable for terrestrial mammals. Because most mammals do not fly, only a few make effective use of the stratified vertical habitat of the forests. The most common mammal in the forests on Konza is the white-footed mouse, a close relative of the deer mouse. As a true forest dweller, the white-footed mouse spends much of its time up in trees and may even build its nest above ground. It is a generalist feeder, consuming green vegetation, fruits, nuts, seeds, and some insects. An average of four young, but as many as seven, are born in the spring; second litters are occasionally produced in the fall. Juveniles have their eyes open in two weeks and are weaned four weeks after birth. Within a week of weaning, they are independent, and females born early in the spring may breed during their first summer.

Fox squirrels are also common in the oak woods, where they are often seen leaping across the forest floor or scurrying up trees. Using their keen sense of smell, they locate nuts on the ground and take

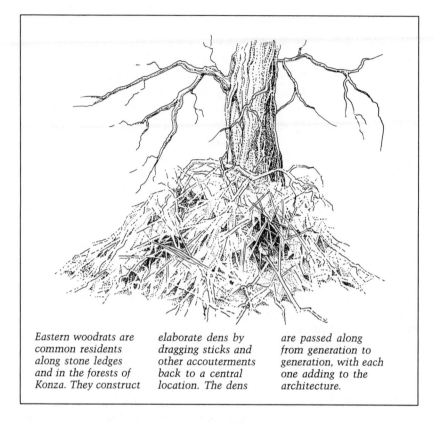

Eastern woodrats are common residents along stone ledges and in the forests of Konza. They construct elaborate dens by dragging sticks and other accouterments back to a central location. The dens are passed along from generation to generation, with each one adding to the architecture.

them to a number of scattered caches, where the nuts are stored for future use. Fox squirrels also consume bark, twigs, buds, fungi, and insects when available. The squirrels stay active throughout the winter, although they remain in their dens during foul weather. The dens are usually located in hollow trees; they are entered through a small opening in the tree trunk, and they are lined with leaves and other insulating material. Courtship between males and females involves conspicuous chases that may go on for several hours. After a gestation period of about forty-five days, one to six (usually three) young are born. The youngsters are slow to develop and may not be independent of the mother for several months. Even then, especially if they were born late in the season, the juveniles may stay with their mother for several additional months before starting their own families during the following summer.

One of the most intriguing rodents on Konza is the woodrat, which is sometimes called a pack rat or a trade rat. These large rodents—individuals can weigh as much as one pound (0.45 kilogram)—are abundant in the forests, especially along rocky ledges, and a few are found in bushes out in the grassland. The rats bring hundreds of sticks, some as long as three or four feet, to a central location in their territories and build a large den, 6 to 8 feet (1.8 to 2.4 meters) across at the base and tapering up to a height of 4 to 6 feet (1.2 to 1.8 meters). The teepee-shaped den provides effective protection against environmental extremes; it also probably deters predators, as it is difficult to dismantle. The core of the den contains a nest near ground level. In late summer and fall, the woodrats store several quarts of vegetation, berries, nuts, and seeds in one or more large chambers above the nest. Although the woodrats remain active throughout the winter, the stored food satisfies their needs during especially difficult times. The dens can become congested when rabbits, shrews, and mice share the facilities.

Although the forests make up only a small portion of Konza Prairie, they serve as a stark comparison to life in the grassland. Whereas the prairie environment is low, compressed, and occasionally harsh, the forest is voluminous, and its inhabitants are somewhat buffered against environmental excesses. Currently, the forests exist only in a swath between the moisture offered by the streams and the grassland fires that prevent the trees from trespassing on the prairie. Within these narrow confines exists a reminder of what Konza looked like several thousand years ago, when oak woodlands dominated the region, and what it might look like today were fires not prevalent across the plains.

6 / Soil and the Belowground Habitat

Centipedes actively hunt among the surface litter and in the dark subterranean world of the Konza soil. They feed on a wide variety of invertebrates, which they sometimes immobilize with a mild venom.

IT IS PROBABLY NOT COINCIDENTAL THAT MAN'S MANY PRIMI-tive cultures, especially those that developed agriculture, viewed the ground beneath their feet as Mother Earth, the point of origin for their ancestors and the source of their sustenance. They knew, as ecologists today are discovering, that the thin skin of the earth's upper crust, the soil, gives birth to the natural bounties of the planet. The soil provides protection, moisture, and nutrients for plants on whose production the remainder of the living world depends. While the sun supplies the fuel that powers the biological realm, the soil provides the ingredients of the recipe for life. The earth contributes many elements to the biosphere, but of its 8,000-mile (12,900-kilometer) thickness, only the outer few feet of crust nourish life. The details of what goes on in the underworld remain sketchy, because it is opaque, and most of the participants are minuscule and secretive. We do know, however, that what goes on below the surface is even more dynamic than what happens aboveground.

Soil is not simply a donation by the planet to the biosphere; it is formed from the interaction, over time, of the base material of the earth with climate, topography, and thousands of organisms. Soil is a milieu of geological and biological ingredients, stirred by various processes that affect the surface of the earth. The initial component is the parent material, the underlying rock of the earth. As the earth cooled from the fires of its birth, the material that emerged from the primordial seas was either sandy water-washed deposits or barren rock that eroded, dissolved, and degraded by weathering. Over time, this original material has mixed and reassembled into basic igneous, metamorphic, and sedimentary rock. The base material may be weathered into smaller pieces on the spot, forming a matrix for subsequent soil formation, or it may be transported by wind, water, or glacial action to another location, where its deposition begins the soil-formation process.

The actual source of the parent material is of interest, but functionally the crucial feature of the incipient soil is its mineral structure. The basic minerals that are important to soil formation are divided into those that contain silicon and those that do not. Most of the nonsilicates are rare or absent in parent material, but where they are abundant, they form major seams of mineral deposits that are sources for primary ores such as iron, gypsum, and bauxite, the source of aluminum. The nonsilicates vary greatly in their solubility, in their susceptibility to degradation, and, hence, in their contribution to soil formation.

The fundamental silicate structure is a pyramid, with oxygen atoms at the four apexes that surround a central silicon atom. These tetrahedral molecules are linked in various ways to form the array of silica minerals that make up most of the soil. The specific nature of the chemical linkages of adjoined silicate molecules determines the crystalline structure of the molecule (such as framework, chain, ring, and sheet silicates) and thus its properties in response to weathering and soil formation. In some minerals, the silicon atoms are replaced with atoms of aluminum, calcium, and potassium; this results in the array of precious, semiprecious, and nonprecious minerals that make up the corpus of the earth. Sheet silicates degrade into clays, whose physical and chemical structure and propensity for bonding with other elements give them a major role in soil formation.

Climate is the second variable that profoundly affects soil formation. It directly alters the parent material and is responsible for the rate at which soil forms. We generally think of atmospheric climate as weather patterns above the surface, but the soil maintains its own climate, which may only loosely relate to what goes on in the air. Air temperature and precipitation do govern the subterranean climate, but that climate is buffered from many extremes that are prevalent in the aboveground environment. Warm temperatures and high levels of precipitation promote soil formation, while cool, dry environments slow the process.

The soil is warmed by direct radiation from the sun, even though almost one-third of the sun's energy is reflected by the earth's surface. Soil is also warmed by convective currents that blow over its surface and by simple conduction: warm air makes warm soil. An extremely minor amount of heat is produced in the soil by metabolism in organisms, by volcanic heat, and by radioactive decay, although this is the major source of heat deep within the core of the earth. Soil heats up more slowly where the sun's rays strike it at shallow angles, which occurs toward the poles. The soil is cooled by low air temperatures, especially when it is windy, by evaporating water, and by shading. Such factors as cloud cover, snow cover, day length, latitude, reflection (albedo), and vegetational cover all complicate the relationship between climate and the soil environment.

Warm temperatures speed up the chemical and biological processes in the earthen matrix, thus promoting soil formation. As a general rule of thumb, physiological reactions increase a little over twofold for each 20-degree (11-degree Celsius) increase in temperature, whereas nonbiological chemical reactions increase two- or threefold over the same range of temperature. Low temperatures retard these processes, in some cases slowing biological reactions to imperceptible rates. If temperatures are low enough to cause the soil to freeze, trapped water will expand, pushing soil particles apart and breaking up larger rocks, an important process in soil formation.

Precipitation directly affects soil formation by the actual force of falling rain and the degradation that accompanies erosional runoff. Water that enters the soil influences the physical and biological processes through its role as the universal solvent, so called because many chemicals easily dissolve in water. As water percolates through the soil, it moves soluble elements to areas where plants and animals have access to them, or it carries the elements deep underground and ultimately into the ground-water system. Moisture is essential to all of the biological activities in the soil; even though some plants and animals can survive long droughts, their impact on soil formation is severely curtailed under these conditions.

Topography is also an important factor in soil formation. The lay of the land is affected by episodes of uplifting and down faulting and by the erosional powers of water. As the terrain changes shape, its capacity to capture and retain water changes. For example, much more water runs off a steeply sloped face than from a flat surface, where it has a chance to seep in. Furthermore, loose stones on steep slopes inevitably tumble downhill, and even small particles gradually work their way downhill under the force of raindrops and the footfalls of animals. The orientation of the slope face is also critical to its temperature regime. In the Northern Hemisphere, south-facing slopes receive direct sunlight in the winter, thus melting snow and warming the surface, whereas north-facing slopes are shaded until spring. Extended exposure to the sun tends to dry out south-facing slopes, making them more arid than slopes that face northward.

Virtually every terrestrial form of plant or animal, from microbe to mammal, has an impact on soil formation. Scientists are only beginning to learn the ways in which organisms affect soil processes on Konza, so details are incomplete at this point. It is clear, however, that biological processes are important in adding organic matter to the basic lithic (rock) contribution, thereby promoting the cycling of nutrients and essential elements throughout the system. Some of the biological effects are physical, simply moving incipient soil from here to there, while other effects are mediated through the metabolic processes of plants and animals.

Because as much as 60 percent of the biomass of plants exists underground, they are a major influence on soil formation. The ponderous power of roots causes a redistribution of soil particles. If a growing root tip enters a small crack in a rock, the root may even split the rock as the growing shoot inexorably widens the gap. Roots also function as binding agents, holding soil together and reducing erosion. Roots are continually borrowing nutrients and moisture from the soil, returning them when they die or when the plant tissue is processed through a decomposer. Microbes are attracted to various exudates of roots, thus increasing microbial activity and enhancing soil formation. Aboveground plant parts intercept rainfall, preventing it from reaching the soil, but they also shade the soil and reduce wind flow, thus slowing evaporation and heating.

The ambient conditions within the soil are buffered from environmental extremes, making this a somewhat benevolent habitat. This, plus the accumulation of nutrients in the soil, attracts many animals to the belowground habitat. The animals consume living and dead plant material and other animals, thus speeding the dynamics of nutrient and mineral processing in the soil. Animals as large as badgers excavate the prairie surface, mixing and aerating the soil. Insects, especially their larvae, and earthworms course through the matrix, feeding on detritus and preying on innumerable smaller inhabitants. Tiny mites make substantial contributions to soil formation, as do nematode worms. Bacteria and fungi do the final processing of organic matter, returning biologically manufactured material to its elemental state, ready for recycling.

The last essential ingredient in soil formation is time. Scores of centuries are required for bedrock to become soil. Slowly, a substrate that is compatible with life takes shape, and microbes move in. Their action further alters the material, eventually providing just enough nutrients for plants that specialize in depauperate habitats. These plants, in' turn, increase the quality of the soil when they die and leave their remains for subsequent generations. This natural succession may continue until the original sere is replaced by an advanced, relatively stable biotic and abiotic constituency. At this stage, the soil remains dynamic, but succession is replaced by a dynamic equilibrium that is only disrupted when either long-term changes in the weather or dramatic geologic events knock the system off track and into a new domain.

The ways in which some soil-forming processes affect the parent material are known, but it is impossible to integrate all the potential interactions simultaneously and conceive of the results. Therefore, ecologists use computers to simulate the processes; this yields results that are quite robust. More detailed simulations, taking into account all of the physical and biological factors that influence soil formation, await not only additional empirical information from the field but also more powerful computers that can manage the massive amount of data inherent in such analyses.

There is no discrete point at which bedrock becomes soil. Soil formation is an ongoing process, yielding to gradual alterations of the biogeochemical matrix. At any one time, soils can be characterized by their physical and chemical properties that pertain to the success of plants and animals that inhabit them. For example, soils that are high in clay (i.e., very small silicate particles) retain more water than do sandy soils, whose large interparticle spaces let water percolate through, but it takes more sucking power on the part of a plant to extract water from clay soils. The amount of water in the soil that is available to plants lies between the total volume of water that the soil can hold (its field capacity) and the wilting point (that volume of water which is too low to maintain internal water pressure in plants). Pure sandy soils have a low field capacity, which is caused by the large spaces between sand particles that cannot effectively hold water, and the difference between it and the wilting point is small, making such soils precarious for plants. Soils that are intermediate between sands and clays exhibit the greatest field capacity and the greatest difference between field capacity and wilting point, thus producing a maximum range across which plants can survive. Many other qualities of soils that relate to their suitability to support life are contingent on the physical properties exhibited by the components of the soil. Roots and the melange of animals that live in the soil "breathe," so soil must have spaces between the particles that will allow the movement of air belowground. The degree to which soil can be compressed, reducing the interparticle spaces, affects the passage of air and regulates the success of subterranean organisms. The abundance and sizes of rocks in the soil also impinge on the movement of roots and many underground animals. While plants and animals are coping with the physical features of soil, they are concurrently altering its characteristics by their own activities.

Two major types of soil dominate Konza Prairie, although many other minor types also occur there. The flat uplands and portions of the slopes are from the Florence soil series, which is composed of a silt and clay mixture called a loam and fairly large pieces of chert, a type of flint that gives the Flint Hills their name, which may make up 70–80 percent of the soil. The upland soils form a thin veneer, usually exhibiting a top soil less than 1 foot (30 centimeters) thick and a subsoil no more than 20 inches (50 centimeters) deep. The soils were formed *in situ* from weathered limestone bedrock, which still exists less than a yard below the soil surface. Florence soils are well drained and are somewhat firm when wet; when dry, they are indurate, thus exacerbating the effects of droughts.

The lowland Tully soils, which are significantly deeper, were formed by alluvial (stream) deposits and soils washed down the adjacent slopes during rainfall runoff. The Tully soils have a 10-inch (25-centimeter) topsoil, similar to the Florence soils, but they contain appreciably fewer chert stones. A lower horizon, about 1 foot (30 centimeters) thick, resembles the topsoil but contains less organic matter. Below that is a subsoil over 4 feet (1.2 meters) thick, composed of silty clay. The Tully soils are very productive, supporting what little farming occurs on the Flint Hills.

Mixed in with both the Florence and the Tully soils are deposits of loess, dust that was produced by the grinding action of ancient glaciers and was blown onto Konza from areas north of the prairie. Konza Prairie also retains small pockets of sandy soils, which tend to host forest plants. West of Konza, sandy soils permit the existence of tallgrass prairie in areas that would otherwise be mixed-grass or shortgrass prairies.

The most pronounced feature of the soils of Konza Prairie is the massive sod formed by the invasive roots and horizontal rhizomes of the dominant grasses. The tangled mass of plant tissue is intricately woven into a mat so thick that it is difficult to push the blade of a shovel through it in places. The roots respond positively to the constant tug of gravity and creep downward in search of nutrients and moisture. Big-bluestem roots commonly extend down more than 12 feet (3.6 meters), although they are densest in the upper 8 to 12 inches (20 to 30 centimeters), and those of several other species may go twice as far. Roots that extend for more than 1 foot (30 centimeters) below the surface are about the diameter of a pencil lead and exhibit some branching, although less than those found closer to the surface. The roots of most plants ramify extensively to take advantage of local concentrations of nutrients. Most of the available nutrients in the Konza soils are concentrated in the upper few inches, so it would seem that the development of a deep root system would be inefficient. A number of plants do delve deeply into the soil, so presumably the rewards are worth the effort.

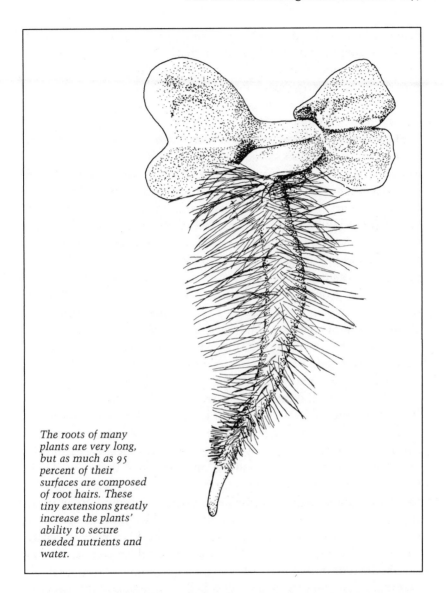

The roots of many plants are very long, but as much as 95 percent of their surfaces are composed of root hairs. These tiny extensions greatly increase the plants' ability to secure needed nutrients and water.

The roots of most of the nongrasses on Konza exhibit a typical growth form of one or more major axes with numerous branches. The roots of other species fan out in a cone-shaped pattern beneath the parent plant, while those that are best adapted to dry conditions have taproots and develop a long, fibrous central root with some branching. There is virtually no room near the soil surface of the tallgrass prairie for the invasion of roots of nongrasses, so the advantages go to those that send their roots below the overlying sod mat. This is not an entirely satisfactory solution, however, as the mat of the overlying grass roots intercepts most of the descending nutrients, making the depths of the Konza soils inhospitable for all but the most efficient plants.

The roots of some species would be miles long if strung end to end, providing a substantial surface through which the plant can secure essential resources. Even more impressive are the millions of tiny root hairs that project laterally from the roots, thus further increasing the surface area. None of the plant species on Konza have been exhaustively studied to determine the extent of root-hair production, but rye, a domestic relative of the grasses, has been analyzed. A single rye plant was found to have 14 billion root hairs, with a total surface area of 4,000 square feet (370 square meters; the size of two large homes). The primary roots had a total surface area of 2,500 square feet (230 square meters), yielding a total surface area 130 times that of the aboveground stems and leaves. The utilization of space by the plant was so efficient that this massive amount of root tissue invaded only 2 cubic feet (0.06 cubic meters) of soil.

Biologists have known for a long time that fungi are common in soils. Most were thought to be parasitic or free living, consuming various organic molecules in the soil matrix. It was also known that a small group of fungi called mycorrhizae form symbiotic relationships with plants. Only recently, however, has it become clear how ubiquitous mycorrhizae are and the important role that they play in the success of some plants. Mycorrhizae function as extensions of root hairs for nutrient-starved plants, expanding the sphere of influence of the root while extracting only a small fee from the plant for services rendered. As roots and their attendant hairs suck up nutrients from the surrounding soil, they create a barren zone about one twenty-fifth of an inch (1 millimeter) wide around the root tissue. Elements that the plants have absorbed will gradually diffuse back into the barren zone, only to be depleted again. A plant that has formed an alliance with mycorrhizal fungi, however, can extend its zone of activity up to fivefold, thus greatly increasing the amount of moisture and nutrients that can be garnered. In return, the plant feeds the fungi a small amount of carbohydrates, which the fungi use in their own metabolism. Apparently, many plants are facultative (optional) users of mycorrhizae, only maintaining them when they are especially stressed for a critical nutrient. Furthermore, when plants face drought conditions, they sever their commensal (mutually advantageous) relationship, cutting their losses and waiting out the drought.

It is likely that almost every species of plant on Konza relies on mycorrhizae. In greenhouse experiments, clones of big bluestem that have been inoculated with mycorrhizae produce over eighty times as much tissue as plants that have grown in sterile soil. It appears that the fungi primarily assist prairie plants in securing phosphorus, which is especially low in Konza soils. In fact, a big-bluestem seedling will not grow in Konza soil unless it is either fertilized with phosphorus or inoculated with mycorrhizae. Mycorrhizae have been found on the roots of forbs at a depth of more than 7 feet (2.1 meters), well below the zone of decomposition that retains most of the nutrients in the soil. This suggests that the forbs may rely on the mycorrhizae to scrounge what few nutrients occur at that depth. It is also possible that the fungi send their own growing stalks (called hyphae) up into the nutrient-rich decomposition zone to abscond with nutrients or to plug directly into the grass rhizomes, thereby serving as nutrient bridges between grasses and forbs. Regardless of the exact nature of these relationships, it is clear that mycorrhizae play an essential role in the success of prairie plants.

Another important symbiotic relationship exists between plants and a specific group of soil bacteria that have the ability to "fix" atmospheric nitrogen, that is, to convert it from the unusable form found in the atmosphere to a form available to plants. Nitrogen is the one major element used by plants that is not derived from the weathering of rocks, and its concentration is known to directly affect the success of plants. The nitrogen-fixing bacteria enter the root hairs of plants while they are still seedlings. The entry of the microbes causes the plants to produce a filamentous growth tube through which the bacteria invade the underlying root cells. The infection spreads once the bacteria have made their way into the roots, eventually causing the plants to produce numerous nodules that house the bacteria and their nitrogen-fixing enzymes. The host plants must pay a price to sustain their symbionts, but the return on their investment is substantial. Some plants on Konza retain nitrogen-fixing bacteria. Most of these plants are members of the legume, or pea, family;

few grasses are known to rely on these beneficial microbes. Another group of nitrogen-fixing microbes, the blue-green algae, also occur on the prairie, primarily on the surface of the soil. These primitive organisms are usually associated with very moist sites, which indicates that during some seasons (especially spring), the prairie can be very wet.

Numerous other microbes live beneath the prairie, but information on their life styles is meager. They thrive in a world that we cannot perceive and have difficulty even imagining. For example, at the size of most of the microbes, no larger than a few thousandths of an inch, the world is wet and sticky. Molecular tensions pull and tug in every direction, and a raindrop is equivalent to a dam-bursting deluge. These tiny organisms can retreat into cysts and spores to wait out hard times, and then they explode in abundance, sequestering resources and altering the environment in a manner that belies their size. Their strength is in their numbers—millions and billions of single cells or small colonies participate in an economy of scale that makes them a potent force on the prairie. Several million bacterial cells reside in a pinch of fertile Konza soil, and between one to five thousand pounds of bacteria occur in one acre (0.4 hectares) of the prairie. Fungi frequently make up an even greater fraction of the microbe population of the soil. Other microscopic inhabitants include algae, which require sunlight for photosynthesis and hence must occur near the surface, and protozoans, single-celled animal-like creatures; but bacteria and fungi are by far the most abundant.

As is the case with most organisms, the distribution of microbes is limited by their requirements and tolerances. Each specific type resides in that portion of the soil column which provides it with the appropriate nutrients and moisture. Conversely, their distribution may be limited by physical features of the soil, such as particle size or the acidity within specific soil sites. These tiny organisms have very few internal systems to maintain a chemical balance, so they tend to take on the chemical characteristics of their surrounding environment. Thus, they must migrate to the appropriate location, or else the local conditions will cause their death; migration and selective death eventually lead to a zonation of microbes within the soil, corresponding to physical and chemical characteristics.

The soils of Konza Prairie are teeming with animal life. Most of the animals are visible to the naked eye, although some imagination may be required to pick them out—the smaller forms resemble particles of soil, and only their movement gives them away. The distribution of these animals, like that of microbes, is determined by the availability of resources; therefore, most of them are concentrated in the upper few inches of the soil. As small ectotherms (animals whose body temperature is determined by the ambient temperature), they are at the mercy of the surrounding environment. Most are active between 65 and 90 degrees Fahrenheit (18 and 32 degrees Celsius) and require well-aerated soil; their success is limited in soggy areas.

The underground fauna is not only abundant, it is also quite diverse and contains contributions from a wide spectrum of families. Four major groups of animals are involved: the parasitic and free-living roundworms (nematodes), earthworms, various arthropods (primarily mites and insects), and a few vertebrate species. The nematodes and the arthropods are the most diverse, containing representatives of numerous guilds, including species that consume detritus, vegetation, microbes, and each other. Earthworms ingest organic and inorganic material. A few vertebrates also take advantage of the subterranean environment for shelter in burrows and for food.

Nematodes are among the most abundant organisms on the planet. It has been said that if the earth's surface could be digested away, leaving only the nematodes, the outlines of its topography and inhabitants could be discerned from the silhouettes produced by the residual nematode populations. Although this notion is untestable and certainly spurious, it gives some idea of what biologists imagine to be the ubiquity and abundance of this taxon. On Konza, nematode densities reach astounding levels—as many as 500,000 per square foot (5.4 million per square meter) in the upper 8 inches (20 centimeters) of soil during their peak abundances, and these estimates do not even include forms that are parasites on other animals. The densities appear to be seasonal, fluctuating from the peak in autumn to lows of 200,000 per square foot (2.2 million per square meter) in a dry summer. Almost one-half of the nematodes in the tallgrass prairie feed on fungi and are facultative herbivores (able to eat vegetation but not specialists). Another one-third are obligatory herbivores, considered by many to be parasitic because a portion of the worm extends into the plants as it sucks the juices out. Less than one-fifth of the nematodes are consumers of microbes, whereas a small fraction are considered predators or omnivorous scavengers.

Nematodes exhibit a relatively simple life cycle. Females lay eggs singly or in clusters, some of which are encased in a mucous cocoon. The eggs hatch and go through several stages, sometimes referred to as larval stages. Technically, these are not larvae, as they do not metamorphose but simply grow into adults. Usually the second- or third-stage juveniles must penetrate a plant to gain resources before they continue their development. In some species the sexes are separate, but in many, individuals are hermaphroditic. Although the hermaphrodites possess reproductive organs for both sexes, they still exchange sperm between two individuals, albeit in both directions, rather than just one.

The arthropod fauna in the soil is usually divided into macro- and microarthropods. The macroarthropods include herbivores (such as certain beetle larvae, cicada nymphs), predators (such as centipedes and predaceous insects), and detritivores (or detritus feeders—such as millipedes and many types of fly larvae). The microarthropods, which, as the name implies, are significantly smaller, are composed of several groups of mites, springtails, and other minute insects. Most of these tiny animals feed on microbes that adhere to litter produced aboveground and belowground. Aboveground arthropods, which can be seen day or night on Konza Prairie, total about 50 pounds per acre (56 kilograms per hectare); the obscure belowground arthropods, which are virtually never seen, may be two to ten times more abundant.

June beetles (June bugs) make up 90 percent of the mass of herbivorous macroarthropods in the soil on Konza. Adult June beetles are quite common on the Great Plains, where they frequently congregate around porch lights in early summer. They are large, ponderous fliers, which emit a warning buzz as they lumber in for a crash landing on a wall or window screen. The adults feed primarily on vegetation, and they may overwinter in the soil before laying their eggs the next season. The larvae, known as white grubs, can be extremely damaging to crops and lawns when their infestations reach epidemic proportions. They are voracious root feeders; during one outbreak several decades ago, the skin of the tallgrass prairie could be peeled back like a shag rug over soil where white grubs had severed the grass shoots from their underground rhizomes and roots. The grubs go through several instars, reaching the diameter of a little finger before pupating. The life cycle of June beetles may take two to four years, meaning that several generations are represented underground at any one time, which increases their impact on the plants. Attempts have been made on Konza to analyze the effect that these creatures have on the plants, but so far the modest decreases in grub densities that have been attained have not resulted in measurable increases in plant productivity.

Click beetles make up a minor fraction of the herbivorous beetle population on Konza. These insects get their name from their propensity for snapping two segments of their exoskeleton together, thereby producing a sharp snap while flipping themselves into the air. The adults feed on vegetation and flowers; but the larvae, which are known as wireworms, are subterranean feeders. The larvae of leaf beetles are also abundant in the soil, but these herbivores apparently have a minor impact.

During warm nights the sonorous buzz of cicadas is a constant reminder that it is summer. When adult cicadas reach high densities and chorus synchronously, the experience can be painful to the human ear. Only males "sing"; actually the sound is produced when strong muscles cause stiff ribs to bend rapidly over a resonating chamber, producing a buzzing sound. Cicadas are among the largest insects on the prairie, occasionally reaching two inches in length. They have very long life cycles; the minimum known is two years, but most are at least four years. Other forms, known as the periodical cicadas, have cycles of thirteen and seventeen years. At first, these seem like peculiar numbers. Two features of these lengths, however, keep potential predators from synchronizing their reproduction with the abundance of cicadas. One is the relatively long absolute length of the life cycles—very few potential predators have similarly lengthy life spans. More importantly, the lengths of life cycles are prime numbers; they can be divided only by one and themselves. Thus, the cycle of abundance cannot be divided into multiples of shorter life cycles, allowing predators to occasionally score big on the periodic outbreaks. Any predator that has a typical one-year life cycle must wait thirteen or seventeen years to utilize cicadas, or the predator must have a matching cycle. The only organisms known to match the life cycle of the periodical cicadas is a fungus that infects the

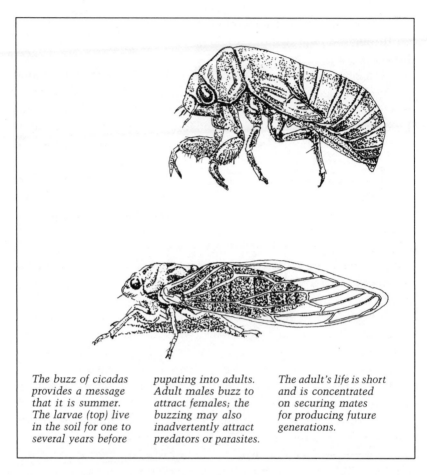

The buzz of cicadas provides a message that it is summer. The larvae (top) live in the soil for one to several years before pupating into adults. Adult males buzz to attract females; the buzzing may also inadvertently attract predators or parasites. The adult's life is short and is concentrated on securing mates for producing future generations.

genitals of male cicadas before being passed on to females during mating. The vast majority of the cicada's life span is spent in the larval stage. The adults live for a month or so before depositing their eggs on the stems and branches of woody vegetation, usually injuring the terminal portion of the shoot in the process. The eggs hatch after several weeks, and the larvae enter the soil for the duration of their long development to adulthood. The larvae use their piercing, sucking mouthparts to attach themselves to a root, where they will remain, if undisturbed, for many years. They molt several times throughout adolescence, eventually climbing up on a twig for their last molt before becoming adults. The larvae may have a severe impact where they occur in high densities, and the egg-laying stage can cause extensive damage to aboveground plant parts.

Millipedes are the primary macroarthropods that feed on the organic debris of the prairie. Although their name means "a thousand feet," the abundance of limbs is an illusion. Millipedes actually have two pairs of legs per body segment, making a total of more than 160 legs in some species. Adults lay eggs in moist soil, where they hatch within a few weeks. The young millipedes are similar in body plan to the adults, but have legs only on the anterior segments; additional pairs of legs are added during subsequent molts until the full complement is attained. Both the adults and the larvae spend almost their entire lives within the litter layer and in the upper soil horizons, where they may reach densities of over two hundred thousand per acre (about one-half million per hectare).

The larvae of some fly species, primarily deer flies, are also abundant detritivores on Konza, but their small size minimizes their overall impact. Termites are occasionally encountered in excavations on Konza. Termites are colonial insects, living in large subterranean settlements where they exhibit a caste system involving a king and queen, the most reproductively active members of the colony, and a variety of workers. Supplementary reproductives assist the queen and can also reproduce under certain circumstances. The worker caste consists of nymphs (early developmental stages) and nonreproductive adults that do various chores around the nest. The soldier caste is the most formidable; soldiers have massive jaws and nasty dispositions, which serve their role as protectors of the realm. The insects feed on miscellaneous woody debris, which on Konza is primarily the dead rhizomes of grasses.

The scourge of the underworld is the predaceous centipede. These wormlike creatures are distantly related to the millipedes but possess none of the more benign habits of their relatives. Each body segment bears a single pair of legs, for a total of fifteen pairs in most species; the hindmost pair is frequently directed straight back, producing the malevolent appearance of a forked tail, whereas the anterior pair is often modified into poison-bearing "jaws." Centipedes feed on insects, spiders, and other small animals, using the poisons in their jaws to paralyze their prey. Centipedes spend most of their lives in the soil or under logs and litter, from which they make frequent forays in search of prey.

The microarthropods on Konza, which are primarily mites and springtails, also exist in several functional guilds. There is a high correlation between the amount of litter that reaches the soil surface and the density of these creatures in the soil, suggesting that they rely on this resource, either directly or indirectly. No doubt, a substantial number of the mites feed on litter, although some are parasitic and others consume fungi. The remaining species are ferocious predators that prey on the scavenging forms. Very little is known about the life cycles of mites; preliminary surveys of Konza indicate that nearly one hundred species are present, but this is probably a significant underestimate. Springtails are primitive insects that get their name from their ability to spring into the air, using their appendages for propulsion. They are primarily detritus feeders, utilizing the large quantity of litter produced on the prairie. Microarthropods occur on Konza in astounding densities, reaching nearly 2 billion per acre (5 billion per hecatre). There is some indication that their populations are adversely affected by frequent burning, which reduces the litter available to detritivores.

Earthworms constitute another prominent member of the underground community on Konza. Several species of native earthworms occur there, and Konza has recently become the home to introduced European and Chinese forms. These species probably immigrated to North America along with the Europeans, who brought with them their favorite potted plants in soil from the Old World. When the plants were planted in North America or when they died and the soil was tossed out, its residents took up citizenship in the prairie. Several of the introduced forms still occur primarily near residences on Konza, suggesting that they were part of very localized introductions. One European species, however, has spread well beyond any possible introduction sites to inhabit most of Konza. Earthworms reach astonishing densities of almost 5 million per acre (12 million per hectare). Although two-thirds of them are the native prairie forms, the European species is somewhat larger, so the two types contribute equally to the total tonnage of earthworms, roughly 150 pounds per acre (168 kilograms per hectare), or a total of almost 650 tons (590,000 kilograms) on Konza.

Earthworms ingest soil and chemically extract specific organic nutrients. The material passes through the gut and is deposited as a cast on the surface or belowground. The excreta are themselves quite nutritious, even though some of the riches have been removed by the earthworm, and may serve as nutritional hot spots for microbes. Most earthworms on Konza reside in the upper few inches

The brightly colored milk snakes are harmless to humans. Most of them feed on other snakes or lizards.

of the soil, where organic resources are concentrated. One introduced species occurs at a depth of about 15 inches (38 centimeters), while some of the European immigrants feed on the surface at night, ingesting fallen litter. Earthworms are hermaphroditic, with each individual retaining both male and female gonads. While mating, they exchange sperm and deposit fertilized eggs into a mucous cocoon secreted by the clitellum, the expanded glandular collar about one-third of the way down the length of the worm. The eggs hatch within the protective cocoon and emerge as small worms, which continue to grow throughout life. Their importance extends beyond the processing of organic matter, for they are significant earthmovers, turning the soil over and aerating it in a way that promotes its suitability as a habitat.

The vertebrate fauna is puny compared to the array of invertebrates, but most of the vertebrates are large and have an obvious impact on Konza. Several types of snakes and a number of species of rodents burrow into the soil, using it primarily as a residence rather than as a cafeteria. The excavations mix and aerate the soil, increasing biotic production underground, but few of the effects have been adequately investigated. Some excavations result in tailings that are deposited on the surface, where the barren mounds become attractive germination sites for seeds. Pocket gophers, which spend almost their entire life burrowing through the root zone, are not common on Konza, for the same reason that plowing was not common—the soil is too shallow in most places to support their activities, except in the deeper lowland soils and at a few locations on the uplands. Where pocket gophers do occur, however, they are known to decrease overlying vegetation from 25 to 50 percent by ingesting plants and covering them with the residue of the excavations.

If you walk through the prairie in summer, you will rustle up a few grasshoppers each step, and you might rouse a vole, or even a deer; a century ago you might have seen a herd of bison. After scores of days of walking, you might see a predatory hawk secure a meal after diving on a rodent, and you would certainly be attacked and parasitized by chiggers. But if you were able to peer into the soil directly under a single step, you would see thousands of such interactions for each footfall. If you could listen in, you would hear the munching of thousands of tiny mouths feeding on miscellaneous detritus, and perhaps the voices of a hundred individuals being attacked by predators and parasites. In numbers of individuals, numbers of encounters, and maybe even pounds of flesh, the mysterious, opaque underground world is the most dynamic habitat on the tallgrass prairie.

CYCLES

"What goes 'round, comes 'round." Every molecule in the universe is part of a cosmic cycle. It is hypothesized that our universe began its most recent expansion as a miniscule wad of mass which exploded in the Big Bang and has continued its expansion for 20 billion years or more. Most physicists believe that the universe will stop expanding eventually and that it will collapse back upon itself before expanding again for the next hundreds of billions of years. Each cosmic cycle (we don't know what the previous one was like, or even if there was a previous cycle) reshuffles the elemental deck, redistributing atoms into new configurations. This is an example

of a temporal cycle, one in which events occur over some regular interval. We know of many other astronomic cycles, such as the wobbling of the earth on its track around the sun and the bobbing of our solar system up and down within the Milky Way galaxy. Closer to home, we experience the seasonal cycle, which is the result of the earth's taking one trip around the sun, and the cycle of night and day, which is caused by the spinning of the earth on its axis. Temporal cycles, especially those that have periods within one or a few generations of plants and animals, greatly influence the pattern of life on earth.

Spatial cycles involve the movement of atoms within the biosphere through a chain of events that may eventually bring them back to the same location. It would be convenient if these were fairly simple cycles, with one step always leading to another; but in fact, the pattern is highly ramified, with many alternative paths for the participants. Some of the cycles are primarily physical, depending on the sun, the earth, or winds to drive them. For example, the water cycle requires evaporation from the soil, water surfaces, and the leaves of plants. This process is driven by solar heat and is enhanced by winds, which are also driven by the sun. When enough moisture has accumulated in the atmosphere, clouds form; when the atmospheric moisture cools sufficiently, it condenses and falls as precipitation—rain at warmer temperatures and hail, sleet, or snow at cooler temperatures. When it strikes the ground, the water may run off into lakes and streams, from which it will again evaporate. Some water also infiltrates the ground, eventually surfacing as a spring or rising through the roots of plants. Along this route, the soil serves only as a retention system, eventually giving up its load of moisture before being recharged. Some of the water takes minor alternative routes. For example, animals drink water and excrete it in their feces and urine. From there it evaporates, either directly or after infiltrating the soil. Of course, some water is used in photosynthesis, where it is broken down into hydrogen and oxygen, which are eventually incorporated into other biological cycles. The atmospheric component of the water cycle is quite rapid, taking an average of ten to fourteen days to complete. Most water molecules, however, are in the soil or in the great bodies of water on the globe, where they may reside for long periods of time before evaporating and traveling through the atmosphere. Although it is clear that the water cycle is quite complex, it is, in fact, one of the simpler cycles of the biosphere.

Other important cycles involve biological steps that build simple molecules into complex tissues and the subsequent breakdown of the tissues back into the basic elements. All of these cycles also have some rather exotic, albeit minor, routes for the elements. Consider the nitrogen cycle: nitrogen is a major component of proteins, which are building blocks for tissues and for enzymes that expedite the thousands of biochemical reactions in plants and animals. Beginning with tissues, there are several routes that nitrogen can take. While organisms are alive, they regularly give off nitrogenous wastes (for example, urine produced by animals). When the organisms die, their tissues decompose and the proteins are broken down, making the nitrogen available to plants, where the cycle begins anew. Additional nitrogen enters the system from atmospheric sources. Elemental nitrogen makes up almost 80 percent of the air, but it is tightly bound in a chemical form that is not available to plants. For nitrogen to be biologically usable, it must be converted into ammonia, nitrates, or nitrites. Lightning converts atmospheric nitrogen into soluble nitrogen, which is washed into the soil where it is taken up by roots. Specialized nitrogen-fixing bacteria in the soil also transform atmospheric nitrogen into biologically usable nitrogen. Some nitrogen is tied up in oceanic deposits for long periods of time, and a small amount is shed into the atmosphere during volcanic eruptions.

Clearly, this is not a simple cycle, because molecules of nitrogen no doubt end up in the same tissues over and over; but their routes during each circuit are unlikely to be the same. The route through some branches may take only a few years to complete, but if a different turn is made at a critical juncture, hundreds of years may pass before a nitrogen molecule is passed along to the next step.

Other essential elements follow similar circuitous paths. Carbon is the basis of life on earth; therefore it is a major constituent of plant and animal tissue and is an essential component of energy cycles. Like nitrogen, carbon is excreted or passed on to the consumers and decomposers when organisms die. These animals then use the carbon to produce energy, in the process giving off gaseous carbon dioxide, which is incorporated into photosynthesizing plant tissue, which is eaten by animals, ad infinitum. The pattern of assembly, *decomposition, and recycling is a common one in biological cycles, even though each element has a unique pattern, which changes from ecosystem to ecosystem. For example, sodium, which occurs commonly with chloride as table salt, ranges from being extremely abundant in oceans and certain deserts to being relatively rare in portions of the tallgrass prairie. While plants apparently do not require sodium, animals do. Hence, the behavior of animals may be influenced by localized resources that are high in sodium. Other elements have properties that similarly influence the abundance and the distribution of biota, but the details of the dynamics of elements vary considerably.*

The law of conservation of energy declares that no energy is lost when it changes from one state to another. For example, machines produce mechanical energy and also give off a substantial amount of energy in the form of heat, which is caused by friction between moving parts. The sum of the energy produced (mechanical plus heat) equals the amount put into the machine, even though we may consider that the portion transformed into heat is "lost." On a universal scale, the heat is not lost; it is radiated into surrounding objects and eventually into space. A similar circumstance holds for biological "machines." When a deer consumes a leaf, some of the energy obtained is turned into growth, but a significant portion, up to 90 percent, is eventually lost as body heat. Thus, even though energy is not lost in the cosmic equation, it does not cycle in biological systems; it must constantly be replenished. In our solar system, the biological world would quickly grind to a halt if the sun quit pumping life into the biosphere via plants and photosynthesis. Imagine Konza Prairie in the absence of sunlight: all of the existing plant material would be consumed by herbivores, which would then die. Their remains would be consumed by decomposers, which would eventually suffer an identical fate. The end of life might take scores of years, but the outcome would be certain in a dark, cold world without sunlight.

An essential step in biological cycles results from the creative processes of photosynthesis wherein elements are combined, in the presence of the sun's energy, to form plant tissue. After passing through plants and occasionally one or more animals, the elements enter the decomposition phase of a cycle. There is usually some initial physical degradation of the dead tissue or a simple leaching of chemicals out of the tissue, followed by the actions of large scavengers such as insects. Once the material has been broken down into very small particles, mineralization takes place, with microbes and fungi chemically subdividing the organic material into its basic elemental components. From there, the cycle starts anew as the minerals are incorporated into subsequent production regimes of plants.

Knowledge of the paths that cycles take and of the relationships between the various phases of cycles yields pertinent insights into the functioning of ecosystems. Such knowledge has inherent heuristic value to ecologists as they analyze how organisms adapt to the energetic and nutritional constraints they encounter. The insights also provide important practical information about our own involvement in the biosphere. Empirical measurements of the relationships between phases in biogeochemical cycles have been incorporated into computer models which can be manipulated in ways that the real world cannot be. We can ask simple "what if" questions about perturbations in the biological economy before they actually happen, allowing us to anticipate where problems might occur in time to prevent disastrous results. Research currently being done on Konza, an ecosystem that is relatively unaffected by recent (in evolutionary time) disturbances, will provide baseline information for comparisons with other more stressed areas. Our knowledge remains embryonic, but we are, at last, getting a glimpse at the major physical and biological processes that influence the biosphere.

7 / Streams

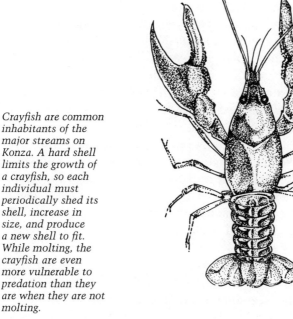

Crayfish are common inhabitants of the major streams on Konza. A hard shell limits the growth of a crayfish, so each individual must periodically shed its shell, increase in size, and produce a new shell to fit. While molting, the crayfish are even more vulnerable to predation than they are when they are not molting.

STREAMS MAKE UP ONLY A SMALL FRACTION OF KONZA PRAIrie, but their influence exceeds their geographic bounds. Streams form distinctive and intriguing habitats within the prairie, and their tributaries and springs offer a reprieve from the arid prairie where trees and their hydrophilic cohorts can coexist next to the prairie proper. Furthermore, the flowing water continually erodes the limestone and shale strata, thus slowly changing the face of Konza.

Shane Creek and Kings Creek are the major streams on Konza, with the latter being the larger. These drainages are among the few pristine creeks remaining in the Great Plains whose headwaters originate on minimally disturbed prairie and therefore serve as important benchmarks by which to judge other more adulterated bodies of water. Streams are actually small subsets of an entire watershed, a geologic basin whose focus is the stream at its base. The Kings Creek watershed covers more than twenty-six hundred acres, with the two main channels of the north and south branches totaling more than five miles in length.

Kings Creek flows through three distinct habitat types in its short run through Konza. It originates in the upland prairie, and over half of its route lies in the grassland. Slightly over one-quarter of its length is through a mixed prairie/shrub habitat in which grasses and taller vegetation overhang the water course. The remaining portion of the creek flows through the gallery forest, which shades the creek and pilfers much of its water through tree roots. These habitat distinctions are important, because streams mirror the terrestrial environment through which they flow. Kings Creek starts out relatively pure, containing only low concentrations of a few minor elements dissolved in the water as it seeps from the ground or falls as rain. The adjacent habitat contributes miscellaneous organic and inorganic matter which imbues the water with the local flavors of each habitat. The three habitats through which Kings Creek flows are especially distinct, and each makes characteristic contributions to the creek.

Where does the water for Kings Creek come from? The immediate sources are rain that falls directly into the channel, seepage from underground reservoirs, and runoff from adjacent surfaces of the watershed—a rare event. Water is bestowed on these local sources from all over the globe, as weather fronts collide, mix, and separate. Evaporation from the earth and its bodies of water produces water vapor, which accumulates in the rivers of air that circle in our atmosphere. When warm air, which can hold more moisture than cool air, collides with a cold air mass or is forced up to cooler altitudes by a mountain range, the moisture condenses and falls as precipitation. In mid-continental North America the prevailing atmospheric flow is from the west, but most of the moisture is wrung from the westerlies by the Rocky Mountains. Most of the moisture that falls on Konza, in both summer and winter, is sucked up from the warm Gulf of Mexico. Water rapidly cycles from its terrestrial existence to its atmospheric phase; therefore any molecule that lands on Konza has probably traveled around the globe thousands of times, perhaps even visiting Konza on one of its earlier trips.

When the soil is very dry, the first water that falls may run off, just as a dry sponge sheds water. When slightly moistened, however, the soil can absorb tremendous amounts of water. Once the soil becomes saturated, most of what strikes the ground cannot be absorbed, so it flows downhill into the creek beds on the floor of the watershed. The soil continues to absorb water, but as it does so, water that is already in the soil is displaced, producing springs and seeps that contribute to the water flow.

Predicting the water level in the streams and tributaries on Konza is about as difficult as predicting the weather. The uncertainty originates with the irregular pattern of rainfall and is complicated by the conditions of the soil and the vegetation at the time of the rain; therefore, both the quantity and the sequence of rainfall significantly influence the flow rates of streams. Even though there is a general pattern of thunderstorms in the spring and early summer, a dry period in midsummer, and relatively little precipitation in the winter, the exact amount and the exact pattern of rainfall and stream flow are impossible to predict. As an example, the flow rate in Kings Creek in 1979 reached a peak of about 100 gallons (380 liters) per second in early April and tapered off until late August, when the flow ceased at the gauging station. In 1980 the flow went from near zero to almost 800 gallons (3,000 liters) a second in one rainstorm in late March. Subsequently the flow tailed off, with only one minor peak in early June. The first third of 1981 was dry, but during the remainder of the year, there were several peaks of flow, including one major pulse in late June and another in early August. It is clear that for at least these three representative years there were no obvious patterns in the flow of Kings Creek.

The headwaters of Kings Creek and Shane Creek drain a smaller area than the lower reaches, and the rock strata there are not as deep as those surrounding the lower stretches. This limits the amount of water available to the upper reaches and makes flow there the least predictable along the watercourse. Water is an ephemeral resource where these young drainages etch the landscape. Farther downstream the prairie/shrub sections of the streams exhibit intermittent flows, which last longer than those upstream but still include periods when no water flows. The lower reaches have water for most of the year; even when there is no actual flow, deep pools persist for months.

The velocity of water in Kings Creek varies tremendously, ranging from a few inches per second in pools at low volume to 10–15 feet (3–4.6 meters) per second in riffles during floods. Peak rates of flow can be ten or twenty times the base rates of flow, and usually reach their maximums within an hour or two after a major storm. During one year of analysis, which was a relatively wet year, storms that increased the flow rate of Kings Creek more than tenfold occurred five times out of twenty-nine storms. Peak flow that was five times the base rate occurred six times, while fourteen storms produced flows that were double the base rate. The four remaining storms increased the flow rate less than twofold. Clearly, large storms that generate high water volumes and high flow rates are relatively rare, but when they occur, they have a dramatic impact on the stream environment.

The velocity of water that passes a point is influenced by several features of a stream. Obviously, the volume of water is important, as larger volumes move at faster rates—up to a point, although water that is dropping straight down reaches the final speed regardless of the volume that is falling. The gradient of the stream channel also affects velocity; steeper gradients yield higher velocities and send water careening down the channel. For any given volume and gradient, the velocity of water flow varies with the configuration of the stream bed. Wide, deep stream beds usually produce slow-running water, confirming the adage "Still water runs deep." Where the channel narrows or runs over riffles, the pace quickens, and the water cascades and ricochets through the stream course.

The gradation of velocity in a stream has an important influence on the stream's substrate. Fast currents generate tremendous forces, carrying large cobbles and dislodging boulders. As the velocity slows down, the heavier items fall out, until only the finest particles are suspended in the slowest moving water. In this manner, the velocity of the current functions as a sieve, sorting out particles along the stream course according to their weight. Only the largest stones inhabit the faster stretches of a stream, where it is narrow and quick. Sand bars, which are composed of fine grains of sand and silt, are the residue of a declining stream flow where the water dropped its last load of material.

Water velocity indirectly affects the stream community through its effects on the stream bottom and directly influences what types of plants and animals can gain purchase in particular reaches of a stream. If the velocity is too great, prospective residents will be swept downstream. Conversely, low rates of flow may not carry enough food or oxygen to underwater organisms, excluding them from pools and other areas that receive low volumes of water.

We tend to think that a stream runs through a valley, but the valley also runs through the stream. Tiny windblown particles to large pieces of debris, such as logs, limbs, and leaves, are blown or fall into the stream as it passes through a habitat. Processes within the stream produce an organic milieu that is constantly mixed by physical action and is altered by withdrawals and deposits made by inhabitants in the water. A portion of what is carried in the current is stored along the banks or in the stream bed, while part of the load is irretrievably lost downstream. These processes suggest four basic features of stream dynamics. The first is the importation of elements into the stream. A second involves processes that go on within the stream itself, adding to, subtracting from, or otherwise altering the importations. A third feature is the storage of material in or along the dry bed, or in inaccessible reaches of the stream. The final feature is the exportation of material from the stream channel. Debris that enters a stream and is not consumed along its course makes its way through the stream and river systems to lakes or ocean basins. For example, material that is exported from Kings Creek flows first into McDowell Creek, then enters the Kansas River, the Missouri River, and, finally, the Mississippi River, which deposits its load in the Gulf of Mexico. Some material is exported laterally from a stream, either blowing or washing up on the banks, where it remains until it decomposes, burns, or returns to the stream.

Importations to a stream are basically of two kinds—elements that are dissolved in the water and particulate matter, which either sinks or is suspended in the aqueous matrix. Dissolved organic material actually consists of individual molecules of matter that have been chemically dispersed in the stream's water. Particulate matter is larger, although it, too, can be quite small, and it is dispersed physically, rather than chemically. Suspended particles either are tugged down by gravity, or they float up, according to their buoyancy. The dissolved material can enter directly with rainfall: for example, rain always contains nitrogen and miscellaneous material that is wafted into the atmosphere with the rainstorm. Rainwater that falls on vegetation or the ground picks up an additional load of dissolved elements and flushes them into the stream. On Konza, the concentrations of dissolved elements are always higher in rainwater that falls through vegetation than in "pure" rainwater, which falls directly into the stream—in some cases, five to ten times higher. The prairie/shrub reaches consistently provide the lowest concentrations of dissolved elements in rainwater, primarily because so little of the vegetation overhangs the stream's channel. The gallery forests contribute the greatest amount of dissolved organic material in precipitation, especially when snow sits on leaves for hours or days, slowly absorbing chemicals from the leaf surfaces and dripping them into the stream. A third source of dissolved material is the leaching of elements in the soil as water percolates down through the soil and emerges as a spring, but very little is known about this route of nutrient importation to the stream.

Particulate organic matter (POM) contributes significantly more to the nutrient budget of Kings Creek than does dissolved organic matter (DOM). The smallest particles enter as windblown dust or other airborne detritus, and thus their importation is greatest on windy days and during windy seasons. Substantially larger particles also fall into the creek, including leaves, branches, and entire trees. Trees take a long time to decompose; in the meantime, they produce bottlenecks behind which debris accumulates, producing a dam that can spawn a temporary pool. Falling leaves from plants along the stream make the largest contribution to the imported particulate matter. Regardless of the source or size of the material that enters the stream, its vital fluids are quickly leached away, and its tissues disintegrate under the attack of biotic and physical forces in the stream, which in turn provide sustenance for the inhabitants of the stream.

As expected, the leaves of grasses are the major organic import in the upland prairie reaches of Kings Creek. Within the prairie/shrub sections, a greater variety of leaves is introduced, including grasses, honey locust, sumac, buckbrush, oak, and elm. Leaves of hackberry and bur oak, plus woody litter from all trees, constitute almost 60 percent of the litter fall in the gallery forest, with leaves from miscellaneous trees and shrubs contributing the remainder. Not surprisingly, over three times as much organic material falls into the stream as it flows through the gallery forest than is imported during its run through the upland reaches; the intermediate prairie/shrub stretches contribute even less.

Although most of what enters the stream falls directly into the water, lateral import from the banks contributes as much as a quarter of the total deposits. As is the case with direct deposition, lateral input varies with the quantity of material available, the velocity of the wind (the primary agent for lateral deposition), and the particular stream-side habitat. Very little lateral importation occurs in the grasslands, where wind-woven grass stems serve as nets, capturing leaves before they can blow into the headwaters. The gallery forest, however, produces many leaves, and the understory is sufficiently open to allow them to blow into the stream from the adjacent forest floor.

Each year, tons of material either drop into Kings Creek or are imported laterally. The timing of deposition is highly variable, but the large contributions from the gallery forest during autumn outweigh all other imports combined. For example, during autumn the deposition of bur-oak leaves into Kings Creek increases tenfold over deposition rates during the other seasons, and the total litter fall may increase six- or eightfold. The dominant prairie grasses do not spontaneously shed their leaves in the fall, so any grass leaves that do fall into the water must be knocked in by wind, precipitation, or animals.

If the only thing that happened in streams was that leaves fell in and floated to the sea, the habitat would be relatively uninteresting biologically. Fortunately, the deposition of dissolved and particulate matter is accompanied by an array of processes that alter these ingredients in important and intriguing ways. The dissolved organic matter that enters is readily available to stream inhabitants and is quickly snapped up by microbes that float in the water or adhere to the surface of submerged objects. Bacteria that inhabit the headwaters of Kings Creek can survive on leached extracts of grass leaves, but they cannot survive on leachates (leached material) from downstream oaks. This suggests that the upstream forms have never encountered oak leaves and have not had the opportunity to adapt to the presence of those leaves' contributions in the water. The down-stream bacteria populations, which encounter leachates from both the distant upstream grasses and the local oak leaves, can survive on either. Nitrogen is in great demand by stream inhabitants; any nitrogen that enters the creek is quickly taken up by local popula-tions, and almost none is washed downstream. Experiments in Kings Creek have shown that during the summer growing season, upstream organisms may actually limit the growth of algae downstream by ex-tracting virtually all of the nitrogen before it reaches the downstream populations. If nitrogen is added downstream, where the upstream inhabitants cannot abscond with it, luxuriant mats of algae form.

Particulate matter also undergoes significant changes during its downstream journey. Physical and biological factors collaborate to break down the particles into smaller and smaller pieces. Larger animals take a bite and leave crumbs for the smaller animals, and so on down the line, until only the tiniest pieces remain. At each step, the rending of tissue spills more organic juice into the water.

The degradation of leaves begins as soon as they hit the water. The initial step is the leaching out of chemicals from the surface and the interior of the leaf. Highly soluble chemicals go into solution in the stream and are quickly mixed with the other components of the stream by diffusion and physical agitation. As leaves float on the water, they are buffeted through the riffles and miniature rapids, beginning their physical breakdown. Once they have become waterlogged, they are subjected to further abuse, lying in leaf packs on the stream bed, where water flows over and around them, peppering them with silt, sand, and stones. The physical decomposition of leaves is affected by the velocity, the temperature, and the load of the current.

Coincident with the physical breakdown of leaves in the stream is an attack by biotic factors. Leaves, which already carry their own microbial baggage, are further inoculated with microbes that spe-cialize in breaking down particulate organic material. Bacteria and fungi possess enzymes that begin the digestion of the leaf, in some cases invading the tissue and consuming it from the inside out. The numerous aquatic insect larvae also begin to degrade the leaves, al-though insects are not thought to be as important in Kings Creek as they are in other streams. Some investigators believe that the initial attacks of insects occur only after fungi have made the leaf surfaces

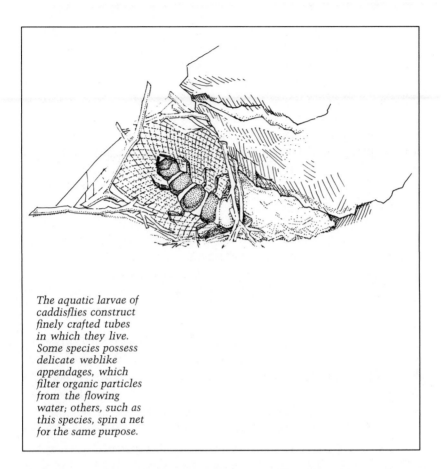

The aquatic larvae of caddisflies construct finely crafted tubes in which they live. Some species possess delicate weblike appendages, which filter organic particles from the flowing water; others, such as this species, spin a net for the same purpose.

palatable, giving the fungi the same role on the leaf that peanut butter serves for bread. Insect larvae are classified into several functional guilds in streams, with shredders being the first to attack leaves. As their name implies, shredders are responsible for physically breaking leaf material into smaller pieces while extracting the nutrients that the shredders require. Although shredders do not appear to be abundant in Kings Creek, they are represented by the naiads (aquatic nymphs) of stoneflies and the larvae of crane flies.

Shredders take their share of the particulate matter and pass the remainder on to the filterers, insects that use nets—either anatomical features or webs spun from a silklike material—to snare the fine and ultrafine crumbs left by the shredders. In Kings Creek this role is taken by the larvae of caddisflies and black flies, but their impact is minimal, because this guild is poorly represented in King's Creek compared to other types of streams. Instead, 98 percent of the aquatic insects in Kings Creek are scrapers, which graze on the accumulated detritus and mats of fungi and bacteria that grow on submerged rocks. Scrapers, such as the larvae of mayflies and true flies, have evolved elaborate anatomical and behavioral traits that allow them to scrape their sustenance from the rock surfaces. Many live directly in the swiftest currents and attach themselves to rocks by means of hooks, suckers, or other forms of attachment and slowly plow their mandibles over the surface, taking in mouthfuls of the accumulated glop.

The shredders and the scrapers are sloppy feeders whose foraging provides many morsels for other organisms. Their waste products and carcasses also enter the flow, adding nutrients that can be exploited by microbes and other creatures. Furthermore, the larvae are preyed upon by a legion of predators, including the larvae of stoneflies, caddisflies, and dragonflies, the adults of some species of beetles, and fish.

Not everything that falls into Kings Creek is equally susceptible to physical and biological degradation. Large pieces of wood may take decades to break down, whereas fine organic matter, and especially dissolved organic matter, is quickly incorporated into the energy or construction budgets of microbes. Even the leaves of different species of plants decompose at different rates. The leaves of oaks and sycamores are especially resistant to decomposition by insect larvae; both their physical toughness and the chemicals that they contain, which are known to deter consumers, probably play roles in slowing their decomposition rates. In fact, experiments in Kings Creek have revealed that virtually all of the loss of weight by oak leaves throughout the first several days of submersion results from leaching and not from the actual disappearance of tissue. Elm leaves are much more easily decomposed, and hackberry leaves disappear the most quickly from the stream beds.

The position of leaves in the stream also affects the rate at which they decompose. Those that happen to sink in the deep pools of Kings Creek are not subjected to the pounding absorbed by leaves that land in riffles where water velocity is so much greater. In addition, riffles support larger populations of the insect larvae—presumably because the swifter current contains more oxygen and carries more food over a shorter period of time than does slower water—and more microbes wash by, thus providing a greater opportunity for inoculation. As an example of this positional effect, leaves of chinkapin oak and hackberry lose almost twice as much weight in riffles as they do in nearby pools over the same time period.

The indigenous stream processes are not entirely destructive; the biological breakdown of every piece of organic matter is accompanied by the survival and success of the decomposer. In addition, aquatic algae carry out photosynthesis where sufficient light reaches the water. Photosynthesis is greatest in the upper portions of Kings Creek, where no overhanging vegetation intercepts the incoming sunlight. Within the closed canopy of the gallery forest, the aquatic algae have the same problem in securing light energy as their terrestrial relatives have in the adjacent undergrowth of the forest.

A substantial amount of organic matter is stored each year along Kings Creek. When the creek floods, huge amounts of organic debris are flushed from sites where it had been ensconced for months or even years. As the flood subsides, material that had been carried from upstream settles out along the stream bank, much as tea leaves do on the edge of a cup, until the next storm tide. Some of the lateral deposits will eventually be knocked or blown into the base flow of the stream, and some will decompose where they lie. Near the headwaters of Kings Creek, most of the storage is in grass leaves. In the prairie/shrub section, wood becomes an important storage component, and in the gallery forests, over 95 percent of the storage takes the form of slowly rotting wood and tree leaves. An unknown amount of organic matter is stored as deposits of tiny (in some cases, microscopic) particles in the interstices of the cobbles, pebbles, and silt of the stream bed. If storage sites remain moist, even though not submerged, the organic detritus is subjected to further decomposition by bacteria and fungi before it is resuspended in subsequent storm surges.

The final process in stream dynamics is the export of material that has not been used or stored—"Use it or lose it." Of course, what is exported from one stretch is imported to the next section downstream, but once dissolved or particulate matter has passed by any one segment, it is essentially lost to it forever. In this sense, the stream is a continuum, with characteristic deposits, withdrawals, and changes occurring along portions of its course. For most organic material, stream flow is a one-way street, with export being downstream. However, organisms that are powerful swimmers, such as fish, can move against the current and revisit upstream reaches over and over again. Some insect larvae crawl upstream against the current, and the adults of other forms no doubt fly upstream to lay eggs after emerging at downstream sites. If there were no such upstream migration, there would presumably be a net downstream movement, and all organisms would end up at the mouth of a river after being flushed downstream over many generations.

At times, the concentration of dissolved organic matter that is exported from Kings Creek is similar to that for other streams in North America, but it varies greatly in response to the pattern of stream flow. While a stream is flowing at its base rate, the populations of decomposers can build to match the rate at which nutrients are supplied, effectively extracting much of what is available before it can be exported. When, however, a stretch has been either dry or flowing at a reduced rate for some time, organic matter accumulates in the stream bed and along the banks. A subsequent flood would quickly flush most of the stored organic matter downstream before the aquatic community could mobilize to use it. After a storm surge, the stream bed may be scoured clean, leaving very little material for the base flow of the stream to export or for organisms to consume until further deposits shall have been made.

At base rates of flow, Kings Creek exhibits some of the lowest values for the export of particulate organic matter found in North American streams. The primary reason is that very little particulate organic material is introduced in the first half of the stream's route, where the grassland gives up its leaves grudgingly. Through the gallery forest, where deposition is greater, there are relatively few insect shredders to break leaves down into smaller particles. Thus, much of what falls into Kings Creek may fail to decompose before the next storm surge can flush it downstream, exporting it forever from the system. It would be very difficult to measure the amount of particulate matter that is exported during storm flows—many of the "particles" are large enough to destroy most measuring devices—but the amount is probably substantial. There is also no way to estimate how much organic matter is exported through ground water that leaves the stream through the soil.

Accurate measurements reveal how little organic matter is exported from Kings Creek. Just as revealing, however, is a quick glance into the pristine stream. The water, when not influenced by a storm surge, is as clear as the air itself. Under such conditions the water is swept clear of much of its content by the creek's residents. The check-and-balance system that the stream fosters keeps input and outflow in a dynamic equilibrium. Many events can disrupt the stability—such as floods, landslides, and sudden blooms of algae. The stream always, however, dampens such digressions and proceeds steadfastly downhill to the sea.

COMPETITION

When resources are plentiful, life can be completely satisfactory for many creatures. During seasons or years when vegetation is lush, prairie animals have more than enough to eat and plenty of places in which to hide. Under such conditions, the number of individuals tends to increase, quickly reaching the capacity of the habitat to support the expanding population. When populations extend beyond the carrying capacity of the habitat or when resources collapse below previous levels, pressure to survive begins to mount, and life becomes more stressful and tenuous. If demand greatly exceeds supply, the results go far beyond simple inconvenience, and many individuals do not reproduce, or they may even perish in the face of decreasing food, space, or shelter. At this point, competition between individuals for the limited resources intensifies; ultimately, the individuals that have the morphological, physiological, or behavioral specialities that increase their chances of securing sufficient resources will be the ones most likely to survive and at least to have the opportunity to reproduce. Competition may involve direct, overt action, such as fighting, or a more diffuse form that entails the efficiency of acquiring limited resources. If the competition is among individuals of the same species, the survivors will have traits that tend to adapt them to their habitat at that particular time. Thus, through the natural selection of individuals, the entire population becomes more closely matched to its environment.

If the competition occurs between members of two different but ecologically similar species that overlap broadly in their distribu-

tion, the species themselves will tend to adapt to the prevailing environmental condition through the adaptations of their individual members. Because members of the same species share genetic information with each other through interbreeding, each species as a group will tend to specialize on a portion of the available resource spectrum. This can eventually lead to further separation between species in their environmental requirements and can result in a form of peaceful coexistence if the species diverge far enough to limit competition during subsequent bottlenecks. This process of speciation makes it appear as though changes happen "for the good of the species"; in fact, however, the adaptive characteristics of the species are mediated through the ecological success of its individuals.

To understand how competition might structure a stream community in Kings Creek, imagine two species of caddisflies using nets to catch organic particles that are floating down Kings Creek. There is a broad range of particle sizes in the creek, but those that are too large to be handled by the larvae are swept clear of the nets, and particles that are too fine slip through the mesh. Should there be a decline in the amount of intermediate-sized pieces available to each individual, perhaps because fewer particles are being produced upstream or because the number of caddisflies that use the particles has dramatically increased, there may not be enough to go around. Under these circumstances, any individuals that have constructed nets with smaller meshes could trap the finer particulates and thus could acquire an advantage over those individuals that had intermediate-mesh nets. A similar advantage would accrue to individuals that could capture pieces of leaves at the larger end of the scale, leading to a divergence in sizes of nets among the two species which previously had spun similar-sized nets. As long as the intermediate particle sizes were limiting to some degree, any divergence that promoted the use of an otherwise unused portion of the spectrum of particle sizes would be favored. Over many generations the two species might diverge in their particle-size specializations until they reached a balance at which both could survive.

Ecologists have attempted to quantify the degree to which species must diverge in order to coexist. Theoretical models indicate what some limits should be, but empirical evidence that tests the predictions is meager. Nevertheless, there is evidence that the selective forces of competition tend to organize some communities into discrete guilds, based on ecological specializations. In the example of the caddisflies, there could be small, medium, and large species which inhabit different reaches of a stream and spin nets of different sizes. Such differences in size might reflect the evolutionary compromises made to solve past pressures of competition.

We tend to imagine that closely related species are most likely to compete directly, and this may often be the case. Two species of caddisflies that have similar-sized nets are likely to acquire similar-sized particles, thus increasing the chance for competition when resources become limited. When this occurs, slight changes in mesh size may accommodate the coexistence of the two species. (Remember that coexistence is not the "goal" of this process; it is simply the outcome when members of each species adapt to the available ecological opportunities.) Thus, to determine how two closely related species have resolved their competitive interactions, we may simply be able to look for obvious ways in which they differ—in the example of the caddisflies, they would be very similar except for the size of their net mesh. But what happens when very distantly related species compete? If we ask, "In what way do they differ?" the answer may be "In every way except that they eat the same thing." For example, on Konza, insects, birds, rodents, and, eventually, decomposers may compete for seeds. The organisms differ in many ways, and no one trait is likely to hold the key to the resolution of their competition for food. Instead, the solution comes from the suite of characteristics that the competitors possess, from their physiological tolerances and requirements to the time of day and the season of their activity. Because such differences are so diffuse, an understanding of competition between distantly related organisms is very difficult.

Plants and animals are surrounded by a swarm of potential and actual competitors. Much of what we see as the structure of biological communities—the neat and tidy niches of community inhabitants—are reflections of past competitive interactions that have been resolved by specialization. If we attempt to measure the degree of competition within contemporary biological communities, we may find none, especially in cases where the issues were settled a long time ago. As one author has noted, we see these communities in the light of the ghost of competition past. There is no rest for the weary, though, for as soon as one set of competitors has been accommo-

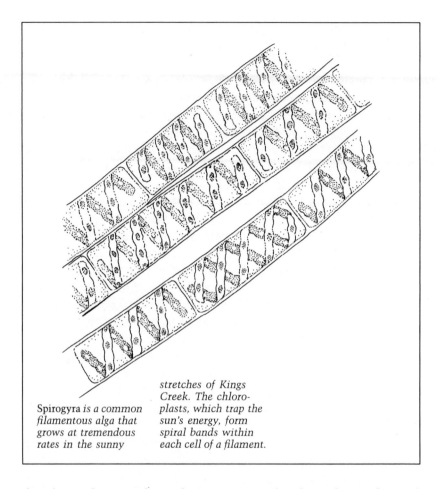

Spirogyra *is a common filamentous alga that grows at tremendous rates in the sunny stretches of Kings Creek. The chloroplasts, which trap the sun's energy, form spiral bands within each cell of a filament.*

dated, another stands ready to negotiate for the rights to limited resources.

Relatively few plants are actually rooted in Kings Creek and emerge up into the air. Horsetail, a very primitive plant, occurs sparsely in moist areas. Cat-tail, a ubiquitous aquatic form, can be found in sunny stretches that stay damp even when they don't carry running water. Some grasses and sedges grow in the stream channel near the headwaters of Kings Creek, and populations of introduced watercress are abundant near some seeps. Several species of speedwell inhabit the streams of Konza, lying just below the water surface, with their roots extending into the stream bed. Watercress is not common in the streams, but it does occur at a few sites. The most abundant plants in Kings Creek are the ubiquitous green algae, primitive single-celled or colonial forms that float in the water. *Cladophora* and *Spirogyra* form massive filamentous mats that cover slow-moving water in the open reaches where sunlight is plentiful. Farther downstream, where shade is deeper than sunlight is bright, simple algae called diatoms predominate. Although a few aquatic insects and other small creatures live in the rich carpets of algae that form over the surface of streams, algae are low in nutrition, and very few animals eat them.

Water is slow to cool and slow to warm, so the temperatures in streams remain fairly constant over the course of a day, as compared to the ambient air temperatures. Seasonally, Kings Creek ranges from freezing to near 80 degrees Fahrenheit (27 degrees Celsius) in still pools on hot days. The moderate temperatures, coupled with the supply of available organic matter in the current, make Kings Creek an attractive habitat for an assortment of creatures. Most groups of insects have some members that are aquatic, and some entire groups are inhabitants of streams. Most are aquatic only during their larval or nymphal stages; they emerge into the air or onto land as adults. As noted, aquatic insects can be divided into functional guilds, groups that share a similar *modus operandi* in the stream. Those that share similar niches tend to converge on characteristic body patterns. For example, the members of several groups that inhabit the swiftest-flowing reaches are flattened and streamlined and possess an array of attachment devices for clutching the substrate. It would be difficult for them to come to the surface for a gulp of air, so most of them have gills to extract oxygen from the water. The larvae of a few species of insects can swim or walk against the current, but most float or crawl downstream to disperse, to escape predators, or to find greener pastures. Some fly larvae rappel downstream by attaching a silken cord to a rock and playing the line out until they reach their destination.

The larvae of true flies (Diptera, or "two wings," referring to their two pairs of wings, one of which is nonfunctional), which include crane flies, black flies, and mosquitoes, are also abundant. Crane-fly larvae, some of which feed on decaying vegetation, look like small aquatic caterpillars, but they metamorphose into adults that are more than 1 inch (2.5 centimeters) in length and resemble overgrown mosquitoes. The larvae of at least fifty species of midges inhabit Kings Creek as larvae; many are scavengers, but almost all of the functional groups of aquatic forms are represented among the midge larvae. When their populations reach extremely high densities, they serve as a smorgasbord for a variety of consumers, from other insects to an assortment of fish. The adults are small, fragile flies that frequently emerge synchronously in large swarms from the pools of Kings Creek. Black-fly larvae attach themselves to isolated substrates in Kings Creek, where they have been known to reach densities of over six thousand per square foot (sixty-two thousand per square meter). The larvae filter out sustenance from the stream flow and are quite innocuous, but the airborne adult flies inflict brutal bites in their attempts to secure a meal of blood.

Among the most graceful insects that frequent Kings Creek and its tributaries are dragonflies and damselflies. Both groups lay eggs in or near the water, where the nymphs go through three molts before emerging as adults. At the time of emergence, the nymphs crawl up onto the land and extricate themselves from their prepubertal cases. They appear rather unkempt and lethargic for the first thirty minutes, until they can unfurl their wings, allowing them to dry and stiffen. As adults they are acrobatic fliers, hovering like helicopters before darting off to challenge an intruder or intercept a potential mate. The males secure territories and lure interested females in for mating. The pair may stay *en copula* for hours, as the male transfers sperm to the female. Females will mate with more than one male, and the sperm of the last suitor is the most likely to fertilize the eggs that a female lays. Consequently, after copulating, a male usually stands guard over his mate until she lays their fertilized eggs, preventing any other males from interrupting and negating the investment made by the first male.

Some insects inhabit Kings Creek throughout their life cycle. Perhaps the most obvious are water striders, which skate across the thin, elastic film of surface tension produced by the attraction of water molecules to each other. These "true" bugs use small forelegs to capture and manipulate their prey. Rows of fine hairs on the last two pairs of legs support the weight of the insect (were these legs to penetrate the surface tension, the insects would plunge below the water surface) and also function as oars for propulsion. Water striders communicate by tapping out signals with one leg, thus sending rip-

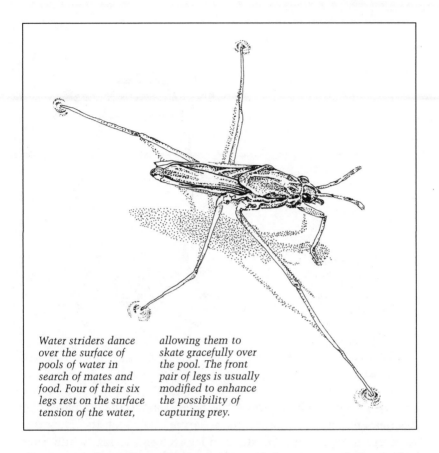

Water striders dance over the surface of pools of water in search of mates and food. Four of their six legs rest on the surface tension of the water, allowing them to skate gracefully over the pool. The front pair of legs is usually modified to enhance the possibility of capturing prey.

ples across the surface. The intensity and the pattern of the ripples convey messages about territorial or mating interests.

Kings Creek also plays host to relatives of the water striders, including water boatmen and backswimmers. Using their rear pair of legs for paddles, most water boatmen forage for algae, although a few feed on other insects. The adults have no gills, so they must periodically visit the surface to gulp air, sometimes taking a bubble of air with them to use like an aqualung underwater. As their name implies, backswimmers swim upside down, using their very long rear legs as oars. The insects are especially aggressive, sometimes attacking large prey and sucking out their body fluids until the victims die.

Several families of beetles frequent the pools and riffles of Kings Creek. One species of whirligig beetle, so named because of its habit

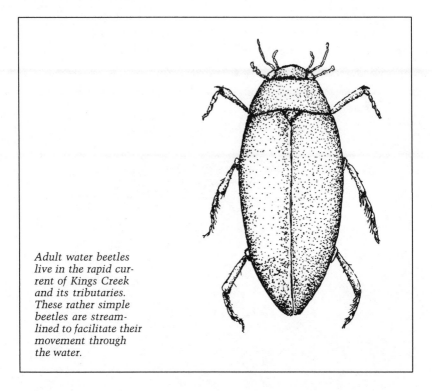

Adult water beetles
live in the rapid cur-
rent of Kings Creek
and its tributaries.
These rather simple
beetles are stream-
lined to facilitate their
movement through
the water.

of swimming rapidly in circles, has been found in the drainage. The beetles are aggressive predators as larvae and as adults. They use severely flattened middle and hind legs for propulsion, while their slender forelegs assist in capturing prey. Several species of crawl- ing water beetles have been collected in Kings Creek. These beetles look like typical terrestrial beetles, although they are streamlined in response to the stream's current. The adults feed on algae, but the larvae are predaceous. Two of the largest beetle families in Kings Creek are the water scavenger beetle and the predaceous diving bee- tle. The former is represented by more than a dozen species. The larvae are consumate predators, but the adults are benign scavengers. The adults periodically rise to the surface of a pool and obtain an air bubble, which they enclose in a silvery sheath on the underside of the body. The predaceous diving beetles are a very large group, with a well-deserved reputation for being assassins in streams. Sometimes called water tigers, they are known to take on a variety of prey, in- cluding small fish. The beetles can reach one and one-half inches in length, and they possess sicklelike jaws. Prey are pinched in the insect's mandibular vice, and the victim's juices are sucked out through hollow channels in the jaws.

A number of creatures related to insects are found along Kings Creek. Most are quite small, but the largest are two species of crayfish. These crustaceans begin life as eggs attached to the posterior appendages of females. The young hatch and go through several molts, reaching an inch or more in size during the first year. They live for at least two years, eventually reaching three to five inches in length, with pincers that are nearly as long. Individuals space themselves out over the bottom of pools in Kings Creek, occasionally posturing or actually fighting over territories. The largest combatants are usually dominant, although the holder of a plot of stream bottom may have an advantage over an interloper, even if the resident is slightly smaller. Crayfish are scavengers; they will even eat their own molted shells. Numerous other crustaceans reside in Kings Creek, including amphipods and isopods. The former are approximately one-quarter of an inch long and resemble small shrimp; most of them are scavengers, feeding on the detritus of the stream. The aquatic isopods in Kings Creek look like their terrestrial relatives—pill bugs, or "rolypolies," which characteristically curl up into an armored ball when disturbed. The aquatic forms are blind; they live in the dark under stones and waterlogged wood and leaves, where they crawl about in search of miscellaneous organic debris to consume.

Free-living (i.e., nonparasitic) flatworms and roundworms have been collected in Kings Creek, as have horsehair worms. Members of the earthworm family are occasionally associated with the stream flow. Miscellaneous snails and freshwater clams make minor contributions to the faunal diversity of Kings Creek.

We usually think of fish as typical inhabitants of streams. Almost a dozen species have been collected from Kings Creek, and several more are likely to inhabit the lower reaches of the drainage. The upper sections, where the water runs cool and clear, host several species of minnows. The southern redbelly dace is one of the rarer species inhabiting Kings Creek; its distribution is limited to a small portion of the Flint Hills, but it can be locally abundant where it does occur. Conversely, the red shiner is one of the most widely distributed and hardiest species of minnow in North America. It occurs in all types of streams, from clear and cool to warm and turbid. It seems to take

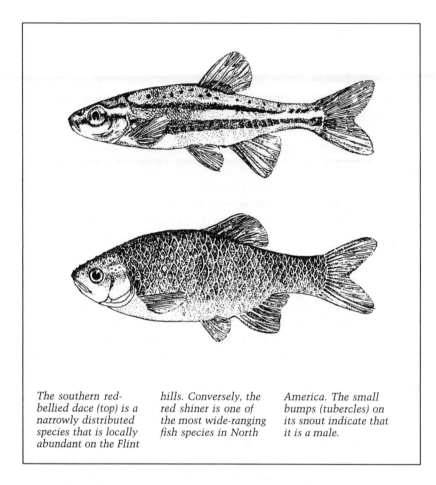

The southern red-bellied dace (top) is a narrowly distributed species that is locally abundant on the Flint hills. Conversely, the red shiner is one of the most wide-ranging fish species in North America. The small bumps (tubercles) on its snout indicate that it is a male.

advantage of the demise of other species, moving in where more sensitive fish have been decimated by changes in the aquatic habitat. Stonerollers are also common. As their name implies, these fish scavenge over small stones in the stream bed, scraping off the thin film of accumulated organic matter with their broad, flat mouths, which are located on the underside of their heads. Only one member of the perch family, the orangethroat darter, inhabits Kings Creek. Other species of fish probably enter Kings Creek, especially at high water levels, when they can invade from downstream.

Although the frogs and toads on Konza are concentrated in the man-made ponds and shallow roadside ditches during the breeding season, some individuals use the pools of Kings Creek as sites for courtship and breeding. The same is true for the painted turtle and the common snapping turtle, the only two aquatic turtles known from Konza Prairie. The common snapper, which grows to about a foot in length, prefers pools with sandy or muddy bottoms, where dead logs or other structures that can be used for sunbathing emerge from the water. It feeds on almost anything, including aquatic plants, insects, crayfish, earthworms, clams, snails, fish, frogs, salamanders, snakes, other turtles, birds, small mammals, and carrion.

Beavers are the only truly aquatic mammal found on Konza, and they are seen only rarely along the lower stretches of Kings Creek. A river otter was last seen in Kansas near Konza in 1904, so others may occasionally have traveled upstream into the prairie creeks. Muskrats are possible inhabitants, but they have not yet been sighted on Konza. Many species of terrestrial mammals use the resources of Kings Creek, especially as drinking water. Their hoofprints or paw prints are common in the feculent mud of the stream bank, leaving evidence of the previous night's activities. Raccoons forage along the edge for crayfish, snails, and clams, leaving the spent shells of their prey littering the banks, and skunks root about in search of an assortment of morsels.

We think of islands as parcels of land ringed by vast oceans, but in every sense of the term, the streams on Konza function as islands of habitat. The streams are surrounded by the fringe of woodland and an ocean of grass. Most of the plants and animals that live in such fresh-water islands are prisoners, their mobility being restricted to the long downstream corridor. The ribbon of aquatic habitat becomes fragmented as portions of the watercourse dry up and leave isolated pools; during the next storm flow, the pools reunite, again forming a single, continuous habitat. Streams are not characteristic prairie habitats, but they are characteristic of tallgrass prairies: they are the bows on a landscape that is wrapped in prairie.

8 / Patterns in Time

Thunderstorms are common visitors to Konza Prairie, especially in the spring, when contrasting weather fronts collide spectacularly over the central plains. Along the edge of a storm the rain may evaporate before it can reach the ground, but at its epicenter, a thunderstorm can drop several inches of rain or hail in a few minutes.

WHEN WE THINK OF KONZA PRAIRIE, WE IMAGINE THE PAT-terns exemplified by grasslands, forests, and streams. Such spatial patterns can be recognized in an instant, even though their specific characteristics vary from site to site—indeed, differences in compo-sition and spatial patterns are what distinguish habitats from one another. In addition to these obvious spatial conformations, we are also aware of distinct time frames that yield patterns on the prai-rie. Most temporal patterns occur across all habitats, although their length and biological consequences may differ. Virtually all habi-tats on earth have some portion of a twenty-four-hour day divided into segments of daylight and dark, but the absolute amount of each varies between locations and throughout the year. The other obvious time frame on earth relates to the seasons. These, too, vary in length and effect; but everywhere on land, cool seasons alternate with relatively warm seasons, or wet seasons with dry ones. Depending on the latitude, the difference between them may be slight—for example, in the tropics, which are always warm, and at the poles, where it is always cold. In between, at the middle latitudes of the temperate regions, tremendous fluctuations in temperature occur seasonally—as much as 140 degrees on Konza (78 degrees Celsius). Because of the extreme environmental contrasts provided by day and night or by the changing seasons, few plants or animals can adjust to all conditions. Thus, most have evolved to take advantage of one portion of the time resource and to tolerate or avoid the remaining, less equable portion. Even in the underground world of Konza, which is buffered against the environmental extremes aboveground, the residents are subjected to the effects of day and night and the seasons.

Aging is one important temporal pattern that is not cyclical. As individual organisms age, they change physiologically and morphologically on their way through senescence to death. Many features conspire to set a limit on how long an organism can live, so there is not much raw material for natural selection to work on in order to extend life spans. The best that can happen in relation to aging is that there be a period in the lifetime of an individual when all of its faculties reach a peak at the same time, enhancing the individual's chance of finding a mate and successfully reproducing. Life spans vary greatly on Konza, from a few minutes for some microbes to thousands of years for clones of plants.

Aging generates specific sequential patterns in individual organisms. For example, young plants and animals spend much of their time and energy growing to a size that will allow them to compete successfully with others in the population. Once an effective size has been reached, investments are shifted to reproduction, which is usually accompanied by a reduction in the growth rate of the individual. In general, individuals that are breeding for the first time usually produce fewer successful offspring than do more experienced breeders, while the oldest individuals begin to decline in their fecundity as past physiological expenditures take their toll. In most populations of organisms other than humans, individuals die fairly soon after they become reproductively senescent. Although these are general patterns for both plants and animals, the absolute amount of time associated with each portion of the life cycle varies. For example, long-lived grasses such as big bluestem can wait years for suitable conditions to reproduce, while an annual species has no options and must respond to the resources available in the current year, regardless of their suitability. Insects such as tent caterpillars quickly pass through their larval stages on the way to adulthood, while many insects that have aquatic larvae or nymphs spend years in that life stage, only to emerge as adults, to mate, and then to die in a few days. Patterns associated with aging in an individual are reflected in the characteristics of the entire population. For example, if the age structure of a population at any one time is dominated by young individuals, the population can be expected to undergo rapid growth as the cohort of juveniles matures and reproduces. Conversely, if a population is dominated by elderly individuals, it will experience declining numbers, which will be characterized by death rather than reproduction.

Although there is little that organisms can do to adapt to the inevitability of aging, they can take advantage of other time patterns that are cyclical in nature. The clearest examples involve the activity patterns of animals, which reflect the times of day and the seasons that are best suited to success. For example, many animals are active at night, when predators are less effective and when temperatures are more benign. Furthermore, because of the rigors of winter, most animals concentrate their activity in the other seasons.

Daily and seasonal patterns are astronomical in origin. Daylight occurs over the half of the earth that is in direct sunlight at any one time. The other half is in the shadow of the earth itself and experiences night conditions. We do receive some sunlight at night; most of it is reflected from the moon, except during a new moon and eclipses, and a tiny portion is reflected from distant planets and is produced by other stars, which, like our sun, generate their own light, rather than reflecting ambient light. Seasons result from the tilt of the earth on its axis in relation to the sun; summer occurs in the hemisphere that is tilted toward the sun, while winter occurs in the hemisphere that is farthest from the sun. The hemispheres alternate between summer and winter as the earth travels around the sun. Other celestial properties of the earth's path through the heavens— such as the slightly elliptical shape of its orbit, which causes it to be closer to the sun during some seasons than others, and its wobbling on its axis—contribute to long-term variations in the severity of the seasons between years, centuries, and millenniums.

Very few animals on Konza are active both during the day and at night. Rather, they concentrate their activity during a specific portion of the daily cycle. Several selection pressures in the environment are responsible for biases toward daytime or nighttime activity. One of the most important factors is predation—many animals have evolved so as to be active during that portion of the day when they are least vulnerable to predation. For example, most species of mice on Konza are active at night, thereby avoiding such diurnal predators as snakes and hawks. Although other predators (such as owls and coyotes) are active at night, the rodents are probably more difficult to locate in the darkness.

Temperature and humidity also affect animal activity. If the days are too hot and dry or if the nights are too cold, animals may be forced to shift their activity to periods that are less stressful. Turtles sunbathe during the day to warm up, which allows them to carry on their feeding and mating activities, whereas certain insects would overheat in the same intense midday sun and therefore must confine their activity to evenings.

Another major influence on daily patterns of activity is the availability of food. Herbivores and granivores (seed-eating animals) could feed around the clock, as their resources are always available. These types of foragers do, however, exhibit distinct activity patterns, suggesting that they choose to forage when their efficiency is highest. For example, seed-eating birds primarily feed during the day, when they can more easily spot seeds on the ground, even though seeds are available throughout the night. Actual availability also influences when animals are active—for example, animals that feed on food that is produced at specific times of the day would be ill advised to remain active when food was not available, because metabolic costs and the chances of encountering a predator would continue, while the animals would have no income to offset the expense. On Konza, plants that are pollinated by insects pay a small reward of nectar to visitors that carry the host's pollen to another plant. The nectar is usually produced during a certain time of the day, and specialized pollinators must be active when the nectar is available. There is constant pressure on the pollinators to synchronize their foraging period with the nectar-production pattern of the plant, as it would be disadvantageous to arrive too early, when no nectar was available, or too late, when competitors had already sipped the flower dry.

The relationship between pollinators and the plants that they pollinate is the result of evolutionary negotiations that have been going on for centuries. The origin of such interdependence presents a hen-and-egg conundrum, as it is not clear whether the plants first produced nectar at a specific time and lured the pollinators into concurrent activity or whether the plant gradually shifted its time of nectar production to match other requirements, such as temperature or sunlight, of the pollinators. Regardless of the sequence of events, the resultant pattern represents the best solution to a series of problems presented by the nectar-producing plant and the nectar-seeking animal. The solution is not likely to be perfect for either, but if the two participants must rely on each other for survival and reproduction, concessions must be made by both.

Plants also have activity patterns that are dependent on the daily cycle, although the patterns are primarily related to their physiology rather than to movement. The most obvious feature of a plant's activity is its reliance on sunlight for energy to drive photosynthesis. Furthermore, sunlight warms the leaves and the soil, speeding the biological and chemical processes within. At times, however, temperatures may be too hot, reducing the plant's ability to photosynthesize. On the hottest and driest days the valves (stomata) on plant leaves may not open during the day, presumably to reduce water loss; instead, they spread open at night, when humidities are higher and water loss is less severe.

Wind is a constant companion of the prairie. Thus, some plants take advantage of the air movement by timing their release of pollen or seeds to coincide with maximum wind velocities. Plants that use wind as a vehicle to transport seeds may retain a fragile attachment to the seed that can only be broken by a wind above a threshold velocity. This ensures that the seed will be released only under the most propitious conditions for dispersal.

Temperature, humidity, and wind velocities are highly variable on Konza, but they do exhibit recognizable daily trends. Temperature can fluctuate more than 70 degrees Fahrenheit (39 degrees Celsius) in a single day, especially during the fall and spring, when weather patterns are changing dramatically. During the summer or winter, the difference between daytime and nighttime temperatures may be less than 20 degrees Fahrenheit (11 degrees Celsius). Relative humidity usually rises at night; if the air becomes supersaturated with moisture and if the temperature drops sufficiently, dew can form as water vapor condenses on cool surfaces. At daybreak, the temperature begins to rise and relative humidity begins to drop, usually reaching its lowest in late afternoon. Winds that are not associated with particular weather fronts are caused by the differential heating of the earth's surface. The differential is usually the greatest during the peak heating of the afternoon. As the earth's surface warms, low-lying air rises, which causes the surrounding air to rush in, producing a flow that generates localized winds.

Konza Prairie, which is situated at a temperate latitude in the mid continent of North America, is the recipient of the pleasures and problems of all four seasons. Temperatures, humidities, and the availability of water differ substantially between the seasons, so plants and animals on Konza must be able to cope with or to avoid the excesses and take advantage of the more moderate conditions. Of course, what is moderate for one creature may be extreme for another—collared lizards bask in the heat of the sun, whereas similar exposure would be lethal to an earthworm. Winter is the most inclement season, and many year-round prairie inhabitants simply maintain a grim existence throughout the winter, subsisting on what they can scrounge or on survival rations that have been stored during autumn. Other organisms cease their activity for the duration of the season, emerging only after conditions become more favorable. Many insects exhibit this type of avoidance by remaining in resistant stages, such as eggs, until spring. Still others migrate to more benign environments and return again in the following season, a pattern that many birds follow. The remaining organisms do none of these; instead, they succumb to the rigors of the off season, dying before the prairie can return to a less inimical state.

Although there are four seasons on Konza, biologically there may only be three—brown, white, and green. These three colors represent three phases in the degree of biological activity on the prairie. Brown is the season when the vegetation has not yet greened up (early spring) or has lost its coloration (late fall), indicating periods of reduced activity. The white season is winter, when snow, freezing temperatures, frozen soil, and ice bring biological activity to a virtual halt. Finally, there is the green season, the spring and summer, when almost all of the creatures on Konza burst forth in fits of growth, activity, and reproduction.

There is no beginning or ending to the seasonal cycle. Spring, however, has come to represent a new beginning in most life cycles, and so it is an appropriate starting point. There is almost an audible sigh on the prairie as winter releases its grip and as spring flushes. Until plants begin to shoot skyward and animals emerge, resources are still somewhat scarce; but the oppressive blanket of cold begins to lift, and the sky clears, letting in the warming rays of the sun and reducing the threat of death. There can still be episodes of death-dealing cold, but by late February the average daily temperature—an average of the maximum and minimum temperature for the day— rises above freezing. Freezes are still possible into mid April, but they become less and less probable by the equinox. Most plants take their cue from the warmth to begin their spring and summer growth. Roots that had been quiescent while surrounded by frozen or near-frozen soil slowly absorb water as the soil defrosts. The warmth allows the cells in shoots of seasonal early birds to multiply, caus-ing the stalks to penetrate the soil surface and to begin gathering the sun's photons. As more and more plants emerge from the icy clutch of winter, there is a cascading effect, with animals rousing to take advantage of newly available resources. These events reach a frenzy of activity at the boundary between spring and summer, which ultimately reveals the spectacular fertility of Konza Prairie.

Because the seasons represent cycles of environmental conditions, plants and animals can use proximal cues to "predict" what con-ditions are going to be in the short term. If over several days or weeks the daily temperatures—maximum, minimum, average, or any combination—are increasing, plants and animals can anticipate that spring is forthcoming. The opposite pattern, one of decreasing temperatures, would signal the coming of fall and winter. These are fairly reliable predictors of seasonal changes, as long as the period over which the samples are considered is long enough to override any brief dips or peaks in temperature. For example, the temperature on any one date in spring may vary 50 degrees Fahrenheit (28 degrees Celsius) between years, but the average daily temperature for any one month probably varies no more than a few degrees between years.

For organisms that can detect light, the length of day (or photo-period) is the most accurate and least variable indicator of the changing seasons. From the beginning of winter—late December in the Northern Hemisphere—the days get longer and the nights get shorter until the first day of summer, when the pattern is reversed. At the two equinoxes—the beginning of spring and of fall—days and nights are of equal length. Many plants and animals can apparently sense the changing patterns of light, so they respond accordingly. Birds unconsciously detect shortening days and prepare to fly south for the winter, while lengthening days may prompt them to move back northward. Animals that hoard food, such as squirrels and woodrats, use the shorter days of autumn as a cue to begin harvesting the season's bounty and packing it away for the chill of winter. Plants, too, rely on the length of days to indicate when it is time to invest in new growth in the spring or to resorb their nutrients in the fall. Changes both in the length of days and in temperature are a direct result of the astronomical events that generate the seasons, so they are ideal indicators of incipient seasonal changes.

Moisture can also serve as a cue to spring activity, but it is significantly more variable than the other two more reliable indicators. It is possible that plants are primed to grow in the spring by temperature and by length of day, but that they do not actually proceed until sufficient moisture is available. Some seeds require more than one good rainfall to germinate—a process called vernalization—presumably to minimize the chance that a freak storm will trigger germination at an inauspicious time.

Spring possesses all of the physical, abiotic ingredients that are necessary to promote growth and reproduction, so almost all organisms on the prairie initiate their reproductive efforts in concert. The reproductive dormancy that characterized winter gives way to a burst of hormones, which rekindle the procreative notions of prairie residents. It may seem that the melodies of newly arrived birds herald the advent of spring itself, but the more reasonable explanation is that males are attempting to dissuade interlopers from infringing on their territories while at the same time persuading females to consort with them for the purposes of mating. This explanation in no way takes away from the approbation with which the enthusiastic vocalists greet the new season.

Summers on Konza Prairie range from a relatively cool, moist refrain to conditions that are characteristic of the edges of Hades. In its gentler form, summer can provide a cornucopia of resources and

Sunflowers seem to honor their namesake by constantly turning toward the sun as it sweeps overhead.

opportunities for the residents of Konza. Individuals may succumb to the competitive and predatory interactions that are common to the tallgrass, but few lose out to the summer in a benevolent year. Conversely, summer may be host to severe droughts and wilting temperatures that suffocate life day after day. With no moisture and with desiccating heat and winds, summer can sap the vigor from the prairie, leaving it limp in the wake of the thermal onslaught. Under such conditions, many die, and most have no opportunity to rear offspring. When several drought years are strung end to end, as in the dust-bowl days of the 1930s, the prairie withers. The ground is left barren by shriveled or deceased grasses, and the soil cracks open in the face of incapacitating conditions. If summer conditions are mild, prosperity abounds, but one of the major environmental sieves through which successful prairie residents must pass is the virulent droughts that irregularly visit the prairie in the role of the Grim Reaper.

By late September on Konza the days are getting shorter, and the temperatures are declining, unmistakable signs that winter is approaching. After the hectic spring and summer, autumn is the season that allows the inhabitants of Konza to relax and admire their handiwork of the preceding months. There is still work to be done to prepare for winter, but the monumental efforts required to raise offspring are tapering off, and the pace is less frantic. Big bluestem and other grasses are transferring resources garnered during the summer into protected underground vaults. Insects are preparing to wait out the winter as resistant eggs, larvae, or, occasionally, adults. Many other animals are seeking shelter that will suffice for winter; those that remain active for the winter, such as woodrats, begin to cache seeds, fruits, and bark for use during the season when no fresh food is available.

As autumn proceeds, the prairie begins to look as though it had been sprinkled with cinnamon and nutmeg. Fall is a subtle season, lacking violent weather and the ecological confrontations that marked the frenzy of spring and summer. The progeny of the year's reproductive effort have left or are leaving home, further reducing the pace. By late fall, frosts presage the arriving winter; the average minimum temperature falls below the freezing point in late November. Winter can arrive at any time with a premature blast from the north, so most Konza inhabitants have their winterizing chores accomplished by late autumn.

Winter is the harshest season for prairie residents. Its length and severity cannot be accurately foretold, so those that overwinter on or under the prairie must rely on the clues available in the subsequent spring to tell them when it is safe to come out. Some small animals will remain inactive all winter, turning down their body's thermostat to conserve energy; this leaves their bodies cold and seemingly lifeless, but in this listless state the discomfort must be minimal. A few Konza residents, such as the jumping mouse, use torpor to avoid the excesses of winter. Torpor is a physiological strategy that incorporates the short-term lowering of body temperature with occasional rousing for feeding and for the excretion of wastes. While the animal is torpid, its metabolic costs are significantly reduced, and it can live through the winter on a fraction of the rations it would otherwise require—turning down the thermostat in your house at night accomplishes the same goal. True hibernation, which requires putting on enough fat to support minimal physiological activity while sleeping through the winter, is not known on Konza, although jumping mice hibernate in other areas. Insects, especially overwintering larvae, enter a state known as diapause, a form of arrested development that can only be broken when a period of low temperatures is followed by more favorable conditions.

Animals that remain active during the winter must constantly search for whatever meager resources are available, and they must be prepared to seek shelter during the worst conditions. The winter may be cold and damp, the worst combination for those that must endure its ravages, or mild, with occasional sunny warm days and little precipitation. During some winters the temperature will stay below zero for more than a week, leaving the recesses of the prairie littered with casualties and severely debilitating those that do survive. Even so, success during the worst winters is measured, not by the condition of those that survive, but by survival itself. If there is a blanket of snow covering vital resources, the difficulties of extended cold periods are compounded. Add to that a strong north wind that is sending snow crystals hissing over the frozen surface, and the ingredients for a tragedy exist.

Because of these conditions, coupled with the meager availability of food, many populations are limited by winter mortality rather than by the activities of spring and summer. Even though overall activity is curtailed in winter, the noose this gelid season engenders is tight. The prairie issues no guarantees to winter residents.

WEATHER ON KONZA

Konza Prairie lies equidistant from the North Pole and the equator and halfway between the two coasts of North America. This geo-

*graphic position yields a typical mid-continental weather pattern,
which is characterized by warm, moist summers and cool, dry winters. Furthermore, Konza exhibits extreme fluctuations in temperature and moisture between night and day and between seasons, as
well as substantial deviations from the average values for temperature and rainfall between years. The highest average maximum temperatures on Konza occur in July and August, when approximately
two-thirds of the days climb above 90 degrees Fahrenheit (32 degrees
Celsius) and maximum temperatures of 110 degrees Fahrenheit (43
degrees Celsius) may occur. The lowest average temperatures occur
in January, with minimums of − 35 degrees Fahrenheit (− 37 degrees
Celsius), but freezing temperatures can be expected from October
through mid April. Summers can be oppressively hot, and winters
can be very cold; but the spring and autumn seasons on Konza are
long and pleasant.*

*An average of 32 inches (813 millimeters) of precipitation falls
on Konza Prairie annually. Although there is great variation in this
amount from year to year, there is a 98 percent chance that at least
66 percent of the average amount of rainfall will occur in a given
year. Two-thirds of the moisture falls from May through September.
Winters are usually dry, although it is not unusual to have 4 to 10
inches (10 to 25 centimeters) of snow sometime during the winter.
The annual average snowfall is approximately 20 inches (508 millimeters), yielding a scant 2 inches (5 centimeters) of actual water.
Annual evaporation from a nearby reservoir averages more than 53
inches (1,346 millimeters); this is almost twice as much as falls in
an average year, so there is the potential for a net deficit of moisture on Konza Prairie. Such a deficit would occur if the rain fell
evenly throughout the year and stayed near the surface of the soil.
The rainfall pattern is quite variable, however, providing more rain
during some seasons than can evaporate. Some of what falls does
evaporate directly from the soil, but much of it remains trapped
between soil particles, where it is consumed by thirsty plants and
evaporates from leaf surfaces.*

*The forces that drive weather systems within the atmosphere
are extraterrestrial, primarily emanating from the heat of the sun.
They exert their influence through rivers of air that flow within the
atmosphere, causing air masses to circulate around the globe. In
the temperate mid-continental regions of the Northern Hemisphere*

the major weather patterns move from west to east in the form of cyclonic and anticyclonic masses of air revolving around low- and high-pressure cells, respectively. The weather at a specific location is determined by which edge of the swirling mass passes nearby. Air masses, especially those associated with high-pressure cells, produce fronts that also move in an easterly direction. The cyclones and the anticyclones and their associated fronts collide and ricochet their way across North America, leaving their imprint as they pass by Konza.

Air masses that move from the Pacific Ocean onto the North American continent carry substantial amounts of water, most of which is lost as the moisture-laden air rises over the Sierra Nevada and the Rocky Mountains, then cools, thereby reducing its capacity to hold moisture, and finally drops its load of water before reaching Kansas. Thus, rather than receiving rainfall that is carried on the easterly flowing air masses, Konza must rely on the arriving weather cells to suck warm, moist air up from the Gulf of Mexico as the cyclones or anticyclones pass over Konza. This occurs more frequently as spring progresses; the northerly migration of the sun, which is caused by the tilt of the earth, steers the paths of the air masses farther north, bringing Konza under the influence of tropical high-pressure zones, which spin in a clockwise direction and shunt moisture northward. When the warm, moist air from the south collides with the cooler air arriving from the northwest, the local air flow can become extremely unstable, which can produce violent thunderstorms. These storms, which are common on the prairie in spring and early summer, are formed when the cold air, which is more dense than warm air, wedges under the warm air, thus forcing it up, where it cools and releases its moisture. This process is amplified by the sun's heating the earth's surface and its overlying air, thus speeding the already rapid rise of the moist air. Thunderstorms usually affect small areas and are of short duration, but they can deposit several inches of rain in a few hours. Along their edges, curtains of moist air spill out, streaking the sky with virga, or rain that evaporates before it strikes the ground. Under certain circumstances, Konza can be released from the grip of northerly flowing moist air in late summer, thus causing deep droughts.

Thunderstorms are most common in the heat of late afternoon; they rarely occur after midnight, when the earth is no longer warm

*enough to cause large air masses to rise and thus promote the dif-
ferences in temperature between the cool and warm air masses.
Nevertheless, thunderstorms can occur at any time if two strongly
contrasting cold and warm air masses collide. Thunderstorms develop rapidly; their anvil-shaped cumulus clouds boil up over 50,000
feet (15,240 meters) and veil the trailing lightning and thunder. In
their first appearance they seem to be peeking over the horizon, but
their ultimate configuration belies their innocuous birth.*

*The paths of cyclones and anticyclones in winter tend to cause
extremely cold air masses to dive into the mid continent. Cold air
holds significantly less moisture than warm air does; for example,
air at 0 degrees Fahrenheit (−18 degrees Celsius) can hold only 4
percent of the moisture that air at 80 degrees (27 degrees Celsius)
can accommodate. Any moisture that is carried onto the North
American continent is wrung out by the mountains to the west;
this results in extremely dry air invading Konza during the winter.
Although the winter sky may not contain enough moisture to rain
or snow on Konza, it often retains a dark, brooding aspect for days.*

*The prairie can be characterized by its weather extremes as much
as by its norms. The most consistently extreme weather occurs in
conjunction with spring and summer thunderstorms. Under specific conditions, intense clashes between warm and cool air masses
spawn tornadoes. These terrifying cyclonic clouds produce winds
higher than 400 miles per hour (644 kilometers per hour) and generate tremendous gradations in air pressure between their center
and their margins. They dip unpredictably from the sky and snake
along the ground in a swath from one hundred to several hundred
feet wide and up to dozens of miles long. As catastrophic as these
fierce winds are, they are so infrequent as to have no impact on the
average weather conditions of Konza.*

*Even storms that do not spawn tornadoes are capable of produc-
ing destructive winds. Gusts approaching 100 miles per hour (160
kilometers per hour) occur along the shearing interface between
air masses. Torrential rains, perhaps lasting only fifteen minutes,
cause localized flooding. Lightning that emanates from the clouds
can set prairie wildfires and may strike prairie sentinels, destroying
those few trees that extend above the landscape. Hail is frequently
a by-product of tempestuous thunderstorms. It forms when falling
droplets of water are lofted back up into the thunderstorm cloud*

to an altitude where the temperature freezes them. If the frozen water becomes captured by vertically revolving cells of air, it may fall and rise a number of times, picking up water on each descent and freezing another layer during each ascent until it becomes too heavy to be carried aloft once again. Most hail is pea-sized, but hailstones the size of baseballs frequently fall in the vicinity of Konza each year. The falling hail carries the seeds of its own destruction, as the downdrafts caused by the ice's dropping from the sky quickly squelch the requisite rising air, thus limiting the production of hail to a brief time span. During the minute or two that hail falls, however, it can be deadly, thrashing the prairie with punishing blows.

Several times during the winter, Konza experiences a quick freeze that is caused when a blast of arctic air plunges into the midsection of North America. These rapidly moving fronts cause temperatures to drop from 20 to 40 degrees Fahrenheit (11 to 22 degrees Celsius) in twenty-four hours. The skies are frequently crystal clear; the sun belies the painfully intense cold. Under certain circumstances, the frigid air is accompanied by blowing snow, thus producing a blizzard that is capable of lacerating plants and animals with flying shards of ice and sapping the warmth from an unprotected victim. The wind greatly amplifies the effect of the cold; in still air, a thin layer of air, warmed by the body, covers the skin of an animal; but as wind speeds increase, this insulating layer is whisked away, exposing the skin to an extreme temperature gradient that quickly robs the body of heat, perhaps even plunging the core body temperature to fatal depths. As an example, a 35-mile-per-hour (56-kilometers-per-hour) wind at 50 degrees Fahrenheit (10 degrees Celsius) has the same chilling power as no wind at 0 degrees Fahrenheit (−18 degrees Celsius). Of course, the opposite effect can occur in the summer: when air temperatures rise somewhat above normal body temperature, the wind actually increases the heat gain by the body. In humans, this is somewhat offset by the cooling effect of sweat evaporation, but most organisms do not sweat. Winter is harsh on Konza; the severity and length of the eruptions of excessively cold weather can be the key to survival or death by prairie residents in any given year.

The variation in daily and seasonal weather patterns is one of the most endearing features of Konza Prairie. Nothing is more dramatic than to watch the anvil of a thunderhead precede a storm onto the prairie before unloading its cargo of rain, thunder, and lightning. Autumns are glorious on Konza, especially when seen from a ridge at sunset as fading sunlight, shining on the clouds, casts a chiaroscuro over the panorama. Even winter can be beguiling, when a dusting of snow covers the rumples on the landscape, smoothing out the creases and suggesting a softness that is uncharacteristic of this season. But the seasons are not just for our appreciation. They can be reality squared for residents that must face daily challenges that are as unpredictable as they are extreme. Many ecological processes affect populations of plants and animals in direct proportion to the number of individuals in them. But mortality that is linked to seasonal extremes shows no such logic; under the harshest of conditions, plants and animals perish individually, without regard to the fate of their neighbors.

9 / Konza Today

Perhaps the most characteristic animal of the North American prairies is the bison, which once ranged in huge numbers across much of the Great Plains. Eventually the bison was almost eradicated by Americans of European descent. It exists today in isolated, managed herds and will soon be introduced to Konza Prairie to serve as a native grazer in research projects.

THE TALLGRASS PRAIRIE IS A SUBTLE AND GLORIOUS PLACE that can be appreciated by everyone, regardless of how much they know about biological matters. The undulating waves of chest-high green grass and the twinkle of dew-laden leaves in the morning sun stimulate all of our senses, awakening a passion for the natural world even if we have no inkling of what causes such phenomena. Indeed, some people would suggest that an intimate knowledge of how something works somehow diminishes its charm, relegating it to a simple deterministic consequence of a mechanical universe. But ignorance is not bliss; knowledge of the tallgrass prairie only heightens one's appreciation of the enormous complexity that defines this habitat. The awesome beauty of the prairie is enhanced, not diminished, by knowledge of the prodigious processes that generate the prairie ecosystem.

Konza is as old as the earth itself. Throughout the centuries it has changed at a snail's pace as physical and biological forces have molded its features. The arrival of Western culture, with its capacity to rapidly alter the landscape, brought the possibility that the natural flow of processes on the prairie might be disrupted. More recent events, however, have ensured that Konza Prairie will remain as protected terrain and a site where scientific investigations can proceed uninterrupted. Thanks to the Nature Conservancy, Lloyd Hulbert, and Mrs. Katherine Ordway, Konza Prairie has been reserved for the future.

A private organization dedicated to the preservation of endangered locales around the world, the Nature Conservancy has long realized that the ultimate threat to living organisms is the disappearance of their habitats through development, agriculture, and wanton destruction. Each organism is part of a population, which, in turn, is a component of the local community. This means that the preservation of a whole community, rather than of specific species, is the most appropriate way of safeguarding the environment. The conservancy's efforts have been directed, therefore, toward the purchase of endangered habitats. Such parcels of land are usually entrusted to a caretaker; in the case of Konza Prairie, the stewardship rests with Kansas State University. Lloyd Hulbert investigated numerous potential sites, and he is responsible for locating and securing the tracts that constitute Konza Prairie. Mrs. Ordway funded the acquisition.

Through their combined efforts, the preservation of ecologically important land has been coupled with an opportunity for scientific investigations related to particular habitats. In most cases, the results from specific habitats have implications for the biosphere as a whole. In this vein, Konza has been designated Konza Prairie Research Natural Area (KPRNA). Protected lands are especially valuable for research, because long-term experiments can be carried out without fear of intentional or unintentional intrusions. As the human population expands, fewer and fewer areas are available for such studies, making Konza all the more valuable.

Scientists who do research on Konza Prairie are driven by an appreciation for the beauty of nature and by an inquisitiveness about the biological world in general and the tallgrass prairie in particular. Each investigator has his or her own interests, and eventually every nook and cranny will be probed, measured, weighed, or counted in the name of science. Thus, knowledge accumulates, bit by bit, and as scientists share their findings in publications and at conferences, more accurate views of the ecosystem and its inherent biological processes will emerge.

In an effort to organize the acquisition of information about important ecosystems, the National Science Foundation (NSF) has funded approximately one dozen large projects under the aegis of its Long Term Ecological Research (LTER) program. The NSF, which is supported by federal tax dollars, recognizes that many ecological phenomena take decades to reveal themselves; therefore, it has undertaken the LTER program in an attempt to ensure adequate levels of support for analyses of these types of processes. Konza Prairie was a natural choice for such support, both because of its ecological significance and because of the willingness of investigators at Kansas State University to invest the time and the effort necessary to conduct this immense project.

The goal of the LTER program is to investigate a variety of features that characterize specific ecosystems—such as alpine tundra, desert, forest, fresh-water wetlands, and riverlands in addition to the tallgrass prairie—and to provide an opportunity for comparisons to determine which traits the research sites share and which make each unique. More specifically, the LTER program is charged with analyzing several major features of ecosystems, including the levels of biotic productivity within each system. Other primary goals include a determination of the accumulation of organic matter and its relationship to nutrient cycling, how various disturbances impinge in the functioning of the ecosystem, and the relationship between processes of population and of community level and key phenomena of ecosystems. These ambitious goals will require an intense effort for many years.

On Konza Prairie these goals are being pursued through a variety of complex research efforts. To measure the biotic production of the prairie, ecologists harvest vegetation from plots of known area and extrapolate their findings to the entire prairie. Attempts are made to trace the fate of organic matter produced on the prairie as it enters the litter, decomposes, and moves through various elemental cycles. Studies of the effects of specific disturbances, from nutrient and moisture stress to fires and grazing, are being undertaken. Finally, analyses of population and community-level phenomena are being investigated by regularly taking censuses of the densities and distributions of the major inhabitants of the prairie, including plants, subterranean organisms, grasshoppers, birds, and mammals. In addition to the analyses of biotic factors on KPRNA, abiotic factors, such as weather patterns and the flow of water over and through the prairie soils, are being incorporated into the overall research protocols that deal with ecosystem-level processes in the tallgrass prairie.

The basic monitoring of ecosystem processes on KPRNA is embedded in a framework of experimental manipulations. Grasslands are obviously affected by fire and grazing, so the LTER project has been designed to analyze the effects of these processes. From the beginning of the project, it has been clear that the major geographic unit of an ecosystem is a watershed. Although individual organisms may traverse many watersheds, the physical evidence of most prairie processes is confined within the watershed basin; frequently it leaves fingerprints that help to identify the nature and the scope of past events. Thus, KPRNA is divided into its discrete watersheds, and fire treatments are applied according to these boundaries.

Although it is impossible to determine what the natural fire regime was in the past, treatments that fall on either side of the most likely burn patterns have been incorporated into the KPRNA management program. Thus, some areas are left unburned, whereas others are burned every one, two, four, or ten years. Some portions of the research area are burned only after 120 percent of the normal amount of rainfall has fallen; other portions are alternately burned for three consecutive years and then not burned for three years. Criteria for valid statistical analyses of the results require that more than one of each treatment be available for scrutiny, so each of the treatments has at least one replicate. The burning takes place in mid April each year; it is known that the time of burning affects the response of the prairie community, but it would be impossible to duplicate and replicate all permutations of the frequency of burning and the season of burning on the main watersheds. Thus, these experiments are carried out on small experimental plots near the headquarters building.

Of course, it is essential to maintain the proper burn regimes for each treatment. This mandates that random wildfires be controlled and that prescribed burns not escape into watersheds that are not scheduled for burning. To minimize the chances of having fires jump watersheds, fourteen-foot-wide firebreaks are mowed and burned between major watershed units each fall. These areas remain relatively barren of fuel the following spring, when the watersheds that are scheduled for burning come under the torch. If the wind speed is low—usually less than 15 miles or 24 kilometers per hour—and from the right direction, the burning can proceed. Using drip torches, the "eco-arsonists" first lay down a fire line on the leeward side of the watershed to be burned. Bucking the prevailing wind, this thin blaze moves slowly, widening the gap between the incipient conflagration and the adjacent grassland, which requires protection. Once a safety zone of a hundred or more feet has been created, the torchbearers circle around the watershed, eventually igniting the grass on the windward side. At this point the blazing scythe is poised on the backswing. Banking off a moderate breeze, the downwind head fire moves rapidly, consuming virtually everything in its path. While the fire is burning, a squad of firemen hovers around its margins, ready to pounce on any attempted escape. A commander remains in control of the entire operation, thus ensuring a coordinated effort. In addition to those who man the torches, trucks carrying water and pumps remain nearby to quench any unscheduled outbreaks, and a number of helpers follow the fire line with beaters to put out small flare-ups. Even after the primary blaze has subsided, recalcitrant embers may burn for hours or even days, necessitating constant vigilance to prohibit the ignition of wildfires. All of this takes an enormous effort on the part of those involved with KPRNA: more than two dozen workers participate each year, contributing almost four hundred hours of labor just to maintain the prescribed management regimes.

Grazing is the second major experimental manipulation imposed on KPRNA. Cattle have lived on Konza for over a century, and bison, the native grazers on the prairie, were reestablished in 1987. Because the grazers are part of the overall pattern of manipulations on

Konza, they must be confined to specific watersheds. This requires a sturdy barrier, as it is difficult to keep a large bison fenced in. A multistranded fence almost 10 miles (16 kilometers) long has been constructed to persuade the bison to stay in their alloted areas. The fence has 12-foot posts, which are buried 4 feet into the ground, every 60 feet (18 meters) and is strung with high-tensile wire. Every other strand is mildly electrified in an attempt to keep the bison from leaning on or going through the enclosure. Bison will be gradually added to the appropriated watersheds, and their impact will be analyzed and compared to the effects of fire. Other native grazers, such as elk and pronghorn, may eventually be introduced to cohabit with the bison.

A series of important ecological elements is being measured on KPRNA as they respond to the grazing and fire treatments imposed on the site. The question becomes "In response to certain fire and/or grazing regimes, what happens to the . . . ?" The basic question can be completed with any number of responses relating to the biotic productivity of the prairie and to the density and distribution of its inhabitants. Even though this is long-term research, significant patterns are already emerging, as discussed earlier, which reveal how critical aspects of a model grassland interact to generate characteristic patterns.

In addition to the large LTER project, KPRNA serves as a tallgrass laboratory for a number of scientists who are working on individual research projects. Konza is only a fifteen-minute drive from the campus of Kansas State University, making it convenient for investigators to take advantage of the site. Although these individual projects may lie outside the scope of the specific goals of LTER, many are related and rely on the baseline data collected from the LTER monitoring program. The studies involve virtually every major group of organisms that have a significant impact on the prairie. Furthermore, most of the studies reveal something about the general interactions between organisms, making the results pertinent to habitats other than the tallgrass prairie.

Some of the current investigations involve analyses of nitrogen cycling on the prairie; the evolution of flowering times in plants; interactions between aboveground and belowground herbivores, as revealed by the response of plants; miscellaneous aspects of earthworm ecology; and a series of projects dealing with the population characteristics of plants, insects, birds, and mammals. The density and distribution of aquatic insects and the nutrient patterns within the stream flow are being investigated in Kings Creek. Every year, new graduate students, research associates, and faculty members discover scientific questions that pique their interest and lead in unexpected directions. KPRNA has also become a research center for visiting scientists who have discovered the advantages of working in the tallgrass prairie on Konza. As is always the case in science, however, the answer to one question generates ten more questions that beg for a response in the effort to make an empirical characterization of the universe.

The research carried out on KPRNA is designed to minimize the impact of the investigations: it would do no good to dissect the prairie completely, leaving nothing but information to show for the effort. Access and experimental manipulations are tightly regulated, precluding indiscriminate alterations of the habitat. The fires have widespread effects, but they are a natural component of the tallgrass prairie's ecosystem, and their absence would represent a major perturbation. The restricted access to the site serves to preserve the sensitive habitat from unintentional degradation and to minimize the possibility that important experiments, which may have been running for years, are not inadvertently disrupted. Public access to Konza Prairie must be restricted for the same reason that the research activities of scientists are regulated. It is anticipated that there will eventually be an interpretive center associated with the site, which will explain to the public the ecological intricacies of the tallgrass prairie and will describe the research being conducted at the site.

What does the future hold for Konza Prairie? Clearly, one essential function of the facility is to continue to preserve the largest tract of tallgrass prairie left in North America. Like so many treasures, Konza Prairie is a resource whose value is incalculable—it cannot be considered in terms of dollars, and we have no way of estimating what important data remain to be mined from its mother lode of ecological information. The preservation efforts are directed toward protecting the site from ourselves—from attempts to use the property for specific short-term goals that are inconsistent with the long-term preservation and understanding of the habitat. Preservation is an admirable goal; but we must also realize that one of the natural phenomena to visit the prairie will be the gradual change from what it is today to what it will be in the distant future. Konza will remain essentially the same for the next several centuries, but if the atmosphere heats up, lengthening summers and extending droughts, it may become the Konza Desert. Conversely, if the sun dims and the ice sheets slip south again, it may become Konza Glacier. In either case, nature must be allowed to take its course, as interruptions on any scale are inconsistent with the purpose and the value of preservation.

A diverse ensemble of environmental features has combined to promote the evolution of grass plants, which, in turn, have spread into expansive grasslands around the world. It is uncertain whether pressures from drought, fire, or heavy grazing first led ancestral plants to take up the characteristic habit of grasses, but the traits that emerged have proven successful in the face of all three. Grasses can tolerate droughts until moisture arrives, they thrive in the face of incineration, and they carry on a constant evolutionary duel with voracious herbivores. The major anatomical feature of grasses that has directed their evolutionary advance is the protection of the growing meristem near or below the ground surface. This critical tissue, which is responsible for the growth and development of aboveground and belowground stems, is significantly more successful in response to the triumvirate of selective forces than are the growth forms possessed by most nongrasses, whose meristems are exposed in more vulnerable positions. Grasses also maintain a considerable amount of their stem tissue and their stored nutrients underground, where they are not exposed to many environmental hazards. Furthermore, physiological specializations for the translocation and mobilization of nutrients, as well as photosynthetic capabilities, promote the survival of grasses under otherwise harsh conditions.

The success of grasses has allowed them to become the dominant growth form across broad areas of the globe, thus forming vast prairies. Each grassland exhibits distinctive traits, and Konza Prairie is remarkable for its tallgrass community. Other grasses are taller (bamboo, for example), and domesticated grasses, such as corn and wheat, exhibit greater productivity, but the tallgrass prairie of Konza is unique as an integrated, diverse community. At first glance, Konza Prairie appears to be monotonous and bland, because it is dominated by a single species—big bluestem; but in fact, it is a dynamic mosaic of individuals and patches that interact to generate a diverse milieu. The beauty of the tallgrass prairie is subtle, with a texture that can be seen as well as touched, and its grandeur is contained in the hidden activity underneath the grass and below the ground.

Another intriguing feature of Konza Prairie is its youth. Although some constituents have been around for many centuries, their collaboration on Konza is quite recent. Only within the last several thousand years has the tallgrass prairie developed its own identify by incorporating many components that it has borrowed or expropriated from adjacent communities. These are exciting times on Konza. We can imagine that the current residents and various immigrants are vying for their future positions on the prairie. Such interactions should eventually lead to new specialists, including those that will be true products of the tallgrass prairie. We are unlikely to see such changes during our lifetime, but if the past is a clue to the future, Konza Prairie will evolve its own unique set of coadapted organisms that will further distinguish it from other grasslands.

Close inspection of the tallgrass prairie reveals many interesting and novel phenomena, but in the broad view, it also reveals the obvious. The tallgrass community, like all others, is composed of many parts, which interact directly or indirectly to produce the whole. The common analogy is a spider web, in which a tug on any one strand affects all other strands. Certainly, the components that are closest to any disturbance are affected the most, but all strands receive some information that a perturbation has taken place. Should a connection within the network be broken, the configuration of the web would be distorted. Although the web might still be recognized as such, too many tugs or severed strands could lead to dysfunction or even collapse. Konza Prairie is a robust community—many strands connect its inhabitants—but a few misdirected tugs could send the community reeling. For example, the soil and its denizens are responsible for a large proportion of the important processes on the prairie, and any disturbance of this subset of the prairie would alter the community significantly.

Thus, perhaps the most important feature of Konza Prairie is that it is being preserved. By protecting its critical elements from being connected with uses that would destroy its character, the tallgrass prairie should have a chance to survive and prosper. As large as Konza Prairie is, it is still small compared to the original extent of the tallgrass prairie, so we can only hope that it is large enough to allow the continued existence of this exquisite habitat. In addition, Konza Prairie serves as a source for information about how the tallgrass prairie, as well as other habitats, functions. This information can be used to further preservation efforts directly and to make the public aware of the extraordinary value of preserving Konza Prairie. As long as Konza is recognized as a reservoir of beauty and knowledge, its value will be compounded indefinitely.

Common and Scientific Names

This list is designed to provide the scientific names of organisms that are mentioned in the text by their specific common names, such as Brewer's blackbird. Groups of two or more species, such as blackbirds, are not included here, because they would be represented by more than one scientific name. This is a particular concern with the various groups of insects, which may contain hundreds of species in a group. For example, there may be fifty species of black flies on Konza. Some of the larger groupings, such as birds, mammals, and insects, are listed in the index. The common names are in alphabetical order by their full common name—for example, big bluestem, rather than bluestem, big.

Flora of the Great Plains, by the Great Plains Flora Association (Lawrence: University Press of Kansas, 1986), was used as the authority for plants. *Fishes in Kansas*, by Frank B. Cross and Joseph T. Collins (Lawrence: University of Kansas Museum of Natural History, 1975); *Amphibians and Reptiles in Kansas*, by Joseph T. Collins, second edition (Lawrence: University of Kansas Museum of Natural History, 1982); the 1983 checklist of the American Ornithological Union; and *Mammals in Kansas*, by James W. Bee, Gregory Glass, Robert S. Hoffmann, and Robert R. Patterson (Lawrence: University of Kansas Museum of Natural History, 1981), were used for the vertebrates.

GRASSES

big bluestem (turkey foot)—*Andropogon gerardii*
bluegrass—*Poa sp.*
bottlebrush grass—*Hystrix patula*
brome grass—*Bromus sp.*
cordgrass—*Spartina sp.*
eastern gammagrass—*Tripsacum dactyloides*
grama grass—*Bouteloua sp.*
Indian grass—*Sorghastrum nutans*
Junegrass—*Koeleria pyramidata*

Kentucky bluegrass—*Poa pratensis*
little bluestem—*Andropogon scoparius*
prairie cordgrass—*Spartina pectinata*
switchgrass—*Panicum virgatum*
wheatgrass—*Agropyron sp.*
wild rye—*Elymus sp.*
wirestem muhly—*Muhlenbergia frondosa*

NONGRASS PLANTS

American elm—*Ulmus americana*
black walnut—*Juglans nigra*

blue false indigo—*Baptisia australis*
box elder—*Acer negundo*

broad-leaved cat-tail—*Typha latifolia*

buckbrush—*Symphoricarpos orbiculatus*

buffalo bur nightshade—*Solanum rostratum*

buffalo-gourd (coyote melon)—*Cucurbita foetidissima*

bur oak—*Quercus macrocarpa*

butterfly milkweed—*Asclepias tuberosa*

cancer root—*Orobanche uniflora*

catclaw sensitive brier—*Schrankia nuttallii*

ceanothus (New Jersey tea)—*Ceanothus herbaceous*

chinkapin oak—*Quercus muehlenbergii*

choke cherry—*Prunus virginiana*

cluster dodder (choisy)—*Cuscuta glomerata*

cottonwood—*Populus sp.*

curly dock—*Rumex crispus*

currant—*Ribes sp.*

dogwood—*Cornaceae sp.*

field pussy-toes—*Antennaria neglecta*

gay-feather—*Liatris punctata*

goat's beard—*Tragopogon dubius*

goldenrod—*Solidago sp.*

green ash—*Fraxinus pennsylvanica*

ground-plum milk vetch—*Astragalus crassicarpus*

hackberry—*Celtis occidentalis*

heath (white) aster—*Aster ericoides*

honey locust—*Gleditsia triacanthos*

horsetail—*Equisetum sp.*

Illinois bundleflower—*Desmanthus illinoensis*

ivyleaf morning-glory—*Ipomoea hederacea*

Jerusalem artichoke—*Helianthus tuberosus*

knotweed—*Polygonum sp.*

lead plant (prairie shoestring)—*Amorpha canescens*

meadow rose (smooth wild rose)—*Rosa blanda*

milkweed—*Asclepias sp.*

Missouri mammillaria—*Coryphantha missouriensis*

morning glory—*Ipomoea sp.*

musk thistle—*Carduus nutans*

plains prickly pear—*Opuntia macrorhiza*

plains wild indigo—*Baptisia bracteata*

plum—*Prunus sp.*

poison ivy—*Toxicodendron radicans*

prairie ground cherry—*Physalis pumila*

prairie parsley—*Polytaenia nuttallii*

prairie turnip—*Psoralea esculenta*

prickly ash—*Zanthoxylum americanum*

prickly pear—*Opuntia sp.*

purple prairie clover—*Dalea purpurea*

redbud—*Cercis canadensis*

red cedar—*Juniperus virginiana*

red mulberry—*Morus rubra*

river-bank grape—*Vitis riparia*

rough-leaved dogwood—*Cornus drummondii*

sagewort—*Artemisia annua*

sedge—*Carex sp.*

smooth sumac—*Rhus glabra*

speedwell—*Veronica sp.*

stickleaf mentzelia—*Mentzelia oligosperma*

sumac—*Rhus sp.*

sunflower—*Helianthus sp.*

sycamore—*Plantanus occidentalis*
Virginia creeper—*Parthenocissus quinquefolia*
watercress—*Nasturtium officinale*
white prairie-clover—*Dalea candida*
wild licorice—*Glycyrrhiza lepidota*
wild onion—*Allium canadense*

wild parsley—*Lomatium foeniculaceum*
wild plum—*Prunus americana*
wild strawberry—*Fragaria virginiana*
willow—*Salix sp.*
yarrow—*Achillea millefolium*
yucca—*Yucca glauca*

FISH

minnow—*Pimephales sp.*
orangethroat darter—*Etheostoma spectabile*
perch—*Perca sp.*
red shiner—*Notropis lutrensis*

southern redbelly dace—*Phoxinus erythrogaster*
ꞌstone roller—*Campostoma anomalum*

AMPHIBIANS

bullfrog—*Rana catesbeiana*
gray treefrog—*Hyla chrysoscelis/ Hyla versicolor* complex
plains narrowmouth toad—

Gastrophryne olivacea
western chorus frog—*Pseudacris triseriata*

REPTILES

bullsnake (gopher snake)—*Pituophis melanoleucus*
collared lizard—*Crotaphytus collaris*
common snapping turtle—*Chelydra serpentina*
copperhead—*Agkistrodon contortrix*
flathead snake—*Tantilla gracilis*
Great Plains rat snake—*Elaphe guttata*
Great Plains skink—*Eumeces obsoletus*
kingsnake—*Lampropeltis sp.*

milk snake—*Lampropeltis triangulum*
painted turtle—*Chrysemys picta*
prairie ringneck snake—*Diadophis punctatus arnyi*
racer—*Coluber sp.*
slender glass lizard—*Ophisaurus attenuatus*
Texas horned lizard—*Phrynosoma cornutum*
western box turtle (ornate box turtle)—*Terrapene ornata*
western painted turtle—*Chrysemys picta belli*

BIRDS

American kestrel—*Falco sparverius*
American tree sparrow—*Spizella
arborea*
barred owl—*Strix varia*
Bell's vireo—*Vireo bellii*
black-billed cuckoo—*Coccyzus
erythrophthalmus*
black-capped chickadee—*Parus
atricapillus*
blue jay—*Cyanocitta cristata*
Brewer's blackbird—*Euphagus
cyanocephalus*
brown-headed cowbird—*Molothrus
ater*
brown thrasher—*Toxostoma rufum*
common nighthawk—*Chordeiles
minor*
dark-eyed junco—*Junco hyemalis*
dickcissel—*Spiza americana*
eastern meadowlark—*Sturnella
magna*
eastern screech owl (formerly
screech owl)—*Otus asio*
egret—*Egretta sp.*
golden eagle—*Aquila chrysaëtos*
grasshopper sparrow—
Ammodramus savannarum
great horned owl—*Bubo
virginianus*
Henslow sparrow—*Ammodramus
henslowii*
hooded merganser—*Lophodytes
cucullatus*
lazuli bunting—*Passerina amoena*

[Emberizidae]
Mississippi kite—*Ictinia
mississippiensis*
mourning dove—*Zenaidura
macroura*
northern bobwhite—*Colinus
virginianus*
northern flicker—*Colaptes auratus*
northern harrier (marsh hawk)—
Circus cyaneus
peregrine falcon—*Falco peregrinus*
pine siskin—*Spinus pinus*
prairie chicken (greater)—
Tympanuchus cupido
prairie falcon—*Falco mexicanus*
red-bellied woodpecker—*Centurus
carolinus*
red-headed woodpecker—
Melanerpes erythrocephalus
red-tailed hawk—*Buteo jamaicensis*
red-winged blackbird—*Agelaius
phoeniceus*
ring-necked pheasant—*Phasianus
colchicus*
rock wren—*Salpinctes obsoletus*
rough-legged hawk—*Buteo lagopus*
rufous-sided towhee—*Pipilo
erythrophthalmus*
rusty blackbird—*Euphagus
carolinus*
sedge wren—*Cistothorus platensis*
upland sandpiper (formerly upland
plover)—*Bartramia longicauda*
water pipit—*Anthus spinoletta*

MAMMALS

badger—*Taxidea taxus*
beaver—*Castor canadensis*

bison—*Bison bison*
bobcat—*Lynx rufus*

cotton rat—*Sigmodon hispidus*
coyote—*Canis latrans*
deer (white-tailed)—*Odocoileus
virginianus*
deer mouse—*Peromyscus
maniculatus*
fox squirrel—*Sciurus niger*
ground squirrel (thirteen-lined)—
Spermophilus tridecemlineatus
jumping mouse—*Zapus hudsonius*
mammoth—*Mammuthus sp.*
mastodon—*Mastodon sp.*
musk ox—*Ovibos sp.*
muskrat—*Ondatra zibethicus*
peccary (wild pig)—*Tayassu sp.*
plains pocket gopher—*Geomys
bursarius*
prairie vole—*Microtus ochrogaster*
pronghorn—*Antilocapra americana*
raccoon—*Procyon lotor*
river otter—*Lutra canadensis*
short-tailed shrew—*Blarina
hylophaga*
Virginia opossum—*Didelphis
virginiana*
western harvest mouse—
Reithrodontomys megalotis
white-footed mouse—*Peromyscus
leucopus*
woodrat (eastern)—*Neotoma
floridana*

Index

Acorns, 119–120
Aggression. *See* Territories
Aging, 187–188
Algae, 150, 170, 173, 178 (illus.), 179
American elm, 116
American kestrels, 52
American tree sparrows, 99
Amphibians, 15, 89–92, 134–135, 184, 215
Amphipods, 183
Antlions (doodlebugs), 47–48
Aphids, 125, 130–132
Arthropods, 56, 151
   in grasslands, 87–88
   macroarthropods, 152–155
   microarthropods, 155–156
Ash, green, 116
Ash, prickly, 123
Asters, heath, 72, 73

Backswimmers, 181
Bacteria, 47, 111, 125
   nitrogen-fixing, 149–150, 160
   in streams, 169–170
Badgers, 104
Bark beetles, 133
Barred owls, 136
Beavers, 185
Bees, 125
Beetles, 75, 88, 125, 132–133, 152–153, 181–182
Behavioral patches, 51
Bell's vireos, 46
Big bluestem, 8, 44, 64, 71
   effects of fire on, 108, 110, 111, 113

growth cycle of, 65–70
   roots of, 146
Biomass, 62, 107, 110, 115, 143
Birds, 21, 52, 112, 216
   in forests, 135–137
   in grasslands, 94–99
   territoriality of, 53, 55, 56
Bison, 53, 113, 202 (illus.)
   as food, 24, 25, 26, 27
   former extent of, 99–100
   research with, 206–207
   See also Buffalo wallows
Black-billed cuckoos, 46
Blackbirds, Brewer's, 112
Blackbirds, red-winged, 95
Blackbirds, rusty, 112
Black-capped chickadees, 99, 135
Black flies, 171–172, 179, 180
Black walnut, 116
Blister beetles, 75
Bluegrass, Kentucky, 71
Blue jays, 120, 135
Bluestem. *See* Big bluestem; Little bluestem
Blue wild indigo, 75
Bobcats, 104
Bobwhites, northern, 52, 97
Booming grounds, 51–52, 97–98
Bottlebrush grass, 124
Box elder, 116
Brewer's blackbirds, 112
Brier, catclaw sensitive, 72, 74–75
Brome grass, 124
Brown-headed cowbirds, 94, 95–97, 112
Brown thrashers, 46
Buckbrush, 46, 73, 123, 168

Buffalo bur nightshade, 50
Buffalo-gourd (coyote melon), 43, 73–74
Buffalo wallows, 38, 51–52
Bullfrogs, 91
Bundleflowers, Illinois, 73
Buntings, lazuli, 94
Burning, 7 (map), 113, 156, 205–207
Bur oak, 116, 119, 168
Burrows, 56
Butterflies, monarch, 88
Butterfly milkweed, 73

Cactus, 75
Caddisflies, 171–172
Cancer root, 74
Cankerworms, 133
Carnivores, 52, 125, 127–130
Catclaw sensitive brier, 72, 74–75
Caterpillars, 75, 121, 133
    tent, 46, 52, 85–87
Cattails, 178
Ceanothus, 46, 72, 123
Cedar, red, 44, 72, 106
Centipedes, 140 (illus.), 155
Cherry, choke, 46
Cherry, prairie ground, 50, 76
Chert, 26, 145–146
Chickadees, black-capped, 99, 135
Chickens, prairie, 55, 94, 97–99
Chiggers, 87–88
Chinkapin oak, 116, 119
Chipmunks, 83
Chloroplasts, 77 (illus.), 80
Choke cherry, 46
Cicadas, 153–154
Cladophora, 179
Clams, 183
Clayton, A. M., 28
Click beetles, 153
Climate, ancient, 19–20. *See also* Weather

Clones, 44, 61, 64, 67–68
Clover, purple prairie, 73
Clover, white prairie, 73
Cluster dodder, 74
Collared lizards, 53, 55, 92–93
Common nighthawks, 36 (illus.), 95
Common snapping turtles, 92, 185
Competition, 109, 175–178. *See also* Evolution; Natural selection
Copperheads, 135
Cordgrass, prairie, 71, 124
Coronado, Francisco Vásques de, 27
Cotton rats, 103
Cottonwoods, 116, 131
Cowbird, brown-headed, 94, 95–97, 112
Coyote melon (buffalo-gourd), 43, 73–74
Coyotes, 52, 104
Crane flies, 171, 179
Crayfish, 55–56, 163 (illus.), 183
Creeper, Virginia, 123
Crustaceans, 183
Cuckoos, black-billed, 46
Curly dock, 76
Currants, 75
Cycles, 158–162

Dace, southern redbelly, 183
Damselflies, 180
Dark-eyed juncos, 99
Darters, orangethroat, 184
Darwin, Charles, 30
Davis, George, 28
Decomposers, 125–126, 173
Decomposition, 170, 172–173
Deer, 100
Deerflies, 88, 155
Deer mice, 32 (illus.), 100–101
Dens, 56, 138 (illus.)
Dewey, C. P., 28

Dewey Ranch, 28–29
Dickcissel, 52, 53, 94, 95–96
Dinosaurs, 16, 17, 60
Disturbances, 38, 49–51, 205
Diving beetles, 182
Dock, curly, 76
Dodder, cluster, 74
Dogwood, rough-leaved, 73, 123
Doodlebugs (antlions), 47–48
Doves, mourning, 94, 95, 112
Dragonflies, 180
Drought, 26, 59, 105
    and forests, 117, 118
    and plants, 65, 149
    in summer, 194–195
Dung beetles, 88
Dutch elm disease, 117, 133

Eagles, golden, 94
Earthworms, 112, 151, 156–157, 183
Eastern meadowlarks, 52, 53, 54 (illus.), 94, 95, 112
Eastern screech owls, 136
Egrets, 94
Elder, box, 116
Elk, 100
Elm, 117, 168, 172
    American, 116
Energy
    cycles, 160–161
    from sunlight, 62, 66, 190
    See also Photosynthesis
Erosion, 39–40
    ancient, 11, 13, 14, 16–18
Evolution, 30–35 *See also* Competition; Natural Selection
Extinction, 17, 22–23

Field pussy-toes, 73
Filter feeders, 171–172
Fires, 8

effect of, on forests, 116–117
molding grasslands, 49, 50, 51, 59, 104–113
    See also Burning
Fish, 183–184, 215
Flathead snakes, 94
Flatworms, 183
Flickers, northern, 99
Flies, 88, 155, 171–172, 179, 180
Flint Hills, 6 (map), 8, 100, 183
    plant species in, 70, 72, 76
    soils in, 145–146
Floods, 51, 173
Florence soil, 145–146
Flowering, 67–70, 75
Foraging, 125–130, 189
Forbs, 43, 60, 72–73, 111, 113, 149
Forests, 39, 40, 115–139, 169
    ancient, 19–20
Fort Riley, Kans., 27
Fossils, 9 (illus.), 10, 13–15, 60
Fox squirrels, 137–138
Frogs, 90–91, 134–135
Fungi, 148–149, 150, 170

Gallery forests. *See* Forests
Galls, 130
Gammagrass, eastern, 71
Gay-feather, 72
Geologic history, 10–21
Germination, 65–66, 70, 193
Glacial period, 18–22
Goat's beard, 76
Golden eagles, 94
Goldenrod, 73
Gophers, plains pocket, 158
Gopher snakes, 94
Grama grass, 71
Grape, river-bank, 123
Grasses, 72, 108, 150, 168
    biology of, 58 (illus.), 59, 62–64, 209

Grasses (*continued*)
  C_4 versus C_3, 81–82
  effect of fire on, 110–111
  origin and evolution of, 17, 18,
    59–60, 105
  types of, 71, 124, 213
  See also Big bluestem; Tallgrass
Grasshoppers, 83–84, 112
Grasshopper sparrows, 94, 95
Grasslands, 5, 20, 41, 59–114, 115,
  209
Gray treefrogs, 134–135
Grazing, 5, 8, 64, 105
  effect of, on grasses, 59–62
  research on, 7 (map), 206–207
  and shrub layer, 121
Great horned owls, 136
Great Plains, 5, 8, 18, 65, 164
Great Plains skinks, 92
Green ash, 116
Ground-plum milk vetch, 73
Ground squirrels, 103

Habitats, general, 37, 39, 40, 41, 164
Hackberry, 133, 168, 172
  as dominant forest community,
    116, 117, 118, 119–120, 121
Hail, 199–200
Harriers, nothern, 99
Harvest mice, 101–102
Hawks, 56, 99
Heath asters, 72, 73
Henslow sparrows, 53
Herbivores, 35, 52, 60, 189
  effect of fire on, 111–112
  versus carnivores, 121, 125,
    127–128
Home ranges, 52–53
Honey locust, 123–124, 168
Hooded mergansers, 94
Horsehair worms, 183
Horsetail, 14–15, 178
Hulbert, Lloyd, 2, 28–29, 203

Illinois bundleflower, 73
Indian grass, 71, 110
Indigo, blue wild, 75
Indigo, plains wild, 73
Insects, 57, 74, 75
  in forests, 130–134
  in grasslands, 83–87, 88–89
  seasonal responses of, 191, 196
  in soil, 152–156
  in streams, 170–172, 179–183
Isopods, 183
Ivy, poison, 122–124
Ivyleaf morning-glory, 76

Jays, blue, 120, 135
Jerusalem artichokes, 75
Johnson, W. D., 28
Juncos, dark-eyed, 99
June beetles, 88, 132, 152–153
Junegrass, 71

Kansas State University, 2, 28–29,
  39, 203
Kentucky bluegrass, 71
Kestrels, American, 52
Kings Creek, 57, 164–175, 178–185,
  208
Kingsnakes, 94
Kites, Mississippi, 94
Knotweed, 72
Konza (Konza Prairie Research
  Natural Area)
  area and topography of, 2, 7
    (map), 37, 39–40
  history of, 2, 27, 28–29, 203–204
  number of species on, 39, 70, 72,
    83, 89
  research on, 106, 113, 204–208
  seasonal changes on, 190–196,
    197
  soil types on, 145–146

Landon, Mrs. Elizabeth Cobb, 29

Lazuli buntings, 94
Lead plant, 75
Leafhoppers, 130
Legumes, 74, 149
Leks (booming grounds), 51–52, 97–98
Lichens, 38, 47
Licorice, wild, 74, 76
Lightning bugs, 89
Limestone, 38, 40, 47, 146
    deposition of, 11, 13, 15, 16 (illus.)
Litter, 107–109, 124, 155, 156, 169
Little bluestem, 71, 110, 113
Lizards, 53–55, 92–93, 135
Locust, honey, 123–124, 168
Loess, 146
Long Term Ecological Research (LTER), 204–208

McDermand, Frank R., III, 28
McKnight, Dr. David, 28–29
Mammals, 83, 216–217
    ancient, 17, 21–22
    in forests, 137–139
    in grasslands, 99–104
    around streams, 185
Mammoths, 21, 22, 24, 25, 26
Marsh hawks (Northern harriers), 99
Mayflies, 172
Meadowlarks, eastern, 52, 53, 54 (illus.), 94, 95, 112
Meadow rose, 74
Mentzelia, stickleaf, 50
Mergansers, hooded, 94
Meristems, 59, 63, 67
Mice, 32 (illus.), 100–103, 113, 137
Microbes, 109, 126, 128
    in soil, 144, 150
    in streams, 169, 170
Midges, 180
Milkweed, 45–46, 89

butterfly, 73
Milkweed seed bugs, 45–46
Millipedes, 155
Minnows, 183
Mississippi kites, 94
Mites, 87, 125, 155–156
Mixed-grass prairie, 5, 6 (map), 65, 71
Moisture, 40, 63, 82, 143, 193, 198–199
Monarch butterflies, 88
Morning-glory, ivyleaf, 76
Mosquitos, 49, 125, 179
Mosses, 124
Moths, 75, 133
Mourning doves, 94, 95, 112
Muhly, wirestem, 124
Mulberry, red, 117
Muskrats, 185
Mycorrhizae, 148–149

National Science Foundation (NSF), 204
Native Americans,
    artifacts of, 23–27
    diet of, 26, 75–76
    prehistoric, 22–26
    tribes of Konza, 27
Natural selection, 107, 126, 128
    in activity patterns, 189–190
    for bird eggs, 96–97
    by grasses, 60–62
    and seed dispersal, 41, 43, 46
    See also Evolution
Nature Conservancy, 2, 29, 203
Nectaries, extrafloral, 74
Nematodes, 125, 151–152
Nests, 56
Nighthawks, common, 36 (illus.), 95
Nightshade, buffalo bur, 50
Nitrogen, 70, 78, 109, 120, 149, 170
    cycle, 160

Northern bobwhites, 52, 97
Northern flickers, 99
Northern harriers (marsh hawks),
99
Nutrients, 70, 120, 128
from fires, 108–109
in soil, 38, 146–149
in streams, 168–172, 174

Oaks, 117–121, 168, 172
bur, 116, 119, 168
chinkapin, 116, 119
Onions, wild, 75
Opossums, 104
Orangethroat darters, 184
Ordway, Katharine, 2, 29, 203
Otters, river, 185
Owls, 56, 136

Parasites, 125
Parsley, prairie, 75
Parsley, wild, 73
Patches, 41–57
Pheasants, ring-necked, 97
Phosphorus, 120, 149
Photoperiod, 192–193
Photosynthesis, 64, 68, 76–82, 125
in the biological cycle, 161–162
under different light conditions,
107, 108, 111, 116, 118, 173
Pine siskins, 99
Pipits, water, 112
Plains narrowmouth toads, 134
Plains pocket gophers, 158
Plains wild indigo, 73
Plants
activity patterns of, 189–190
ancient, 14–15, 20
dicots versus monocots, 60–62
effect of fire on, 74, 110–111, 113
nongrasses, 72–75, 147
as patches of habitat, 43–47

and soil formation, 143–144
around streams, 178–179
used by Native Americans, 75–76
Plums, wild, 46, 75, 86, 123
Poison ivy, 122–124
Pollen, 18, 20, 41, 42 (illus.), 70
Pollination, 46, 74, 119, 189–190
Prairie chickens, 55, 94, 97–99
Prairie cordgrass, 71, 124
Prairie ground cherry, 50, 76
Prairie parsley, 75
Prairie turnips, 75
Prairie voles, 101 (illus.), 102
Precipitation, 5, 109, 142, 164–165,
168, 197
Predation, 125, 129–130, 189
Prickly ash, 123
Prickly pear cactus, 75
Projectile points, 23 (illus.), 24, 26
Pronghorns, 100
Pullman Cattle Company, 28
Purple prairie clover, 73
Pussy-toes, field, 73

Raccoons, 104, 185
Racers (snakes), 94
Rainfall. *See* Precipitation
Rats, cotton, 103
Rat snakes, 94
Red-bellied woodpeckers, 136–137
Redbud, 73, 118
Red cedar, 44, 72, 106
Red-headed woodpeckers, 137
Red mulberry, 117
Red shiners, 183, 184 (illus.)
Red-winged blackbirds, 95
Reptiles, 16, 89, 92–94, 135, 215
Rhinoceros beetles, 132
Rhizomes, 58 (illus.), 108, 110, 149
of grasses, 44, 62–64, 67–68
Ring-necked pheasants, 97
Ringneck snakes, 94

River-bank grapes, 123
River otters, 185
Rock wrens, 94
Rocky Mountains, 17–18
Rodents, 100–103, 113, 137
Root hairs, 110, 147, 148
Roots, 58, 62, 67, 110, 143–144, 146–148
Roses, meadow, 74
Rough-leaved dogwood, 73, 123
Rough-legged hawks, 99
Roundworms, 183
Rufous-sided towhees, 46–47
Rusty blackbirds, 112
Rye, 148
Rye, wild, 124

Sagewort, 73
Sandpipers, upland, 95, 112
Scrapers (aquatic insects), 172
Sedges, 72, 178
Sedge wrens, 95
Seed bugs, milkweed, 45–46
Seeds, 43, 50, 64, 65, 66 (illus.), 72, 76
Shane Creek, 164, 165
Shiners, red, 183
Shortgrass prairie, 5, 6 (map), 64, 65, 71
Shredders (aquatic insects), 171–172, 174
Shrews, 56, 103–104
Shrubs, 40, 46–47, 72, 73, 86, 116–117, 121–123
Silicates, 60, 61 (illus.), 141–142, 145
Siskins, pine, 99
Skinks, Great Plains, 92
Skunks, 104, 185
Slender glass lizards, 135
Smooth sumac, 73, 168
Snails, 57, 183

Snakes, 56, 94, 135
Sod, 64, 146–147
Soil, 38, 44, 118, 165
    effects of fire on, 107–108, 110
    formation of, 141–145
    types and features of, 145–146
    underground fauna in, 150–158
Southern redbelly dace, 183, 184 (illus.)
Sparrows, 53, 94, 95, 99
Speedwell, 178
Spiders, 87
Spirogyra, 178 (illus.), 179
Springtails, 156
Squirrels, 103, 120, 137, 193
Stickleaf mentzelia, 50
Stomata, 82, 111, 118, 190
Stoneflies, 171
Stonerollers, 184
Storms, 186 (illus.), 198–200
Strawberries, wild, 75
Streams, 163–175, 178–185
Succession, 20, 50, 117, 144
Sumac, 46, 75
Sumac, smooth, 73, 168
Sunflowers, 43, 74, 194 (illus.)
Switchgrass, 71
Sycamore, 116, 172

Tallgrass, 44, 152–153, 161
    characteristics of, 8, 64–65, 83, 185, 210–211
    extent of, 1–2, 5, 6 (map)
    and fire, 104–106, 108, 110–111, 113
    soil of, 146, 148
Temperature, 82, 187, 190–192
    of soil, 142, 143
    of water, 179
Tent caterpillars, 46, 52, 85–87
Termites, 128, 155
Territories, 53–56

Texas horned lizards, 93
Thrashers, brown, 46
Ticks, 87, 125
Tillers, 64, 67, 110
Toads, plains narrowmouth, 134
Torpor, 195–196
Towhees, rufous-sided, 46–47
Trails, 51
Tully soil, 146
Turnips, prairie, 75
Turtles, 92, 185

Upland sandpipers, 95, 112

Vetch, ground-plum milk, 73
Vireos, Bell's, 46
Virginia creeper, 123
Voles, prairie, 101 (illus.), 102

Wallace, Alfred E., 30
Walnut, black, 116
Water beetles, 182
Water boatmen, 181
Watercress, 179
Water cycle, 159–160
Water pipits, 112
Water scavenger beetles, 182

Water striders, 180–181
Weather, 77, 196–201
Weeds, 76
Weevils, 75
Western box turtles, 92
Western chorus frogs, 134
Western wheatgrass, 71
Whirligig beetles, 181–182
White-footed mice, 103, 137
White prairie clover, 73
Wild licorice, 74
Wild onions, 75
Wild parsley, 73
Wild plums, 46, 75, 86, 123
Wild rye, 124
Wild strawberries, 75
Willows, 116
Wind, 169, 190–191, 199–200
Wirestem muhly, 124
Wood-boring beetles, 125, 132
Woodpeckers, 136–137
Woodrats, 56, 138–139, 193, 195
Wrens, 94, 95

Yarrow, 73
Yucca, 75

DATE DUE			